Mark Rave

Plays: 3

Shoot/Get Treasure/Repeat,
Over There, A Life in Three Acts,
Ten Plagues, Ghost Story, The Experiment

Shoot/Get Treasure/Repeat: 'Extraordinary pieces, which start with satire or absurdity and sidle into the sinister or horrific.'
Observer

Over There: 'It almost amounts to a Lehrstuck, but without any condescension or priggishness in its didacticism.'
Financial Times

A Life in Three Acts: 'The mixture of anger, compassion and emotional rawness here, combined with a rigorous lack of sentimentality, strikes me as admirable.' *Telegraph*

Ten Plagues: 'Startlingly effective . . . the tokens of the plague – a raised circle of marks on the body – and the tokens of love become entwined in a world in which a kiss can bring death.'
Guardian

The Experiment: 'Crammed with slippery language, it evokes a vortex of atrocity from fairytales to Mengele and Medea.'
The Times

Mark Ravenhill's previous work includes *A Life of Galileo*; *Ten Plagues*; *Ghost Story*; *Nation*; *The Experiment*; *Over There*; *A Life in Three Acts* (co-written with Bette Bourne); *Shoot/Get Treasure/Repeat*; *Ripper*; *pool (no water)*; *Dick Whittington and his Cat*; *Citizenship*; *The Cut*; *Product*; *Education*; *Moscow*; *Totally Over You*; *Mother Clap's Molly House*; *North Greenwich*; *Some Explicit Polaroids*; *Handbag*; *Sleeping Around*; *Faust is Dead*; and *Shopping and F***ing*.

MARK RAVENHILL

Plays: 3

Shoot/Get Treasure/Repeat
Over There
A Life in Three Acts
Ten Plagues
Ghost Story
The Experiment

with an introduction by the author

B L O O M S B U R Y
LONDON · NEW DELHI · NEW YORK · SYDNEY

Bloomsbury Methuen Drama

An imprint of Bloomsbury Publishing Plc

50 Bedford Square
London
WC1B 3DP
UK

1385 Broadway
New York
NY 10018
USA

www.bloomsbury.com

Bloomsbury is a registered trade mark of Bloomsbury Publishing Plc

This collection first published in 2013

**Shoot/Get Treasure/Repeat, Over There, A Life in Three Acts,
Ten Plagues, Ghost Story, The Experiment**

Shoot/Get Treasure/Repeat first published by Methuen Drama 2008
Reissued with additional material 2009
Copyright © Mark Ravenhill
Over There first published by Methuen Drama 2009
Copyright © Mark Ravenhill
A Life in Three Acts first published by Methuen Drama 2009
Copyright © Mark Ravenhill
Ten Plagues first published by Methuen Drama 2011
Copyright © Mark Ravenhill
Ghost Story first published by Methuen Drama 2013
Copyright © Mark Ravenhill
The Experiment first published by Methuen Drama 2013
Copyright © Mark Ravenhill

Introduction copyright © Mark Ravenhill, 2013

Mark Ravenhill has asserted his right under the Copyright, Designs
and Patents Act, 1988, to be identified as author of this work.

British Library Cataloguing-in-Publication Data

A catalogue record for this book is available from the British Library.

ISBN: PB: 978-1-4725-1034-1
ePDF: 978-1-4725-0775-4
ePub: 978-1-4725-1299-4

Library of Congress Cataloging-in-Publication Data

A catalog record for this book is available from the Library of Congress.

Typeset by Country Setting, Kingsdown, Kent CT14 8ES

Contents

Mark Ravenhill
Chronology

September 1996   *Shopping and Fucking*, Out of Joint and the Royal Court Theatre (Royal Court Theatre Upstairs and national tour)

April 1997   *Faust is Dead*, Actors' Touring Company (Lyric Hammersmith Studio and national tour)

February 1998   *Sleeping Around*, a joint venture with three other writers (Salisbury Playhouse, transferred to the Donmar Warehouse and national tour)

September 1998   *Handbag*, Actors' Touring Company (Lyric Hammersmith Studio and national tour)

September 1999   *Some Explicit Polaroids*, Out of Joint (New Ambassadors Theatre and national tour)

May 2000   *North Greenwich*, Paines Plough (Wild Lunch series)

August 2001   *Mother Clap's Molly House* (Lyttelton, National Theatre, transferred to the Aldwych Theatre, February 2003)

July 2003   *Totally Over You*, performed as part of 'Shell Connections' Youth Theatre Festival (National Theatre)

March 2004   *Moscow* (Royal Court International Playwrights' Season)

October 2004   *Education*, read as part of 'National Headlines' season of topical verbatim monologues (National Theatre)

August 2005   *Product*, Paines Plough (Traverse Theatre, Edinburgh, and international tour)

February 2006   *The Cut* (Donmar Warehouse)

March 2006   *Citizenship*, 'Shell Connections' (National Theatre)

October 2006   *pool (no water)*, Frantic Assembly, Lyric Hammersmith and Drum Theatre Plymouth (Lyric Hammersmith)

November 2006   *Dick Whittington and His Cat* (Barbican Centre)

August 2007   *Shoot/Get Treasure/Repeat*, Paines Plough (Edinburgh Festival). Won both a Fringe First and a Spirit of the Fringe Award

February 2009   *Over There* (Royal Court)

August 2009   *A Life in Three Acts* (Traverse Theatre, Edinburgh, prior to an international tour, in a production by London Artists Projects in association with Koninklijke Schouwburg/Het Paradijs, The Hague)

July 2010   *Ghost Story* (Sky Playhouse Live, broadcast by Sky Arts)

October 2010   *The Experiment* (part of the Terror Season, Southwark Playhouse)

August 2011   *Ten Plagues* (Traverse Theatre, Edinburgh)

January 2013   Translation of Bertolt Brecht's *A Life of Galileo* (RSC, Stratford-upon-Avon)

Introduction

I wrote *Shoot/Get Treasure/Repeat* as a sequence of twenty-minute plays, each play to be presented separately for each day of the Edinburgh Fringe Festival 2007. I didn't know at first what I was going to write about. I simply wanted to have the discipline of writing a large number plays of an exact length in a concentrated period of time. But then I realised that the festival audience would experience the plays in different ways – some people might see only one of the plays, some might see many or even all of the plays. I decided it would be best if – rather than being entirely separate – the individual plays could also 'talk to each other'.

I didn't consciously pick the 'war on terror' and the invasion of Iraq as subject matter. They simply seemed the only thing at the time which would satisfy the dimensions of the task I'd set myself, that of producing over six hours of theatre. I didn't have any time to do any research for the project. But I didn't feel too bad about that. All the events of the conflict from 11 September 2001 onwards had been repeated and analysed endlessly on twenty-four-hour rolling news. Many theatres had already responded to the war with verbatim pieces based on documentary material. So I reckoned that our problem as an audience wasn't that we didn't have enough information or that we hadn't heard enough opinions. In fact, I thought that we'd had far too much of both and that there was something paralysing, almost undemocratic about that excess.

So the *Shoot/Get Treasure/Repeat* plays take the words and images that were already firmly implanted in our minds by rolling news and verbatim theatre and ask us to look at them in a different way. Maybe they emerge as more tragic, more comic, more epic or more pathetic than they did when presented as 'fact'. I'm not sure. But I hope they don't replicate the job of the journalist, which so much of our current theatre does, but instead bring to our contemporary world something of a poetic and therefore, I believe, a more political sensibility than 'journalism' allows.

You don't have to read or perform the *Shoot* plays in the order they are published here. You can 'shuffle' them in different sequences or just choose a few at random. There is no definitive way of reading or producing these plays. Of course there never has been a definitive way of reading or producing any play. But sometimes in the past people have spoken as if there were. Hopefully this foolish idea is on its very last legs.

Every play I write is normally a reaction against the last one I wrote. Probably to the audience and the reader they seem more like a continuum but to me it's always an attempt to start again, to do something different. After the 'epic in fragments' of *Shoot/Get Treasure/Repeat* I wanted to do something different with *Over There*. I decided to restrict myself to two characters and, by way of further restriction, to characters who are almost identical to each other, so much so that at some points in the play they become interchangeable. Twins seemed to offer this possibility and also suggested to me the setting of West and East Germany and their reunification.

This time I also did verbatim research – the first time I've ever done this for a play. I spent a week in Berlin interviewing people from all walks of life about their past and present, especially about their different past lives in the West and the East. I was particularly struck, twenty years after the fall of the wall, how separate many of the former Easterners still felt from life in modern Germany. While none of them wanted a return to the repressive aspects of the former regime, most of them spoke with a sense of loss about the better aspects of life in the old East. The former Westerners, however liberal they seemed, were very quick to dismiss this as ridiculous nostalgia. Before I began my interviews I had no idea that there was such a deep schism in the German identity or that the 'post-communist' identity could last for so long. So maybe a bit of journalism can – from time to time – be a good thing for a playwright.

With *A Life in Three Acts* I decided to abandon altogether the transformation of 'research' into 'drama'. I'd known the performer Bette Bourne for several years and had got some sense of his rich life. There's a bit of the vampire in most writers, so I couldn't help wondering if there was a play, a musical, a TV series or a feature film to be made from Bette's stories of his past. But ultimately it seemed to me that none of them would be as good as simply having Bette sit and tell his story. I began a series of long taped interviews, which I then transcribed, edited and structured. Bette and I used this 'script' to re-create our conversations before a theatre audience, initially in three separate 'acts' during the Edinburgh Festival 2009. Hopefully, other people will feel free to use the material to play 'Mark' and 'Bette' in other performances.

The subject of 'plague' was suggested to me by the composer Conor Mitchell as we talked about writing a song cycle together. For several months I went away to read about various plagues in world history, from the Bible onwards, without finding any real purchase on the subject. But when I read Daniel Defoe's *A Journal of the Plague Year* I found my connection with the subject. Defoe's mercantile London felt close enough to my own world to allow a way in. I drew heavily on Defoe (and sometimes on Pepys) to write *Ten Plagues*. I suspect that, at heart, Defoe was an early neo-liberal conservative, that he believed that we are all alone fighting our own corner and that we only get to know ourselves by being utterly alone. This is the man, after all, who wrote *Robinson Crusoe*. So the solo voice and piano of a song cycle seemed right for this theme of solitude.

Reading about plague also led me to more contemporary writing about illness by – among others – Susan Sontag and Barbara Ehrenreich. I was particularly struck by Virginia Woolf's words in her essay 'On Being Ill':

> Considering how common illness is, how tremendous
> the spiritual change that it brings, how astonishing, when
> the lights of health go down, the undiscovered countries
> that are then disclosed, what wastes and deserts of the soul
> a slight attack of influenza brings to light . . . it becomes
> strange indeed that illness has not taken its place with
> love, battle, and jealousy among the prime themes of
> literature. Novels, one would have thought, would have
> been devoted to influenza; epic poems to typhoid; odes to
> pneumonia, lyrics to toothache. But no; . . . literature
> does its best to maintain that its concern is with the mind;
> that the body is a sheet of plain glass through which the
> soul looks straight and clear.

Although there is more literature and drama about illness
now than at the time when Woolf was writing, much of it is,
to my mind, rather sentimental and soapy. I wanted to see
if I could write something tougher and less 'weepy' about
terminal illness and *Ghost Story* was the result, first performed
as a live television drama.

It's a popular trope of postmodern thought that all memory
is unreliable and that there can never be an objective
recollection of any event. While this is undoubtedly true,
it does bother me that there is a real possibility for moral
evasion if everything is subjective. Because still events do
happen, acts of great evil are committed and somebody
carries them out. How to identify evil and its executors
within the slippery subjectivity of our modern world? This
was the nagging question that led me to write *The Experiment*.
Initially I wrote it to be played with the lines split up
between several actors but it has been played (including by
me) as a monologue. Again, there's no fixed way of playing
the text: divide up the lines as you see fit. Plays only really
exist when you as reader and theatre-maker 're-author'
them. These plays were once mine but now you need to
make them your own.

Mark Ravenhill, 2013

Shoot/Get Treasure/Repeat

Shoot / Get Treasure / Repeat was originally developed in association with the National Theatre Studio and Paines Plough, and was first produced by Paines Plough as *Ravenhill for Breakfast* at the Traverse Theatre, Edinburgh, in August 2007. From 3 to 20 April 2008 the plays were presented in various venues across London in a production by the Gate Theatre, the National Theatre, Out of Joint, Paines Plough and BBC Radio 3.

Play One

Women of Troy

A chorus of **Women**.

– We want to ask you this. I want to ask you: why do you bomb us?

– We all . . . All of us: why do you bomb us?

– Yes. Why . . . ?

– Just . . . tell us – why?

– You see. We are the good people. Just look at us. Take a look at us. Take a good look at all of us. Gathered here today. And what do you see? You see the good people.

– I don't get . . . I can't see . . . why would you bomb the good people?

– Can I talk about me? I'd like to talk about me. Every morning I wake up, I take my fruit and I put it in the blender and I make smoothies for my family. My good family. My good partner and my good child. For Thomas and for Zachary. And yet you –

– And me. Every morning I sit down with my good mother, with Marion, and we eat bacon and eggs and pancakes. A good meal. And yet you –

– Me. Every morning I read the paper. I read about the . . . There is suffering in the world. There is injustice. Food is short. This morning a soldier was killed. His head blown off. I am moved about that. I care. As any good person would. And yet you –

– My husband likes to be out early washing the SUV. Every morning washing the . . . which is . . . he washes the SUV every morning. Maybe . . . But still, it's a good car. We live in

a good place. It's a good community. All of our neighbours
are good people. Here, behind the gates, we are good people.
The people you –

–   I only eat good food. Ethical food. Because I believe that
good choices should be made when you're shopping. All of
my choices are good choices. They really are. So don't you –

–   'A good breakfast sets you up for the day,' my father
always said. 'You have a good meal at the start of the day.'
And he had bacon and black pudding and sausages and
sometimes a burger and . . . for every day of his sixty-four
years. He was a good man. I miss him so much. My partner
understands. And now you –

–   I work for the good of our society. Every day I deal with
the homeless and the addicted and the mad and the lost.
They come to me and I try to do what I can for them. I try to
mend their broken wings. I use the arts to heal them. Drama
or dance or painting. We'll . . . well, we'll . . . like we put on a
little play. They all heal. Which is . . . that is a good thing to
do. I'm doing good while you're . . . Do you see who am I?
Do you? Do you see how good I am? As we all are good.
How good we all are. How good freedom and democracy
truly is. So please don't hurt . . .

–   That is wrong. Wrong. Why are you doing this?

–   Why?

–   We are the – no doubt about that – good people.

–   That's right, the good people. The good guys. The
righteous ones.

–   You're just blowing us up like this –

–   It's frightening. It's horrific. It's horrible.

–   Blowing us up. My friend, an old dear friend from the
university, she, oh . . .

–   Come on, hey hey hey, you don't have to, you don't
have to –

–   She was such a good person. She was a truly good person.

–   No no, calm yourself, no –

–   I want to, okay? I want to speak out, okay? Okay? Okay?
Okay?

–   Okay.

–   Because you understand what good men and good people
and good children you are destroying, our civilisation, a
world of good people.

–   Yes.

–   My friend from the university was on the bus that
morning. She was going to the department of political
science. And that fucking – oh sorry – those flames just tore
through her body and she was thrown through the window
and she lay there screaming on the pavement. She was an
angel. That woman, all her life an angel and now she's lying
there screaming, calling out in pain, 'HELP OH HELP OH
HELP OH HELP – '

–   Come on, you don't –

–   I want to –

–   This isn't good for you –

–   No, they have to see, they have to see the good people,
they . . . She was an angel. She was a rock. She . . . she died
in the hospital an hour later of her injuries. And what had she
ever done in her life but good?

–   Our way of life is the right, the good, it's the right life.

–   It's the only way of life –

–   The only way of life. Freedom, Democracy, Truth – so
why? Please why?

–   Why do you bomb us?

–   Please, we want to understand. We want to. Why do you bomb . . . ?

–   I remember when I heard about the bombings, about the wave of destruction, I was . . . I was . . . juicing. Thomas was in the shower, Zachary was watching a DVD. And suddenly flames were engulfing our world. Members of my civilisation were burning up and screaming and dying in pain. I felt what they felt. It was awful and I just sat there and I thought I just honestly thought I sat there and I thought: why would anyone do this to the good people?

–   I took Alex to the school in the SUV. We drove through the gates of our community in the SUV and the news of the bombings came through on the car radio. They stopped the music and they told us about the bombs that were . . . everywhere. Alex began to cry. I mean, what do you do? What do you do? He was seven. I turned off the radio but he screamed out to me: 'Mummy, Mummy, what's happening? Why are they doing this? Aren't we good people?' And I said, 'Of course we are, darling, of course we are, we are very good people.'

–   Good for you.

–   Good for you.

–   Good for you.

–   We know your culture's very different.

–   And that's okay. We accept that.

–   We tolerate, we accept, we celebrate –

–   We celebrate – exactly – we celebrate difference.

–   It's all part of being a good people.

–   It's what makes us the good people that we are.

–   Everywhere. Good good good good good good good good good good good good people. Please, you're good. Of course you are. You must be . . . Please, show me a little good.

–   I want to imagine you . . . Help me. Help me imagine you –

–   I want to imagine you going to the garden centre. I want
to imagine you taking your son and your husband in the SUV
and choosing a – I don't know – a bench. A garden bench.
I want to picture that. Just to see you as . . . normal. But
somehow . . .

–   I want to see you: it's night, it's three in the morning,
maybe your lover is ill and you reach out to him in the night,
your fingers brush his fingers, you touch him and you say 'I
love you' and he says 'I love you' back and there's a little
ripple of fear through you – does he mean it? – before he
reaches out and holds you through the night. I really want to,
I want to see you . . . this is what we do . . . this is what the
good people do. But are you doing it? I can't see that. I want
to see that. But I – oh I can't see that –

–   Of course we've had enemies before, of course we've
fought wars, but I still . . . still . . . I saw the old enemies
drinking coffee, their . . . eating their breakfast . . . I could
picture that . . . I could picture them . . . They had breakfast,
babies, they made love . . . but you . . .

–   Look at me. Look at me. Don't be so strange – just look
at me.

–   Oh.

–   Oh.

–   I see nothing when I look at you.

–   I see . . . darkness. I see –

–   Everything that is . . . you are opposite and – oh shit, this
is hard . . .

–   You are so different.

–   ATTENTION. THERE'S A CAR. THERE'S A CAR
PARKED RIGHT OUTSIDE THE HOSPITAL AND IT'S

PACKED WITH EXPLOSIVES AND IT'S WAITING TO
DRIVE ITS WAY INTO THE HOSPITAL.

– Again?

– This is too much.

– On and on and on and on and on.

– A HOSPITAL WARD HAS JUST BEEN BOMBED.
A MAN CARRYING A BACKPACK WALKED ONTO
A HOSPITAL WARD. IT IS BELIEVED THAT THE
BACKPACK CONTAINED HIGH EXPLOSIVES.
SEVEN PATIENTS AND STAFF DIED IMMEDIATELY
IN THE BLAST, ANOTHER TWENTY SUFFERED
SEVERE BURNS. THE AUTHORITIES HAVE
CORDONED OFF A LARGE SECTION OF THE NEW
TOWN.

– Oh my God.

– Oh shit oh shit oh shit.

– Why have you bombed us? You bastards.

– Why have you bombed us?

– Why have you bombed all those good people? It's just . . .
I can't begin to . . .

– There were people in there, you bastards, people with
cancers and strokes and heart attacks and Aids and dementias
and you have – you have bombed those good people –

– Nurses. Is there a better person than a nurse? I don't
think so. I don't think . . . I think a nurse is the goodest, the
best per-per-per-per, the people, nurses are the best, best
good people, the people, the people, the people, the people
who do the best good, the, the, the the the the the total . . .
they do more good . . . they do good . . . in this whole wide
world and you have blown them apart and you have torn
them apart and you have consumed their bodies in flames.
You cunts, you cunts, you cunts, you utter, you – yeah.

– Look, I'm going to be honest, okay, I'm going to be totally totally honest, okay?

– Do it.

– Just do it just do it just do it just do it just do it.

– You are not a person. I don't see you as a person. I've never seen you as a person. You're a bomb. I look at you. And all I see is a bomb. I see you there now and I see you and I hear you ticking away and I feel frightened and angry and disgusted. That's what I feel.

– I want to forgive you. Is it too late? You've bombed all those . . . Is it too late to forgive . . . Do you understand the idea, the word, I FORGIVE? A nurse burning up. I see it in my . . .

– I want to – okay – I want to . . . We can trade with you, okay? There's natural resources, okay, and let's take the natural resources and let's take the natural resources and let's yes . . . what do you . . . A nurse burning up . . . what do you say, huh?

– Look at you. Tick tick tick tick tick tick. That's all you – you monster – that's all you –

– And there's the multimedia environment, would you like that, bet you would. Come on, yeah? The multimedia environment that would be oooh – freedom democracy democracy freedom the multimedia environment nurse flames – that would be good fun. What d'ya say?

– You EVIL EVIL EVIL EVIL EVIL –

– And shopping. I can give you as many . . . I can bring you as many . . . you really can, I promise you, you can have as many – flames nurse – you can have shops and I have travelled this world up and down and down and up and round and I have not discovered a woman or a man, a man or a woman who does not – nurse nurse nurse – love to shop.

–   Democracy and freedom. Freedom and democracy. I offer them to you. I'm giving them to you. Don't be frightened. Don't be alarmed. Do they seem – nurse in flames – like big difficult words? Well, they're not, they're not, they're –

–   Instincts.

–   Exactly, they are – good, they are human instincts and if you'll just – we can liberate you and then you'll understand, you'll embrace, you'll live, you'll enjoy freedom and democracy. Think of that you'll have freedom and democracy.

–   (*Punches air.*) Hurrah!

–   (*Punches air.*) Hurrah!

–   (*Punches air.*) Hurrah!

–   You can be good people, good persons, good you can you –

–   PLEASE LISTEN CAREFULLY. YOU ARE ABOUT TO DIE. WE HAVE INFILTRATED THIS SITE. A SUICIDE BOMBER IS INSIDE YOUR SITE AND YOU ARE ABOUT TO DIE. MESSAGE ENDS.

–   No! No! No! I'm a good person.

–   Me too. I'm good. I'm good. I'm good.

–   Lord protect us Lord protect us Lord protect us.

–   I love you, Tom. I love you, Zachary. Zac – your paintings on the fridge that I'm so proud of. I love them. Thomas – our evenings of fish and wine and colleagues from the university. Good evenings. You are a good man. I love you.

–   Marion, you are a good mother. Our breakfasts mean so much to me. Our good breakfasts where we talk about the good day that lies ahead. Marion, Mother, I love you.

–   Please. Go to the garden bench. Go the garden bench and sit on the garden bench and think of that day at the garden centre. Such an ordinary day but still a good day, wasn't it? Wasn't it? Wasn't it a good day? It was. I love you.

–   Please don't have too much coffee. Please don't have too much sugar. Please don't – no do, do, do . . . Oh you always were such a good flirt. I love you.

–   Come on, pull the, squeeze the trigger, push the button. We're ready.

–   We're ready now to go. Ready and – at peace, loved. Are you?

–   Ready and we are oh so sure so sure so sure – we are the good people the good people.

–   The good people.

–   The good people.

–   And the Lord made His earth for us, His earth with its resources and its . . . coffee, the bombs, the shops . . . they are for us. For us to use the good people. And we will use them, we will.

–   We stand together now.

–   We stand together stand strong.

–   We are ready for death.

–   Which of you is the suicide bomber? Identify yourself. Come forward. Come forward.   .

A **Man** *steps from the crowd with a backpack on.*

Man   I am the suicide bomber.

–   You can kill us, detonate your . . . blow our bodies apart, rip our heads from our . . . consume us in your flames because we will die a good death.

–   A good death for a good people.

–   A good death for a good people.

–   Hallelujah!

–   Hallelujah!

–   Hallelujah!

–   But if there's good people, don't you see that? If there's good there's got to be there must be – you see?

–   Yes.

–   Bad people. Can't have good without bad. Bad without good. I never thought before. But now I'm . . .

–   The flames burning up all our angels.

–   Maybe you are bad people, yes?

–   Well, maybe that's right, huh? Maybe that's right? Maybe we are the good people and you are the evil, wicked, terrible – maybe you are the bad people.

–   Yes yes yes. Bad people, And maybe eventually the time has come when there's good and bad and the great battle will begin.

–   The never-ending battle of good and evil.

–   And maybe we've been pretending, maybe we've been dreaming, maybe we've been numbing ourselves.

–   Maybe this is the truth about us. And maybe this is the truth about you. Maybe you are evil.

–   I'm sorry to say that. We're sorry to say that. We look at you and we . . .

–   This is the end for us, this is the . . . But this is just the beginning of the war. The good people . . . there's an army of the good people and they're standing up now and they are fighting you and this is a war that is going to go on for ever.

–   For ever.

–   For good. For us this is the end, but for the war it is just the beginning.

–   The war begins.

–   Here.

–   Now.

–   Today.

–   You tear our bodies apart so the great war between good and evil can begin.

–   The beginning. Amen.

Man   Paradise!

Bomb blast. The **Man** *and the* **Women** *die. A great white light that blinds the spectators. Out of it steps a* **Soldier**, *half-man, half-angel.*

Soldier   I have been sleeping. But now I wake. For centuries I roamed the planet and created this world. But then I saw what I had made and I slept. My job was done. But I was wrong. My job was not done.

Freedom and democracy and truth and light – the fight is never done. There are always enemies. We must fight.

He kisses the lips of each of the dead **Women** *in turn.*

Soldier   I promise you that gun and tank and this flaming sword will roam the globe until everywhere is filled with the goodness of the good people.

There will be good everywhere.

And then, every day, peace will be war. Keeping the peace with the gun. It is my destiny.

I open battle.

I declare war.

Begin.

He lifts his sword high and a great army fills the stage.

Kill the bombers. Slaughter our enemies. In the name of the good people – begin.

Play Two

Intolerance

Middle-class kitchen. Breakfast time. **Helen** *sits with a smoothie, a probiotic yogurt and the post. Off, the sound of a DVD of a children's animation.*

Helen This is a mixture of raspberries and cranberries and apple juice.

I used to – there was a lot of caffeine in my gut. And I used to hurt. I really –

Sometimes I would be doubled up with – I would be – I would try to talk to you –

For instance, I might be trying to talk to you – just to tell you that you're lovely or special or –

And suddenly I would shoot with pain.

And I would stop.

I would just stop talking to you.

And sort of –

And I became worried that I was holding in an agony, a –

Oh I don't know, a –

And I ran over and over my life and I realised –

No.

Everything is perfect.

My life has been . . .

A happy family. Grass and swingball and mountains and barbecues.

School was happy. No pressure to learn.

University. I passed. Nothing special but then I'm not . . .

And I met Thomas.

He ticked the boxes that I ticked on the form and a year later we were buying together.

This apartment is lovely.

I once – only once – had an argument with the woman downstairs – but she is now in rehab and it's quiet as the top of a mountain in this apartment.

There's a little more berry than juice in this this morning.

Which in my book is a good thing.

Your very good health!

She drinks the smoothie.

Breakfast. Quiet.

I don't read the newspapers or watch the news or anything.

There's bombs and wars and . . .

They only upset you really and what can you do?

If I'm going to be blown up – so be it.

As long as I'm in the centre of the blast.

Breakfast is my favourite time of the day. My time.

Thomas is in the shower.

Zachary is watching a DVD in his bedroom before school.

And I'm here – with my juice.

I remember the day that I discovered the key. My intolerance.

I felt foolish.

Foolish because I thought my pain must have run deep.

In one session with the – what was the name of that woman who regressed me?

Oh it goes, it goes. Her name has . . .

Anyway, one day she takes me so far back.

I'm with the angels. I am an – I don't even have the words . . .

There was no religion in my school or family or town so –

I am an – I suppose – an archangel. But with Lucifer I am banished.

And I'm supposed to fall into Hell with the rebel army. But I don't.

For some reason –

The whole army – one half of Heaven – is sucked into Hell. And throughout the cosmos you can hear their screams.

They're still screaming to this day. It's just –

It's just –

But for whatever, for whatever, I don't know why –

My fall is disturbed, it doesn't go quite right.

And so I end up in Eden on my own.

I mean in Eden with my wing hanging loose and hurting beside me.

But there's nuts and berries.

But I'm so alone.

No God, no Lucifer – nobody.

I try to tell stories. But stories in Eden for yourself. For eternity.

It's pretty fucking pointless.

Hello! Hello! My wing has broken –

There was once a man who lived by a –

No no no.

The man runs towards her, in his hand the missing –

No no no no.

Fucking pointless.

What's the fucking point?

Day after perfect day on my own with my wing hanging by my side.

So one day I hang myself from a tree.

Ha. Heh. Heh. That seems so silly now.

But at the time when you're being regressed –

I suppose that woman –

Inga! That was it! Inga! She was called Inga!

I had to take antihistamines because of the cats.

I suppose Inga was a charlatan.

Because that woman discovered that I had fifteen previous lives. I lived them all.

But still a year later I was doubling up with pain.

I flew once to a client. I'd flown three hours, she'd flown five. It was her only window that year.

And for the whole weekend I just lay on the bed in the hotel room screaming with the agony.

She'd call up from the lobby every now and then and it took all I had just to push my lips into the right shape for –

Sorry, still in too much pain.

And she'd say –

Not to worry. I can go shopping.

That poor woman.

This place was – I mean it was one of those places where they'd only had civilisation –

It was the first few years.

So the shopping was extremely poor.

God, she must have been miserable.

And by the time I recovered she'd had to go back.

Her little boy's mood swings had kicked in again. His medication needed playing with.

I had wasted both our time.

Acupuncture would take it away for a few days.

Then the pain would be back.

Then I developed a phobia of the needles.

Thomas was so loving through all of this. Thomas is such a wonderful man.

He would anticipate the pain.

He could see it coming in my face and he'd whisk Zachary away and sit him in front of a DVD.

I'm very lucky to have Thomas.

He'll be out of the shower soon.

He teaches political science in the university and travels widely because he thinks in an original way and there's a market for that.

If you have an original idea you can set your price very high.

That's what Thomas tells his students. I don't know whether they listen. But they'll learn.

Some of them come back to him a couple of years after graduation and say –

I've learnt how to sell myself.

And we raise a glass of white wine to them that evening over supper.

Here's to another one finally learning that Thomas is a very wise man.

It takes a few years but they get there in the end.

This is a probiotic yogurt.

The main thing is no caffeine, but I think this plays its part in keeping the pain away.

It makes sense. Active culture in your gut helps to keep you happy.

She eats the yogurt.

I tried acupressure when I got too scared of the needles but it didn't do anything for me. But it seemed to have no effect.

And I became resigned. I said to Thomas: I will be living the rest of my life in pain.

And he said: no no no no.

I suppose therapy in the conventional sense is pretty much . . . over.

I don't understand, but at supper parties in our new apartment when Thomas's colleagues from the faculty would come and I would give them fish that was the consensus.

But I was in pain. Every day. Sometimes for several hours.

Sometimes I wasn't seeing Zachary. We weren't snuggling up together in front of a DVD like a mother and child should do.

For a while I believed that therapist.

Actually, you know, actually a very long time.

When I think, if the time and the money –

I am an unashamedly classic analyst, he told me. So I nodded and there was a couch and it was several years and I went very early and we would –

I mean this was before breakfast. This was very early.

I'd get in the car and cross the city. There would be immigrants in offices cleaning and young people coming out of warehouses where they'd been dancing.

And then there was me going into that big old house from a hundred years ago.

Talking talking talking.

Trying to find some kind of thing in my mind, my memory – something.

When all the time it was my gut that was hurting. But oh no.

And we did.

I mean there was –

I told him about . . .

We did . . .

Oh this is so long ago . . .

It wasn't even my . . .

The time my father would cry about . . .

Hold me and cry about . . .

My father would cry about his grandfather who'd told him about . . .

The camp, you know.

Oh – my gut is still so – maybe a twinge – did I? – but actually, you know, miraculously still . . .

Still calm because . . .

That was the past. That was history. That was the last century.

That was so long ago. I'm not going to pretend that those emotions are my emotions just so just so – just so the –

He was a little shit, that man.

Little fat Jew.

Pain in the gut.

Oh. That shouldn't be happening.

This really shouldn't . . .

I've had no caffeine for, for . . . so many years . . . for three years.

Ooooo-uuughhh-uggggghhhh.

ERRRRRRRRRR! AAGGGGHHHHH!

Oh God. Oh God. Oh God . . .

It's . . .

Shit. Fuck.

This should not be happening.

Ahh.

Long pause.

Better now.

I don't . . . why?

There's nothing to make that –

I shouldn't . . . a Jew is . . .

Jews are . . . wonderful. Jews are . . . people. You know.

Just the whole therapy thing, the whole . . . thing. It wasn't for me.

I just sensed.

And when I read the – when I saw the magazine piece about the caffeine intolerance, I just knew.

I thought: that's me.

I have to reconsider breakfast.

And I did.

And look at me now.

Serene.

It's not my word. It's the word several friends and colleagues have used about me.

You are now a serene person.

Somebody even used the word: reborn.

So I suppose . . .

The shower's stopped. Thomas will be towelling himself.

Silence. Zachary has turned his DVD off. Zachary is getting dressed. Thomas is getting dressed.

My breakfast is complete.

Silence now.

Isn't that wonderful?

My gut is . . . my gut is . . . my gut is . . . so calm.

Look – a postcard from my downstairs neighbour writing from the rehab clinic. I didn't think they were allowed to do that.

She says she's writing to all the people she's hurt and wants to apologise.

She doesn't need forgiveness. But she wants us to know she's working on herself and is determined to be a new people. She means person.

I think I'll put it on the fridge with the spare magnet. Over there by Zachary's painting of the soldier with no head.

Of course, yes, I'd prefer it if his people had heads – but they don't. And that's just the way Zachary sees them. And that's the way he expresses himself.

Each of us is an individual. I won't judge.

She didn't need to do that. She really didn't.

A new person. Well, I look forward to that. She'll be welcome in here if she's no longer dependent. Zachary can read for her.

Thomas? Zachary?

Tom?

Zac?

Gone. No goodbye.

Well – it's late. There's a rush.

I say a little prayer: don't let them be bombed today.

We'll text later. And I'll remind Thomas about the theatre.

I'm going to get new shoes today.

I just feel like it.

UGH. MY STOMACH. I AM A SLAVE TO MY . . .

Such a fucking mystery.

Really thought I was going to be happy.

What can you do?

(I may have a frappa I mean fuck it just fuck it I may have a fucking frappawatsitcino whatfucking ever.)

When you've tried everything – Inga, the little Jew – everything – what can you do? What the the fuck can you do?

Well, there's war on, isn't there? It says on the telly so it must be – the war has begun. We've invaded them.

Now I have zinc and calcium and iron. It's quite a little ritual, isn't it?

But I think they do play a part in – they are doing a part in making my life –

As near as perfect as any life can be.

She takes the tablets.

Play Three

Women in Love

Anna, Dan.

Anna It was the week after the chemo and the radio ended and you were in for observation and I said to you: I've brought you breakfast. I didn't know whether you wanted breakfast. I didn't know whether you were allowed breakfast. But I decided you should have breakfast.

Dan And I said: Thank you for bringing me breakfast.

Anna And I asked: Did you sleep at all? I want you to sleep.

Dan And I said: I sleep all the time. They bring me drugs so I sleep all the time.

Anna And I said: Well, that's good. I'm glad they bring you drugs so that you can sleep. It must be hard to sleep.

Dan And I said: Oh yes. It's hard to sleep in here. People are mad or people are in pain so they call out in the night. Yes. Last night a woman called out that she was an angel with a broken wing.

Anna I laughed.

Dan You did. And I laughed. An angel with a broken wing. And she was lost and would God come and rescue her.

Anna And I said: She'll be one of the mad ones then.

Dan You did: One of the mad ones then.

Anna There's coffee for your breakfast. And I handed you the coffee. It's from a machine. But that's all they had.

Dan And I said: A machine is alright.

Anna There's no sugar, I said.

Dan   And I said: I've got little packets of sugar. I found these. Because I like coffee very sweet. That's what I said.

Anna   And I said: I don't want you having sugar. You shouldn't, you know. Your body. Chemo. Radio. Sugar.

Dan   You did. But you gave me the stirrer.

Anna   Did I? Really? I don't remember the stirrer.

Dan   Oh yes, the stirrer. Definitely the stirrer.

Anna   That's a detail I've forgotten.

Dan   And you said: I'm sorry, it's broken.

Anna   Ah yes!

Dan/Anna   I'm sorry, it's broken, but that's the only one I have.

Both laugh.

Dan   Ah yes.

Anna   Ah yes. Of course I remember the stirrer now. And you poured all the sugar into your coffee.

Dan   I did. And I asked you if you'd brought a newspaper.

Anna   And I said no because a newspaper is too depressing and you won't get better if you're reading newspapers.

Dan   You did say that. And I was angry with you.

Anna   You were angry with me. Which wasn't good for you. And there was a croissant.

Dan   Which also came out of a machine and had a bit of chocolate in the middle.

Anna   I'm sorry I couldn't do any better. Plastic cup and (*laughs*) plastic croissant.

Dan   Ah well.

Anna   Ah well.

Dan   And I said: I need to see the news.

Anna   I said: No.

Dan   And I said: I saw the TV news last night. The invasion.

Anna   And I said: How?

Dan   I had the nurse bring the TV into my room on a trolley, I said.

Anna   The poof nurse? I asked.

Dan   Nancy the Nurse, yes, I replied. Nancy the Nurse wheeled the TV into my room and we watched the invasion on the news together. The desert.

Anna   I didn't have any breakfast myself that morning.

Dan   No you didn't.

Anna   No I didn't. And I said: Nancy Nurse fancies you.

Dan   Do you think so? I said.

Anna   I think so, I said. And I think you flirt with Nancy the Nurse, I said.

Dan   Well, maybe I do, I said, maybe I do.

Anna   Definitely you do, I said. Wheeling in the television. I don't want that to happen. You won't get better if that goes on.

Dan   I said: I like flirting.

Anna   You'll flirt with anything, I said.

Dan   Why else do you think we're together? I said.

Anna   And you reached out and stroked my breast.

Dan   No.

Anna   Oh yes.

Dan   No.

Anna   Yes, definitely yes.

Dan   Funny . . . I don't . . . no . . . no . . .

Anna   You did, I swear to . . . stroked my breast –

Dan   You're embellishing the –

Anna   No. No. No.

Dan   I had the strength? In my arm?

Anna   I suppose you must have done.

Dan   I didn't think I had the strength in my arm. Ah well. What did you feel?

Anna   Well . . .

Dan   Was there . . . ? Arousal?

Anna   Yes. Arousal. The nipple – erected.

Dan   How am I forgetting . . . ?

Anna   Some embarrassment of course. We were in a hospital room.

Dan   Well, fuck that.

Anna   And pride that I'd got you. I'd got you and Nancy the Nurse and the poofter persuasion weren't sticking their cocks / up you.

Dan   No thank you.

Anna   Well, that's how I lost Brendan –

Dan   Of course.

Anna   And relief that your arm could do that.

Dan   Miraculous.

Anna   And anger because you'd smeared chocolate from the croissant all over my top.

Dan   Choccy titties. (*Laughs.*)

Anna (*laughs*)   Choccy titties.

Dan   Mmmm. I said: I saw the TV news and on the TV news I saw – did you see the TV news last night?

Anna   Yes I saw the TV news last night, I said.

Dan   And on the TV news last night I saw the soldier have his head blown off. Did you see that?

Anna   And I told you: Yes I did see the soldier have his head blown off.

Dan   By the suicide bomber. Have you ever seen anything so horrific on your television?

Anna   No I haven't, I said.

Dan   No I haven't either, I said.

Anna   I said: You won't get better.

Dan   I really don't think I did touch your breast.

Anna   Oh yes oh yes. In fact . . . look. Same top. Chocolate still there. See. See.

Dan   My eyes are . . .

Anna   I've scrubbed and I've scrubbed . . .

Dan   My eyes are still . . .

Anna   But the stain won't come out.

Dan   Bring your choccy titty very close, my dear, bring choccy titty for inspection.

Anna   Can you see that now?

Dan   I think so. Maybe a little closer.

Enter **Rusty**.

Rusty   Can I have the TV now?

Anna   Said Nancy the Nurse.

Rusty   The old bitch next door's got a ticket. Her son brings her a ticket with her winning numbers on twice a week.

Anna   Said Nancy the Nurse.

Rusty   It's rollover today and she reckons she's gonna win thirty million. I said to her: What's the point of thirty million, Grandma? The doctors have only given you another week to live, and she says to me: You got to have hope, son, you gotta hope, son.

Dan   And Nancy the Nurse unplugged the television from the wall.

Rusty   I don't know. Is that good? Hoping for thirty million when you've got seven more days on this planet or is it just plain fucking stupid? I throw it out as a question.

Dan   Pondered Nancy the Nurse.

Anna   And out he went with the television. She had the television on very loud next door.

Dan   Did she?

Anna   Oh yes. Don't you remember that?

Dan   No.

Anna   She had the rollover on very loud next door. She was a very old lady.

Dan   I see. I asked you: Were there pictures of the soldier with his head blown off on the cover of this morning's paper?

Anna   And I said: I'm not telling you. I'm not talking about it. I'm not talking about it. And I gave you extra pills: vitamins. Minerals. Zinc. Calcium.

Dan   I had a lot of pills rattling around inside me.

Anna   You did, and I stuffed more down you, but I really, I really – we all have to supplement our diets, you know? We're not getting enough goodness / when when –

Dan   Coffee and croissants from a machine.

Anna   Exactly. Exactly.

Dan   For breakfast.

Anna   It's killing us. Really, so just –

Dan   And I took all the tablets you gave me.

Anna   You did.

Dan   And you kissed me on the lips.

Anna   Did I?

Dan   Oh yes. Always a kiss on the lips after I've taken my pills. You always do it.

Anna   Do I?

Dan   Without thinking about it, yes, you always do. I love you.

Anna   And I love you. Totally. Sometimes I wish I didn't. But I do. I love you totally.

Dan   Thank you.

Anna   With all my, my, my . . .

Dan   Choccy tits.

Anna   With all my choccy tits, yes.

Dan   Choccy tits. Sugar lips and a candyfloss cunt.

Anna   I'm a sugary girl.

Dan   And I said: Let's talk about the university.

Anna   And I said: Oh no oh no oh no.

Dan   Oh yes oh yes oh yes.

Anna   No work until you're better –

Dan   Yes yes yes yes yes yes yes yes yes yes –

Anna   We're not – no – talking about work until you're better. I said that: I said that, no no no. You will not get better, I said, you will not get better if you are worrying about the university.

Dan   And I said: There is no point. Don't you understand? There is no point in getting better if there is not the university, don't you see that? Don't you see? Yes I'm here yes I'm ill yes I'm probably here because of the university, I'm not stupid, I can see that my whole life the stress the pressure the time wasted to make this has made me an ill person but also it's the I am that person and there is nothing there is nothing there is nothing.

Anna   You won't, you won't, I care, I said. I love you. I'm here. I live in a hospital because I love you and you – you love the university YES YOU FUCKING DO – you fucking love this thing and I'm a person and I –

But now it was suddenly written on the wall in front:

> ONLY WOMEN LOVE. MEN DO SOMETHING –
> THERE'S A THING GOING ON THAT'S CLOSE TO . . .
> MEN HAVE A FEELING. BUT ONLY WOMEN LOVE.
> AND YOU WILL GIVE AND HE WILL NEVER . . .
> LIKE A WHALE FLYING TO THE MOON.

Dan   I'm listening to this.

Anna   I know. And . . . ?

Dan   And it's very interesting.

Anna   So of course you, any man, can achieve, of course they can do, of course they've done all this stuff in the world, they've done everything because they don't feel –

Dan   All I asked was that we talk about the university.

Anna   This fucking awful burden of love cut it out. That's the curse. If ever there was a . . . tree of knowledge . . . Eve . . . the apple . . . blah . . . if ever there was the curse . . . this LOVE thing . . . cut it . . .

Dan   Shhh. I kiss you and I say I love you.

Anna   You do. You do. You do. And I kiss you and say I love you.

Dan   So where's the . . . ?

Anna   Sorry. Forgive me. I was unfair.

Dan   I have feelings. Just they don't always . . .

Anna   Hey. Candyflosschocolatelemonade, sir?

Dan   Tell me about the university, I said.

Anna   Alright, I said, maybe we'll do that. A little bit of talk about the university would be alright. I don't want you turning this room into your office.

Dan   I won't. I promise, I said.

Anna   Alright, I said.

Anna   Your eyes were starting to close then.

Dan   No. I don't think so.

Anna   Oh yes. Your head was falling back on the pillow. Your eyes were closing. Your breath . . . it rasped.

Dan   Continue with the research.

Anna   And your head fell back.

And there was silence then.

The lottery had finished in the next room.

And you lay there and the time passed. I put your research away.

Enter **Rusty**.

Anna   Did she win the thirty million? I asked you.

Rusty   She lost her ticket. She can't remember her numbers. She's very old, I replied.

Anna   And I said: Oh well.

Rusty   I told you: She's weeping. I could be a very rich woman and not know it. They'll rollover if I don't claim my prize.

I said to her: You didn't win. Give up, Grandma. Just be happy you've got no memory.

I wish I had no memory.

Anna   I write everything down at the end of the day.

Rusty   And I said: Let it go, dear, let it . . .

People come. They fuck you. You fuck them. You move on. You let them go.

And diseases carry them away and you move on.

Anna   And you? I asked.

Rusty (*laughs*)   I'm blown up, bomb on a bus on the way home tonight, I replied. I go out through the window in a ball of flames. Flaming. Screaming. My life.

Anna (*checking* **Dan**)   Is he alright? He's . . . rasping.

Rusty   He's not doing too badly. He'll be out of here. You should go home. When did you get here?

Anna   Nine-something. Breakfast.

Rusty   Midnight now. Fifteen fucking hours. You go home.

Anna   I'm going to sleep here.

Rusty   His wife phoned, I told you. You didn't like that.

Anna   No: I was fine about that. I've met his wife. We shared a coffee. We're . . . we understand each other now. I asked you: Is there no one in your life?

Rusty   Oh yes, I replied. When he's on leave. He's in the invasion force.

I always wanted a soldier, since I was seven, and now I got one.

Sometimes it's bad. I fart. He thinks it's a landmine.

He gets nightmares. Suicide bombers. I hold him. It's a war on terror, isn't it?

Anna   Do you watch the news? I asked. Don't let him [*Dan*] watch the news.

Rusty   And I said: I keep an eye out. But – I don't. I'm not stupid about this. He won't be for ever.

Anna   And I said: I'm stupid.

Rusty   How much do you love him?

Anna   Everything.

Rusty   You shouldn't. It hurts.

Anna   I know.

Rusty   Yeah.

Screams, off.

Listen, I told you. Listen, she's started again.

Anna   'Oh forgive me, Father, forgive me. My wing has broken and I'm alone in Paradise. I followed Lucifer and that was wrong and take me back.'

Rusty   We laughed: Mad.

Anna   Mad.

Rusty   Listen, I offered. I can smuggle you – don't tell anyone – but there's a couple of spare temazepams. It's hard to sleep in here, I said.

Anna   No thank you, I said. I prefer not to – Western medicine, I said.

Rusty   Uh-huh, I said. And all through the night that woman screamed out for her broken wing and you slept in that chair and there was no bomb to take me away and no news from the the theatre of war and –

Anna   And each of us made it through the night and the morning came and we carried on.

Exit **Rusty**.

Anna   I brought you breakfast – from a machine.

Dan   I love you.

Anna   I know.

Dan   I mean it. Did you bring sugar? I'll need sugar.

Anna   No news today. Nothing happened in the world today. Nothing. Okay? Nothing at all. (*Kisses him.*) And I love you.

Play Four

Fear and Misery

Kitchen. **Harry**, **Olivia**. *They are eating supper. We hear a child's sleeping breath on a baby monitor.*

Harry Do you remember the night Alex was conceived?

Olivia Of course.

Harry Were you calm? That night.

Olivia Calm? Why do you . . . ?

Harry Well . . . Sometimes I wonder if you were really . . . It's important to me that my boy was conceived in total . . .

Olivia Well . . .

Harry As I planned it.

Olivia As you planned . . . Really? Why is it always – ? It doesn't matter. It doesn't matter – Alex was conceived.

Harry In calm. Say it. In . . . Tell me he was conceived in calm.

Olivia Listen . . . it doesn't . . . I love you.

Harry So why can't you . . . ? Whatever it is. Listen. Whatever. We say . . .

Olivia This is . . . It's okay.

Harry Really . . .

Olivia I'm opening some . . . (*wine*). Would you . . . ?

Harry You had to be calm. That's important.

Olivia Well . . . well . . . actually . . . actually . . . I wasn't.

Harry Oh . . . oh. No?

Olivia Sorry.

Harry   Tell me.

Olivia   I can't.

Harry   Tell me. TELL ME. FUCKING WELL – Partners? Partners tell – That is a – you tell me.

Olivia   Well . . .

Pours two glasses. They drink for some time.

Sometimes I'm . . . Sometimes . . . you're inside me. We're . . . making love. We really are . . . making love. But it feels like, it seems like – there's a sort of . . . rape. Sorry. Rape. Sorry. Rape. Sorry.

Long pause.

Harry   Ever been raped?

Olivia   No.

Harry   Ever fantasised about being raped?

Olivia   No!

Harry   So why the fuck, why the fuck, why the . . . spoil the moment our child was conceived? Spoil the . . . In this world of fear why spoil the one . . .

Olivia   Sometimes your eyes like – it's a moment, it's nothing.

Harry   I'm a good man. I'm a kind man.

Olivia   A moment like you don't want to make love but instead make – hate – make . . . like you want to . . .

Harry   Were you ever abused? Your father?

Olivia   There are moments in the past when I've felt for a blink there's a blink of . . . rape and then it's back to love again.

Harry   Do I scare you now?

Olivia   No.

Harry   What are you feeling now?

Olivia   Sorry I said anything. Sorry. I love you – respect you – trust you – I totally totally love you. I do I do I do I do.

Harry   Listen – you're my refuge.

Olivia   And you're . . .

Harry   Cuddle.

She does.

The world out there is so . . . somehow, somehow, when my back was turned, somehow the world turned so bad. And when I come back to you . . .

Olivia   You're keeping us safe here. I know that. I really – I appreciate – my love . . .

Harry   It's nothing. When was the last time the battery was checked on that smoke alarm?

He gets on a chair and removes the batteries.

Olivia   The security. The extra locks. The child locks. Making sure no plug is free. Keeping the mice at bay. I know the work you –

Harry   It's nothing.

Olivia   You work so hard to keep us out of harm's way and I thank you for that.

Harry   These things have to be done.

Olivia   I know, but still . . .

Harry   I'll change these. To be on the safe side. Will we make love tonight?

Olivia   I think we probably will. Yes. We will.

Harry   Will you trust me totally and utterly? Can you promise me there'll be no fear at all?

Olivia   . . . No. I can't.

Harry   Then maybe we won't make love.

Olivia   Alright.

Harry   Other men'd fuck you harder, fuck you harder, smash you harder and then you'd know it's rape, you know that, don't you? Don't you? You think it's rape with me –

Olivia   I don't think it's –

Harry   Then you can bet your fucking bottom fucking dollar that it's more like fucking rape with any other fucking man. OTHER MEN WOULD –

Olivia   QUIET. Shhh. Shhhh now, Alex is sleeping. Alex only got off . . . Quiet. I just got Alex off twenty minutes ago.

Harry   Sorry sorry sorry.

Olivia   It's really important Alex doesn't –

Harry   Of course of course of course. Is he alright? Did he seem alright?

Olivia   I think so, yes.

Harry   Any dreams?

Olivia   Not yet. It's early. He might still . . .

Harry   You didn't let him watch the news? The invasion.

Olivia   Of course not.

Harry   It's very important he doesn't – that's where he got this whole – the soldier dream, the thing, he got that from the news –

Olivia   Listen to him breathing.

Baby monitor. Breathing.

Sounds like he's doing alright to me.

Harry   Yes. He's alright. And what about us? Are we alright?

Olivia (*laughs*)   Let's get pissed.

Harry   If we're frightened of each other . . .

Olivia   I'm not . . . no. Honestly. No.

Harry   What frightens you?

Olivia   Well . . .

Harry   Hold you.

He does.

Olivia   I go to the supermarket and suddenly a woman falls to the floor and says that God has banished her from Heaven and she's broken her wing. She's calling out to me: HELP ME HELP HELP ME OR I WILL HANG MYSELF FROM A TREE! How did that happen? I ran a bath with oils, I lit candles, but still that woman won't . . .

Harry   Was Alex there – in the supermarket. Was Alex there?

Olivia   Alex was with the childminder.

Harry   It's just . . . it's just . . . it's just . . . it's just . . . it's just I think it's so important we keep Alex away from all these terrible things, you know? I can't bear to think of Alex being exposed –

Olivia   He wasn't, he wasn't, he wasn't there, he was . . . he was playing while I was . . . It was terribly disturbing.

Harry   But you're over it?

Olivia   I suppose so.

Harry   Shall we go out with our wine and sit on the bench?

Olivia   The baby alarm doesn't work on the . . .

Harry   Ah well then, ah well.

Olivia   I really think we have to . . .

Harry   Of course.

Pause.

Olivia Do I ever frighten you?

Harry Hah! You've never raped me.

Olivia No, but . . . what do you – ? What scares you about me?

Harry That you won't wash your vagina. That you'll fuck a black man. That you'll have a breast removed.

Olivia . . . God.

Harry I'm being honest.

Olivia Okay.

Harry Maybe I shouldn't have been . . .

Olivia I really never –

Harry YOU CALLED ME A FUCKING RAPIST FOR FUCK'S SAKE. YOU TOLD ME MY SON WAS BORN BECAUSE OF AN ACT OF RAPE.

Olivia I DIDN'T. I DIDN'T. I NEVER DID THAT. I NEVER DID. WON'T YOU – LEAVE IT. JUST LEAVE IT. JUST LEAVE IT . . . Our child was born in love and tranquility and his life will be lived, he will never know, I will do everything I can to make sure he never knows the fear and – that I –

Harry That we –

Olivia We, we have known. We will work together. Keep away from the addicts. The madwomen. The bombers. The soldier with his head blown off. We will keep them away – yes?

Harry Yes.

They stop, listen.

Olivia . . . He's sleeping very well.

Harry Yes.

They embrace.

Olivia   I want Alex to be clever but not so clever that he isn't liked by other children. I want him to fall in love.

Harry   A girl –

Olivia   Or . . . whatever. I want him to be fulfilled. But above all . . .

Harry   Secure?

Olivia   Secure.

Harry   Yes. Secure.

Olivia   Security is the most important thing in this life.

Harry   It is. I want to be with you for ever.

Olivia   And I with you.

Harry   Do you mean that, do you really really really mean that?

Olivia   Idiot. I wash my vagina obsessively. I've never fucked a black man. And my tits are staying put.

Harry   Don't belittle me.

Olivia   Oh please.

Harry   The gypsies are finally moving on. There's been a police thing and they've finally moved the gypsies on.

Olivia   Well, that's good.

Harry   So that's one less bunch to set the car alarm off.

Olivia   Great great. I'm getting a bit sleepy. Early breakfast tomorrow.

Harry   I thought we could make love tonight.

Olivia   Let's see, okay?

Harry   Okay. If you're not sure . . .

Olivia   Alex has pre-school Latin at seven thirty so –

Harry   Of course. Listen, if you want to go to bed. I just want to . . . I need to finish these smoke alarms.

Olivia   I see.

Harry   It's been three months since I last . . . we could burn up in the night. That's one of my worst – this old . . . that we all just burn away in the night. I can't sleep sometimes because . . .

Olivia   You never said.

Harry   Well . . .

Olivia   You should tell me.

Harry   I do, but you're sleeping and I –

Olivia   Still. Tell me. I'll be washing extra hard tonight. Down there.

Harry   Sorry I said that.

Olivia   Is my body so frightening? You're frightened of this? My vagina, my tits, my – fear fear fear.

Harry   Here we go. Here we go. Here we go. RAPIST. RAPIST. RAPIST.

Olivia   SHUT UP. SHUT UP. SHUT UP. SHUT THE FUCK UP.

Alex *murmurs in his sleep.*

Olivia   Oh God, have we – ?

Harry   I'll check on him.

Exit **Harry**. **Olivia** *spots estate agent's details. Reads them.* **Harry** *re-enters.*

Harry   He's asleep.

Olivia   Well . . .

Harry   Everything's okay.

Olivia   Well . . .

Harry   The crack house was raided last night.

Olivia   Oh good.

Harry   We were talking in the – buying my paper – and the police bust their way, exploded it open and rounded them all up and now the bastards are waiting trial. Let's pray it's prison.

Olivia   Well, that's good news.

Harry   Isn't it? Isn't it? Isn't it? I'm sorry if I . . .

Olivia   Doesn't matter.

Harry   I do love you.

Olivia   I know.

Harry   I do love you and I want you to love me. Shall we go to bed? Good for property prices. Gippos moved on. Crackheads moved on. This place is going to rocket.

Olivia   You think so?

Harry   Oh yes, you just watch, this place is just going to totally rocket.

Olivia   We're sitting on a fortune?

Harry   A wise investment. But still, I'm not sure this place, this street, this whole –

Olivia   But . . . Character, history, community –

Harry   Yes, I know

Olivia   Character, history, community – we said, agreed.

Harry   But still I'm not sure. This was fun for us. This was . . . colour. The poor, the ethnics, the, the . . .

Olivia   Gippos on crack.

Harry   Exactly. Exactly. Exactly. Exactly. The gippos on crack. I'm not sure all that – for Alex, for Alex for Alex's future, for the security, for the security of Alex's future.

Olivia   What's this? (*Estate agent's details.*) This was on the . . .

Harry   I printed it off the . . . A new community. Gated community. Good catchment area.

Olivia   A new-build?

Harry   I was just surfing. I think we should consider –

Olivia   I don't want a new-build. You know what I want, know what I want and still you go ahead –

Harry   I was just curious about the possibility.

Olivia   Without even talking to me you go ahead –

Harry   I want I want for fuck's sake, fuck's sake, look around you, look, look – there's . . . they are selling heroin at the station, they are in gangs on buses, they have knives, they are fighting on the streets and now and now and now there are bombs. How can you be – ? How can you wilfully . . . ? It's fucking frightening, it's so fucking –

Olivia   I know, I know.

Harry   And now when I explore, when I think about the possibility, you just –

Olivia   I have to sleep.

Harry   Walk down the street and your eyes are scanning, scanning, never meeting a gaze of course because that would be . . . but scanning. Waiting for the blow to come. The . . . something. Kick in the gut. Bullet in the head. But somehow knowing it will . . . Knowing that, knowing that's . . . inevitable. Knowing that 'they' will attack you. They will steal from you, bully you, humiliate you. They will. They will.

A **Soldier** *covered in blood and mud enters and watches* **Harry** *and* **Olivia**. *They can't see him.*

Harry   I want us – you, me, Alex – to build a wall against . . . Somehow the world out there got full of . . . Somehow there's nothing but hate out there. Aggression. Somehow the streets got filled with addicts who need to steal to get so high they can kill who then come down and want to attack and steal your . . . THE WORLD IS ATTACKING US, THE TERROR IS EATING US UP AND YOU . . . WE NEED GATES. WE NEED TO, TO, TO . . . DRAW UP THE DRAWBRIDGE AND CLOSE THE GATES AND SECURITY, SECURITY, SECURITY, SECURITY. I CAN'T FIGHT THIS WAR EVERY DAY. WAR WITH THE SCUM. THE POOR, POOR DRUG-HUNGRY MENTALLY DERANGED DAMAGED SCUM. I HAVE TO HAVE PEACE. I'M NORMAL. YOU'RE – ALEX WILL BE GIFTED AND WE CAN'T CARRY GUNS EVERY DAY. WE CAN'T. SOMEWHERE JUST TO GROW. WE'VE EARNED THAT. WE WORK.

The **Soldier** *turns and exits to go to* **Alex**.

Harry   WE ARE LOVING – AND I WANT THIS. I WANT THESE GATES. I WANT TO FEEL SAFE BEHIND THESE GATES. THIS IS THE ONLY WAY I WILL FEEL SAFE. BEHIND THESE GATES. SO DON'T YOU – COMMUNITY, THAT'S A LIE. THERE'S NO COMMUNITY. I HAVE NO COMMUNITY WITH THEM. I WILL FIGHT FOR THIS, I –

Alex *screams.*

Olivia   You – Don't you – no – Alex – No, I'm going to him. You – PRICK.

She goes.

(*Off.*) Come on, sweetheart, come on, I'm here, Mummy's here, alright, Mummy's here to hold you, yes, that's right. Did you see the soldier, yes? Oh no. Was he missing his head like . . . yes? Yes, darling, there is a war but it's not our war, we don't . . . There are some of our soldiers, yes, but we don't even . . . we don't want that war to happen and it's a long way away, that war is such a long, long, long way away. Okay? Okay? We're . . . Are you going to go to sleep for Mummy? Will you do that? Good boy, Alex. Night. Night.

She enters. Sits. Long pause. She looks at the estate agent's details.

Olivia   Well . . . maybe.

Harry   Yes?

Olivia   Maybe.

Harry   Look. I did some sums. If we do a week less in the Dordogne, we could rent this place out, the maths is looking pretty –

Olivia   Can I look at them in bed?

Harry   Okay.

Olivia   I'll read it all before lights out. I know. I think maybe you're right, maybe Alex will – maybe a more stable environment.

Harry   You reckon?

Olivia   It's got to, yes – somewhere safer might – he might stop having those terrible – the gated thing might do that.

Harry   I think it might. But if I'm raping you . . .

Olivia   No. Nothing. A few blinks.

Harry   The night Alex was born?

Olivia   No. I'm sure not. Alex was conceived with love.

Harry   That's important.

Olivia   Can we go to bed?

Harry   Let's.

Play Five

War and Peace

Alex, **Soldier**.

Alex And Alex was seven and Alex said to the soldier: Why do you come here?

Soldier And the soldier had no head.

Alex Why?

Soldier And the soldier said: . . . I'm sorry, son.

Alex I don't like you, said Alex.

Soldier I know, said the soldier.

Alex So – just . . .

Soldier I have to, the soldier said.

Alex But Alex said: You're disgusting. You're horrible. Look at you. Ugh.

Soldier Soldier said: I know that, son, don't you think I fucking know that? I fucking know how fucking horrible I am. If I could have my head back again –

Alex Leave me alone, Alex said. I'm perfect.

Soldier My girl's fucking left. My mates in the regiment have gone off, said the soldier.

Alex And Alex said: I'm a perfect child.

Soldier Soldier – I'm . . . it is so horrible. I've been kicking mirrors and windows and that.

Alex Alex – Look at you – blood.

Soldier That is very, very, very old blood. Nothing fresh on me.

Alex   I thought you weren't coming tonight, said Alex.

Soldier   Couldn't keep away, said the soldier.

Alex   Mum and Dad are downstairs, said Alex.

Soldier   And the soldier said: I really want to talk to you. Need to talk to you.

Alex   I could call for them, said Alex.

Soldier   You could –

Alex   Maybe I'll do that. Maybe I will – 'Mum, Dad.'

Soldier   No don't don't don't. Our time, okay? Our time? You told me you liked our time?

Alex   Sometimes.

Soldier   And other . . . ?

Alex   I'm frightened sometimes, Alex told the soldier with no head. He told the soldier with no head: I wee the bed. Last time. Other times.

Soldier   I didn't know that, said the soldier.

Alex   I'm talking to a . . . it's a psychiatrist.

Soldier   What do you tell them?

Alex   Not much.

Soldier   So this is our secret?

Alex   Oh yes.

Soldier   Let's keep it that way, yeah?

Alex   And Alex told the soldier: I draw pictures of you. They think you're a dream. They don't know . . .

Soldier   We agreed this was a secret, said the soldier.

Alex   I know.

Soldier   I'm keeping my side of the bargain, you keeping yours? Yes? Yes?

Alex   Yes, said Alex.

Soldier   Good boy, said the soldier. That is – oh good on you, son, yes yes yes, good boy.

Alex   And Alex said: I am a good boy, everyone says so. What do you do?

Soldier   Girl won't have me. So I sleep in an alleyway, soldier said. Wank and sleep.

Alex   Sounds horrid.

Soldier   The army – it toughens you up, said the soldier. I've seen worse. And then the soldier asked: Can I touch your head again?

Alex   But Alex said: You smell of alleyway.

Soldier   But the soldier said: I really want to . . . tonight . . . I really want to touch your head tonight, son.

Alex   But Alex said: You're so dirty.

Soldier   And the soldier said: Do I look like a monster to you?

Alex   Yes, said Alex.

Soldier   And the soldier said: Fear's okay. That's a good thing, fear is. I've been been scared so many times.

Alex   Yeah?

Soldier   Oh yeah. So many times. Made me a man. I've shat my pants twenty times a day and still carried on fighting. And the soldier said: Join the army, son. No one's a man till they join the army. And he said: I'm just – a bloke, yeah?

Alex   But Alex said: You got no head.

Soldier   Lost fighting the fight . . .

Alex   Which fight? I want to understand the fight. Who are the enemies?

Soldier   But the soldier said: Please. Let me feel your head again. Such a good head. You're a fine lad.

Alex   I'm outstanding. Everyone says so.

Soldier   I'm sure they do and I'm a piece of shit. Oh son, let me touch you.

Alex   Can I hold your gun? asked Alex.

Soldier   After.

Alex   I want to do it now. I play with your gun while you touch my head.

Soldier   That's not what we usually . . .

Alex   I know. But still . . .

Soldier   And the soldier said to Alex: Like the feel of my gun, huh?

Alex   Yeah.

Soldier   Feel like a big man, yeah?

Alex   Yeah.

Soldier   We're all the same: big man with a gun in your hand. How old are you?

Alex   Seven.

Soldier   And then the soldier said: Too young to know it. But you wait – few years you'll feel empty, empty, aching all day, like you lost yourself a long time ago.

Alex   But Alex said: My life is good.

Soldier   Empty, he said. But you always feel finished with this [*gun*] in your hand. Live without food, live without money – you can do it, it's hard but you do it. Live without family, live without friends – that's easy. But live without war? No human being's ever done that. Never will. It's what makes us human.

Alex   Who you killed? asked Alex.

Soldier   Towelhead. Coming for me so . . . Kid only a few years older than you but he's coming towards me with a gun so . . . phut.

Alex   Was that good?

Soldier   It was alright.

Alex   Alex – Give me the gun.

Soldier   Soldier – I gotta touch your head.

Alex   Alex – Gun first. Gun gun gun gun gun gun gun gun.

Soldier   Soldier – You drive a hard deal, don't you? You're a deal driver, son.

Alex   I want to be in the City like my mummy and daddy, said Alex.

Soldier   Do you? Do you? Do you? I can see that, yes.

Alex   Gun.

Soldier   You keep the deal we . . . There you go.

He gives **Alex** *the gun.*

Alex   It's a heavy one.

Soldier   There's heavier than that. Like it?

Alex   Oh yeah.

Soldier   What will you do in the City?

Alex   Hedge funds.

Soldier   I don't know much about –

Alex   They're high-yielding.

Soldier   What a strange little bloke you are.

Alex   No, said Alex.

Soldier   I've got to touch you, son, okay, okay? I gave you my – okay?

Alex   Okay.

Soldier *touches* **Alex***'s head.*

Soldier   And the soldier said: Beautiful hair. Skin. Teeth like . . . These teeth are so fucking good . . . You go to a dentist, we never used to go to a dentist. And he said: You got such a fine head. So beautiful.

Alex   I know, said Alex.

Soldier   One day the girls are gonna fight over you.

Alex   I suppose, said Alex.

Soldier   Oh they will, believe me, son, they will. Girls go for all this. You want a girl?

Alex   Later.

Soldier   That's it. Plenty of time for pussy, yeah? Plenty of time for pussy. Oh yeah . . .

Alex   Will you stop touching me soon? asked Alex.

Soldier   Uh-huh.

Alex   I'd like that, said Alex.

Soldier   You keep playing with that gun. My fingers are disgusting, are they?

Alex   Yes.

Soldier   But you like me, yeah? We're friends, yeah? You told me we were friends?

Alex   I don't know.

Soldier   You told me, son.

Alex   I suppose.

Soldier   You're my only friend in the world. I need you. These nights we have, our secret nights, these are everything I've got.

Alex   I know.

Soldier   So don't you – you got a bit of snot, I'll wipe you.

Alex   It's alright. I don't –

Soldier   I'll wipe you. (*Wipes.*) See, that's alright? That's alright now, isn't it? That's perfect now. The head's just perfect now. We got to look after this head, yeah?

Alex   Yeah. And then Alex asked: Do you want it?

Soldier   What's that?

Alex   Is that why you come here? asked Alex.

Soldier   What you talking about?

Alex   Do you come here, said Alex, because you want my head?

Soldier   The soldier said: You're a mad crazy little kid, aren't you?

Alex   Alex said: I'm a clever boy. I've worked it out. Night after night. You come in. You walk through my wall. Night after night. You want my head.

Soldier   No. Have you told anyone else?

Alex   You want to take my head away, yes yes yes?

Soldier   Oh son –

Alex   You want to take my head and put it on you and go away, that's what you want to do.

Soldier   Son, please –

Alex   I know what you're – well, no no no no no.

Soldier   I need a head.

Alex   Not mine.

Soldier   It's a beauty.

Alex   It's for me. It's for my life. My perfect life. It's not for you.

Soldier   I'm in agony, son. I'm needing I'm wanting a . . . oh please, son –

Alex   MUMMY! MUMMY! DADDY!

Soldier   Oh no, don't you, don't you – I'm bigger than you, I'm a big man with training and –

Alex   DADDY!

Soldier   No, son, don't you fucking –

He covers **Alex***'s mouth.*

Soldier   Listen, son, okay, listen, you listen to what I got to say, this world this country this . . . everything exists because of me, because I go out there and I fight the fucking towelheads.

Alex   Mmmmggguh.

Soldier   And if we can't fight them fucking towelheads then this is over, right – yeah? Yeah? This place, gated community, hedge funds, that's over unless I'm fighting the fighting. You see? You see? You see?

Alex *bites the* **Soldier***'s hand.* **Soldier** *pulls away.*

Soldier   You little fucker. Fucking bit me, you –

Alex   Could have shot you, said Alex.

Soldier   Yeah.

Alex   Boom! said Alex.

Soldier   Yeah.

Alex   You bleeding? said Alex

Soldier   Some, said the soldier.

Alex   Show me.

Soldier   No head – I can't fight, I can't . . .

Alex   SHOW ME.

Soldier *raises hand.*

Alex   Lots. I did that.

Soldier   You proud?

Alex   Oh yes. And Alex said: We want to keep people like you out. Gated community. That's us.

Soldier   You keep me out? You'd like that?

Alex   Maybe.

Soldier   Soldier in your room every night. You wouldn't stop that? Would you? Would you? Would you?

Alex   . . . I don't know.

Soldier   Think this is all yours, but you know, you know . . . See all this? This wasn't always gates. Oh no. This was mine, the soldier said.

Alex   Yeah? said Alex.

Soldier   All this was – there was no gates when I was a kid, when I was your age, fifteen years ago. This was an estate, said the soldier. This was all council, far as the eye could see, beautiful that was, beautiful. Few Asians. They were alright. And we'd play up and down the streets. And we'd play war. Beautiful it was. You stop when your mum called 'Tea' then you'd go out and you'd kill and bomb and landmine till the sun went down and then you'd go into bed and you'd sleep so sound. See my estate? And now . . . Now? My estate. Wiped away. Half of them work in the shopping park. Half of us are freeing the world from the towelheads. Come on. Come on. Come on. Make me happy. Give me your fucking head. Yeah? Please. Yeah? What do you say?

Alex   I . . . I . . . I . . . And Alex pissed the bed.

Soldier   Pissed yourself?

Alex   Not as much as before. And Alex said: Go away now.

Soldier   I need a month, said the soldier. Give me your head for a month. A tour of duty. I hate this world. I get restless. Fight the big fight.

Alex   Alex said: No. Go away.

Soldier   I got to fight. You got to help me. You want your world? You want this life? Want this to go on for ever? Then give me the head so I can fight.

Alex   I don't want to – Get back. No. No. No!

He moves away.

Soldier   And the soldier called out: I've been fighting. I want my reward. You took my estate. I'm fighting for your freedom and democracy . . . I'm fighting for democracy, least you can do is –

Alex   And Alex was angry and he shouted: You keep away from me, wanker. You – you – this is my room, this is my property, my family's . . . I do well in all the SATs . . . I'm gifted . . . We drive an SUV . . . I am so powerful and you're, you're . . . you're scum . . . you eat bad food, you have numeracy and literacy issues, you will never be on the property ladder, you smoke and play the lottery, you're dirt and you don't belong in a gated community. Out, get out, away. You are a monster. You look like a . . . you are a deformed monster. Monster / monster monster monster monster MONSTER MONSTER.

Soldier   Yeah, I'm fucking disgusting, what you gonna fucking do about it? Huh? Huh? Huh? Huh?

Alex   You make me feel sick. And Alex told the soldier: My piss is turning cold on the bed now. You're not human. I am human. But you're not human.

Soldier   I know, said the soldier.

Alex   My world is a safe world and I can't have you in it. My emotional needs.

Soldier   And the soldier said: Fuck you. I am this country. I love this country. I've got a job to do and I'm going to do it. And there's no little cunting kid and his fucking hedge fund going to stop me, see, because all this, this is worth nothing if we're not out there beating the towelheads, then, see, see, see? And the soldier said: GIVE ME THE HEAD!

Alex   Off me. Help!

Soldier   And the soldier held Alex's head and he pulled and he said: I'm never giving this head back, see? I'm going to keep this head for ever. You know what was wrong with wars before? They ended. There was peace. But this one goes on and on and on. It's a war on terror and it goes on and on and on and on. There's no God, see? There's no end day. There's just this war on terror on and on and on and on and on and on and on and on and on and on and and on and on and on and on and on and on and on and on and on and on and on and on and on and on and on and on and on and on and on. What's that? Hah! Hah! Oh good boy, oh good lad. That's it. You shat yourself. Shit everywhere. Hah hah hah hah hah hah hah.

Alex   Fuck off. Cunt.

*He fires the gun, shoots the **Soldier** in the arm.*

Soldier   Fuck. Agh.

*He falls. **Alex** kneels.*

Alex   Is there blood? asked Alex.

Soldier   Coming now.

Alex   Sorry, I just want a – do you want a plaster?

Soldier   That's no fucking good, son. That's as much use as a cunt on a camel. FUCK. FUCK. CUNT FUCK PAIN FUCK.

Alex (*raising gun*)   Don't swear in my room. My rules.

Soldier   Sorry.

Alex   I'm sorry I hurt you . . . See this house? Such a good investment. Be worth a million before you know it. You should go. You don't belong in a gated community – Ugh. You're . . . blood on my duvet now.

Soldier   And my brains are blown across the desert.

Alex   So hard to get cleaners. There's the work. But they're lazy. (*Gun pointed.*) I want you to go now. Go away. Now, or I'll shoot you in the chest. Thank you for coming.

Soldier   It's a hard life, son. But maybe you'll never know that.

Alex   And Alex told the soldier: I'm going to retire when I'm fifty.

Soldier   You're a wanker. I'm a cunt.

Alex   You're rude.

Soldier   I'm a man, said the soldier, and then he said: Goodbye.

Alex   And the soldier went but Alex kept his gun. And the war went on.

Play Six

Yesterday an Incident Occurred

A group of **Speakers**.

   – Good morning/evening.

   – Yesterday there was an assault in this space. An incident occurred of a violent nature.

   – If you saw that incident we ask you to come forward, come forward and make yourself known.

   – We will respect your rights at all time.

   – Your privacy will be protected.

   – But please come forward –

   – Yes. You have rights. Of course you have rights. But you have responsibilities as well.

   – Not reporting, not coming forward, witnessing and not coming forward to report a violent offence is something we take very seriously indeed.

   – Very seriously indeed.

   – Very seriously indeed.

   – You are a responsible citizen. I'm an optimist. I'm a philanthropist. I believe that most of us are inherently good. Most of us are doing our bit for those around us in a way that is inherently good.

   – But there's always the rotten egg.

   – Always there stinking in the barrel.

   – I am a caring person. I care deeply.

   – But we will not tolerate assaults upon our actors, our backstage staff or our front-of-house staff.

–   Why should we? Why should we? Why should we? Why should we?

–   Such attacks, assaults, attacks – by the rotten eggs – are entirely unacceptable.

–   Yesterday a member of the audience stepped forward, stepped forward out of his – it was a man – stepped forward and struck one of our cast members about the head. Our colleague fell to the floor. The audience member kicked him in a frenzy of, kicked him . . . Bones were broken, there was severe bruising, bleeding, internally and externally. The skull was fractured.

–   I was there. I was sharing a scene – it was utterly horrible.

–   We live in a time of terror, of random, violent, horrible, random, pointless attacks. There is a war on. Abroad. At home. Right here.

–   No one is safe.

–   I tried to pull him off. But this man was frenzied. He'd lost his mind. He was overcome with anger and he poured it into the poor broken body of our dear colleague.

–   The attacker was captured by the authorities. We would like to kill him. But we need witnesses.

–   One of you must have been here yesterday. One of you must have just sat there, there, while, while –

–   Sorry to be heavy. Sorry.

–   Of course ninety-nine point nine per cent of the time life is wonderful. Life is great. Life is fabulous. Babies are born. I should know. I've got one.

–   The sun shines.

–   The sun shines and then you sleep in your bed for eight lovely hours next to the man or woman you love.

–   Or both if you are a bohemian.

–   Or both if you are a bohemian. And in the morning there is the smell of croissants as the girl takes them out of the oven.

–   And the children come bouncing on your bed calling 'Mummy! Daddy!'

–   Because children love the world.

–   As we all do.

–   We all do. We all love the world.

–   If only that tiny little point of the population would use the helplines to report incidents and and and –

–   One of you saw yesterday's incident.

–   One of you saw yesterday's incident and is not coming forward.

–   You're not coming forward. And what are you?

–   A rotten egg.

–   You are a filthy – thank you – rotten . . . And you're stinking, stinking, stinking –

–   Stinking out the whole bloody barrel, you, you, you –

–   But we'll, there's something we'll –

–   There is something we can do.

–   We can, we will act against the rotten egg who is not coming forward.

–   We can. We will. This is what we . . .

–   Since yesterday, a commission, a panel, a meeting of minds has been looking into this problem.

–   The problem of the rotten egg. Their chairman reports:

–   A range of options to punish the rotten eggs in a democratic and humane society. And after questioning witnesses and balancing investment and projected incomes, we have concluded that branding is the way forward.

   – Branding is the way forward.

   – Branding with a hot iron is the way forward.

   – So . . . we are seeking the right to brand those who do not report such incidents – with an iron. A bill is being drawn up to go before our elected –

   – Exactly, thank you. There will be branding with an iron. One of you will be –

   – It's an entirely natural process.

   – The iron will be heated to 250 degrees centigrade and you will be branded.

   – Just here [*above the right elbow*]. A livid scar will remain for life.

   – And why not? Why not? Why not? Why do you think you should get away with it? Well, you won't, this way you won't.

   – This way you go to a beach or a cocktail party or a – you sit in the foyer out there drinking your coffee and eating your breakfast roll and you *will* be recognisable to the rest of us.

   – 'There goes a rotten egg.'

   – There goes a – I want to vomit –

   – There goes an – want to kick the cunt – ah oh, tee tee ee en ee gee gee –

   – It is necessary to do these things if we are to live in a civilised society.

   – A society where rights are matched by responsibilities.

   – I'm sure you, as a decent citizen, will join us in welcoming the branding of those who do not come forward. So come forward now – step out of the crowd and come forward now.

Pause.

   – Branding will hurt. We won't pretend . . .

–   You will be a pariah for – ooh – decades –

–   But listen, listen, there'll be forgiveness.

–   Somewhere.

–   There's always kind, liberal, kind, forgiving, liberal, kind people who will forgive.

–   There's always refuge from the mob.

–   There's kindness in the world. There's always liberals.

–   We even fund the liberals (*laughs*) to a small degree.

–   In the report, a third of the study group actually – oh, bit of a surprise – thanked us for the branding.

–   So come on, come on, lone sad, lonely sad man or woman, woman or man, step forward and report yesterday's incident.

–   Step forward now.

Pause.

–   No?

–   No?

–   No.

–   Very well. (*A picture.*) Here's the member of our staff who is this morning critically ill following yesterday's assault. A rib has punctured his lung. There's bleeding in his brain.

–   He's an actor – yes. But he's a person. Above all else he is a person.

–   And like any normal person he has a family.

–   Can't you feel anything . . . ? Empathy . . . maybe?

–   A normal guy with a mortgage and a wife. Just like normal guys everywhere.

–   Good. Good. Good. Starting to feel his pain.

—   Here's a message from his wife. Here's a message written from his bedside by his wife.

—   Will you read it to us?

—   Would you like me to?

—   I certainly would.

—   Then I shall: 'Please punish anyone who witnessed and did not report this terrible assault upon my husband. He is my rock. I have been married to him for twenty years and in all that time he has been a rock. He has never done anything but good in this world. He loves life and treasures everything about the freedom and democracy we enjoy. This morning, as I brought him a cup of coffee, to his bedside, he held out his hand to me and said the words: "I love you." This is my hope. In all the middle of so much evil, love will always continue. I know I've spoken to my elected representative and asked her to ensure the new branding measure is passed without delay and I hope anyone listening to this will do the same. Freedom must triumph. Democracy must triumph. I want these rotten eggs branded. I say it on my website, I'm blogging it to the world, and please read it out to this morning's audience at breakfast: brand them, brand them, brand them.'

—   A very clear voice.

—   An admirably clear voice.

—   It's the voice of the people and it's righteously raised in anger.

—   (*Punches air.*) Hurrah!

—   (*Punches air.*) Hurrah!

—   (*Punches air.*) Hurrah!

News arrives.

—   And listen, I'm hearing . . . reports are coming in . . . ah. Our elected representatives are meeting. A special meeting of the House of Representatives has been called in the light of yesterday's attack. The meeting has just begun . . . the debate has started. The engine of democracy has swung into action.

–   Will a bill be introduced to allow branding to take place?

–   Oh, we're confident of that. It's the will of the people.

–   Will the branding be in public?

–   Will we carry it on prime time? There's an advertising lobby for –

–   Will it be a ticketed event? The Culture Minister says –

–   Will medical and legal supervision be thorough?

–   Or even excessive?

–   Or even excessive.

–   Or maybe the liberals will, maybe they'll chip away with their 'amendments'.

–   As is their right.

–   As is their right. In a democracy.

–   Let's wait and see, shall we? Let's wait and see. But democracy is taking its course.

–   Democracy and freedom and hope and truth.

–   Can I ask that we say a prayer? A prayer – doesn't matter if you're not religious – can I ask that we say a prayer? A prayer that the voice of the people be heard in the House of our Elected Representatives.

–   Well – why not?

–   Why not?

–   Why not?

–   Why not?

They kneel.

–   O Lord, we thank you for your normal world. We thank you for the normal men and normal women who move about this normal city. We thank you for the normal cultural and normal leisure activities we enjoy on this normal day.

–   Blessed be the normal coffee we drink.

–   Blessed be the normal breakfast roll we break and enjoy this morning.

–   And blessed be Vermeer and Monteverdi, the jugglers and the comedians, the *Bacchae* of Euripides and the brilliant new plays that inhabit thy earth.

–   Give us this day an excellent rate of interest.

–   Blessed be this loyalty card.

–   In mall and in retail outlet, online and instore.

–   And cursed be the rotten eggs, those who witness the attacks and do not come forward.

–   Curse them as you once cursed Lucifer and the rebel army as you threw them into Hell.

–   O Lord, send wisdom to our elected representatives.

–   Send our elected representatives the wisdom to pass this legislation.

–   This legislation which will allow us to brand the rotten eggs.

–   Brand them.

–   Brand them for ever.

–   Brand them for ever and evermore.

–   Amen.

–   (*Punches air.*) Hallelujah! Amen!

–   It will come, it must come, that day must surely come. Then there will be fireworks and music and dancing and champagne. And oh, how happy our world will be.

–   A blessed place. A good place. A calm place. A happy place.

–   It's so close. It's just a, a, a –

–   A breath.

–   Yes. It's just a breath away.

A piece of new information arrives.

–   Excuse me, excuse me, excuse, could I . . .

–   We hope that you've planned a day of relaxing activities.

–   I know I have. I've planned a day of incredibly soothing activities.

–   It's a wonderful city. It's bristling with culture. There's comedy and opera and jugglers and – ooh – oratoria. And we should – what's the . . . ? – revel! We should revel in that.

–   Sorry. Sorry. Sorry. Bad bad bad bad tragic bad bad news. We have just heard that – sorry to say – that woman's husband, our colleague the actor, has just died.

–   Really?

–   Really. His internal injuries. Very severe internal injuries. Injuries sustained during the assault yesterday in this space. The assault for which as yet no witness has come forward.

–   I'm incredibly saddened by the unnecessary death of a fellow human being.

–   I am almost inconsolable. I'm sorry, I can't, a moment . . . I . . . oh my Lord. (*Sobs.*)

–   What is it? Come on, come on.

–   I spent – one summer – I never told anyone, but one summer . . .

– Yes?

– We were lovers that summer. Before his wife . . . We spent the summer on a boat drifting across a lake making love under the moon and stars. We read Shakespeare. *The Winter's Tale*. It was so beautiful. We had such a bond. Oh, this is hurting me very very very very deeply. Medication, counselling, what do I do?

– A life lost.

– Words cannot express the grief that any of us feel for that man's death.

– Well – I'm feeling anger. I'm feeling the most incredible anger.

– Then let it out.

– Yes. Let it out. Give voice, give voice, give voice.

– What sort of world is this? Really? What sort of world? We've been silent too long. We've kept our peace while the society, while the . . . while elements, the scum, the cancer, the evil scumming cancer dregs have had things their way. They've stomped all over us.

– Too right.

– Too right.

– Well, I for one have had enough. I've had enough. I want violence. I want attacks. I want the crushing hand. Don't tell me we can counsel them or give them money – we've tried that, I've tried that. I really believed . . . God, to think I really believed . . . But now is the time to strike them, strike them, strike them.

– Yes.

– Yes.

– I'm not going to be inhuman. I'm not going to gas them. But I will lock them all away for ever. Into the darkness, all of you – go. Go. And let the normal people continue on their way. Sorry. Sorry.

–   Please, don't. You were speaking for me.

–   You were speaking for so many of us here.

–   Yes?

–   It's good to remind ourselves there are just a few rotten eggs.

–   Stinking out the barrel.

–   Please, we have to brand people. We have to. It's the only option. It's the only option under the circumstances. Who is your representative? Who are they? Will you be calling them, texting them, emailing them – today? Do it today you must, you must, you must, you must, you must.

–   Democracy is there for you to make use of.

–   Make use of democracy. Let's hear what the backbone has to say.

–   We may lose it, we may lose it. Don't take it for granted. If you don't text or email now and call out for branding, democracy may wither away.

–   Just wither away.

–   And die. Democracy will be dead.

–   It's up to you. Do you love democracy? Or do you hate democracy? Which is it going to be? Contact your representative now. Just text the words BRAND THEM now.

More information arrives.

–   Just a moment while I . . .

–   The city offers a full range of sporting, leisure, shopping and artistic facilities.

–   It's wonderful. It's a range we're very proud of.

–   Justifiably proud.

–   Justifiably proud of. I'm planning a cycle ride, buying a juicer and listening to Monteverdi. What about you?

–   I shall be ambling.

–   Really?

–   Oh yes, ambling with an itchy credit card and a rumbling tummy.

–   Sounds good to me.

–   Sounds brilliant to me. Hah hah. Utterly brilliant.

–   A further message from Marion.

–   Marion?

–   From her husband's – now dead husband's – bedside. Marion, now a widow, sent us this message.

–   'Fuck the bastards. Fuck them. Fuck them. Round them up. Round them all up and take them up to the castle and tie them to a stake and burn them, burn them, burn them. Fuck.'

–   I support you, Marion.

–   I'm feeling what you're feeling and you're speaking for me.

–   Marion adds: 'Please help the authorities. Please put pressure on your elected representatives. Let none of us sleep till we've beaten down every last door and burnt every last piece of scum flesh.'

–   Ah yes.

–   Ah yes.

–   The eloquence of the ordinary man or woman when impelled to act is incredible.

–   We're all incredible, wonderful people, apart from the rotten eggs.

–   And let's not forget that. Let's not forget to celebrate the wonderful, ordinary men and women.

–   The backbone. The backbone should be celebrated.

–   I know I'm celebrating it.

–   We're all celebrating it. We're all celebrating it. We're celebrating the men and women who get up in the morning, get up, drink their coffee for breakfast, then do their bit – do their bit to generate wealth for the ordinary families that make up this society. And tonight those families will be sitting down and sharing some lovely meals together after another normal day. I'm celebrating everything the backbone does.

–   So I'm asking you. Come forward now or be branded. Any witness – come forward. Now.

Long pause.

–   Nobody?

–   Nobody?

–   Nobody?

–   Nobody. Very well, very well, well, the search goes on. Thank you for your time. But one of you is the rotten egg. And we'll find you.

–   We'll find you and we'll brand you hard.

–   Sorry to be heavy. Sorry.

–   Of course ninety-nine point nine per cent of the time life is wonderful. Life is great. Life is fabulous. Babies are born. I should know. I've got one.

–   The sun shines. For instance, yesterday. Yesterday I was at a garden centre. I drove out to a garden centre. And I watched a couple – a man and woman in their thirties and a little boy of about seven – and that couple chose a bench for their garden. Nothing special. An ordinary couple, an ordinary bench. But I was moved. I was very moved by the, the, the . . . moved by the ordinariness of it, you see? Those are the people we don't . . . we don't read about them in the papers. Just the ordinary . . . not thugs, not terrorists, not scum . . . just ordinary . . . and we should hear about them more. Let's hear about them more.

– After all, it's what most of us . . . We are mostly totally normal.

– And hooray for that.

– Hooray.

– One of you here must have witnessed last week's incident.

– There must be a witness.

– A man is dead.

– We now know that there is a dead man and an ordinary woman who has lost her rock. Who's coming forward?

– Which of you saw the attack?

– Come forward.

– Come forward. Now.

– Come forward.

– Come forward now. Now. Now. Now.

Pause.

– No? No?

– No.

News arrives.

– Hang on, I'm getting a . . .

– Me too . . . Oh that is good news.

– That is excellent news.

– A recommendation from the commission. While finding the facts, while asking the questions that matter, the commission decided that –

– And I quote: 'There is a key problem. Your audience is not being monitored closely enough. Would you let these people walk down a street unobserved? Would you let them shop without following and recording? Then why oh why in the name of freedom and democracy are they sitting there unmonitored in the theatre?'

–   So . . . we're installed cameras. In this space. We are installing microcameras in this space.

–   There are CCTV cameras watching you at the moment.

–   There are no . . . None of these cameras is a dummy camera. Every one of these is a real camera. A very real camera. And it will assist us to identify those who witnessed the assault and are failing to come forward.

–   It was the most cost-effective . . .

–   Under the circumstances. How will this work? How will we use this . . . ? Can you explain the . . . ?

–   Certainly. Yes, certainly. We have a team of behavioural psychologists, that is to say a team trained in the psychology of behaviour, who are at the moment behind this wall analysing you for any signs of guilt. Any guilt will be evident in your behaviour and will be made known to us. There will be a dossier on each and every one of you here today and over the next twelve hours we'll be doing an extensive, objective, analytical analysis of each of you.

–   We will identify the innocent. We will identify the guilty. The good. The evil.

–   The backbone. And the rotten egg.

–   Can we just say . . . ? I'd like to say on behalf of all . . . Just say . . . Sorry for any inconvenience this may cause.

–   Sorry.

–   But really, for the innocent what possible inconvenience could this cause?

–   Well, indeed.

–   Indeed.

–   If I was an innocent person – as I am – would I object to
a simple observation by a fully trained behavioural
psychologist? Would I object? Would I? I put the question.

–   Well, clearly . . . no.

–   Clearly not.

–   I would visit garden centres. I would wake to the smell of
coffee and croissants prepared by the girl and I would say to
my beautiful wife: 'I think a visit to the garden centre this
morning.' Would I mind if a camera was watching? Would
I object to observation and analysis?

–   Clearly not.

–   Clearly not. I would have a camera in my car, a camera
in the petrol station, a camera in the quiet corner where I
chose my garden bench. And I would have them there
happily, I would . . . I would . . .

–   Embrace – ?

–   Embrace them. Because here in my heart of hearts, here
in my soul, in my gut, in my head, I am clean, I am clean, I
am pure, I am pure, oh I am sweet and pure.

–   As are we all.

–   As are we all apart from the scum.

–   The scum.

–   The scum.

–   The scum.

–   We'll watch and identify and crush and we'll, oh how
we'll, the time is coming, it's coming now, when the scum will
be wiped away and only the backbone will be left.

–   Hallelujah!

–   Hallelujah!

–   Hallelujah!

–   O Lord O Lord O my God my Father my God thy world will be cleansed. It shall, it shall, it shall. Just as thy Heaven was made free from the sinful ones, just as you cast Lucifer down, so shall our city, our country, our empire be clean, clean, clean, clean.

–   Please don't let the cameras bother you. Act normally. Smile or frown or . . . cry. Yes, you can cry if you want to. Sob. Whatever you feel is appropriate. But in no way should you let the cameras bother you.

–   Why would you?

–   Why would you?

News arrives.

–   Excuse me, I'm getting a . . . something . . .

–   Yesterday I walked by the river. It was a beautiful day. I watched some planes overhead. Some of our brave boys and girls practising for the new surge, and I thought: this is perfect, this is lovely, this is the most perfect day of my life. And I ate linguine in the evening.

–   Oh yes! Yes! Yes! It's been passed. It's gone through on a fair majority. The bill has been passed.

–   Oh that is good news. O my God, O my God, O my God.

–   That's marvellous. That is – oh yes!

–   That is fan-fucking-tastic. That is . . .

–   Democracy and truth democracy and truth democracy and truth democracy and truth democracy and truth democracy and truth democracy and truth.

–   Fireworks and champagne.

–   Champagne and fireworks.

–   Handel, speak for us. Handel, give us thy spirit as we celebrate this moment of history.

–   A dance a dance a dance.

Handel is played as they dance and punch the air.

–   Hurrah for the normal, the normal, the normal.

Dancing ends.

–   We can now brand anyone who witnessed yesterday's incident but does not come forward. Under medical and legal supervision, an iron heated to an exact temperature of 250 degrees centigrade will be applied to the right arm just here until a permanent mark is left.

Information arrives.

–   We're getting a . . .

–   My faith is restored . . . sometimes you think . . . you think . . . democracy is failing . . . you think – I don't know – it's not working . . . Why this vote, this cross on this box? Why? Sometimes you can't . . . until something comes along, something, and hope is, trust and hope and – God bless democracy – hope and trust are reborn.

–   There have been some amendments.

–   Oh. The liberals.

–   Oh.

–   Some amendments were made during the passing of the bill in the interests of a humane society.

–   As we surely are.

–   We surely are.

–   The branding will take place privately. TV crews and ticket holders will not be admitted as had been earlier proposed. And calls for burning at the stake at the castle have been, as they say, 'kicked into the long grass', where they will be considered by a committee.

–   Oh well, still . . . a victory for democracy and humanity.

–   Democracy and humanity.

–   Democracy and humanity. Our core values. Once again they shine through in every act of our enlightened society.

– Marion, the grieving widow, has welcomed the new measures while questioning if they go far enough.

– 'I want them burnt at the stake. I really do. I want to see them scream as the flames encase their fetid bodies and I want to spit on their ashes as they are swept away. I will be campaigning tirelessly for burning at the stake. Join me at my website and let's make the voice of ordinary men and women heard.'

News arrives.

– It is understood that the first brandings are now taking place in a government-recognised but privately owned centre near here. It is private event. There is medical and legal supervision. No tickets have been sold. No TV crews are present.

– So different from our enemies. In our enemies' countries, people are dragged kicking and screaming into public places and they are branded without proper medical or legal supervision.

– Revolting.

– My stomach is turning.

– Turning. There – in the heart of that evil empire – people are burnt frequently at the stake.

– Ugh.

– Ugh.

– Their only crime? Their only crime? What is their only crime? Their only crime –

– It's . . .

– Oh yes.

– Their only crime to stand up and say: 'I am a person. I am my own distinct person. I have my own personality and my own thoughts.' And for this, these people are burnt.

– Disgusting.

– Disgusting.

– Disgusting.

– How they yearn for freedom and light and choice, democratic choice, for rights and responsibilities.

– How they yearn, and how we, many of them, take them for granted.

– This is your last chance. Marion is grieving. Her husband is dead. Yesterday's incident was brutal.

– Come forward now or be branded. Any witness – come forward. Now.

Long pause.

– Nobody?

– Nobody?

– Nobody?

– Nobody.

– I'm getting some. We . . .

– The tapes of today's meetings will be analysed.

– Our behavioural psychologists will identify the guilty.

– Your branding will take place before nightfall.

– We're being joined by . . . BRING HIM IN! BRING HIM IN!

*A **Man** is dragged in by two **Guards**/front-of-house staff. He is very weak.*

– A historical moment.

– This is history.

– This is the first person – correction – the first rotten egg to be branded since the passing of the new legislation. He has been brought straight to us from the branding centre. He has come because he wishes to speak to you. He has words. Well, my friend, now is your moment, now is the moment, now is your time so . . . speak.

Man (*weakly*)   I am a rotten egg. I know that now. I see that now. The mark is here on my arm for all of you to see. Like a broken wing. Please despise me, please hate me. That is your right – and your responsibility. How I wish I could lead a normal life. Paint watercolours. Go fly fishing. Teach my daughter Spanish. Talk online with my friend in Southern Australia. But this will never happen. I am evil and I have been banished from Paradise for ever. This is justice and I embrace it. I did not come forward. I witnessed a violent incident in the New Town and yet I did not come forward. Why didn't I . . . ? For one reason and one reason alone. I am a bad person. There is no point trying to understand me. There is no point giving me money. I am bad bad bad bad bad. Please assist the authorities. Please report violent incidents. Please come forward. God bless the cameras. God bless our elected representatives. Democracy and truth and history and freedom and . . .

He loses consciousness.

–   This city is a lovely place.

–   I think so. I think it's lovely.

–   I may look at some Vermeer, there's a folk band promised in the park and I'm looking forward to Monteverdi enormously.

–   Do you know what I'm going to do? What I'm going to do right now? Right now I'm going to have a great cup of coffee.

–   Oh yes. For most of us it's going to be a fabulous day.

–   What a great world it is. Good morning.

The **Speakers** *leave. The* **Man** *remains unconscious on the floor.*

Play Seven

Crime and Punishment

A **Soldier**, *a* **Woman**.

Soldier   Interview begins 9.32 a.m. (*To* **Woman**.) State your name.

Woman   . . .

Soldier   9.32 a.m. State your name.

Woman   . . .

Soldier   Refusal to state name. You speak English? Do you speak English? Do you speak English? Do you speak English? Speak English. Speak English.

Woman   Speak English.

Soldier   English is spoken. Are you comfortable? Are you comfortable? Are you comfortable?

He raises his gun.

Woman   I am comfortable.

Soldier   Subject is comfortable. 9.33 a.m. I'm talking . . . talking to . . . ? [*State your name.*]

Woman   . . .

He raises his gun.

Woman   A woman who was once a wife and mother and is now a widow.

Soldier   You are comfortable? You have been given coffee and a bread roll. You have received medication. You are feeling tranquil?

Woman   I am comfortable.

Soldier   And almost tranquil. Well, that is good news. That's very good news. Tell me about the dictator.

Woman   He was a very bad man.

Soldier   Of course he was.

Woman   My husband was not allowed to teach. His post was removed from the university. My brother had a hot iron applied to his arm because he wrote in a newspaper.

Soldier   So . . . a very bad man.

Woman   A very bad man.

Soldier   A very bad man.

Woman   But a strong man. Maybe sometimes a country needs a strong, bad man. This is what we debate late into the night: was it better for our poor country to have a bad man but no civil war? So much argument. I think you say frying pan or fire. But I say: in our world, there is a Hell with a Devil in it, below that another Hell with another Devil in it and below that another Hell with another Devil. There are only Hells and we are angels with broken wings and we are all burning in these Hells and which one do we choose?

Soldier   Your mouth is pornographic.

Woman   I'm sorry.

Soldier   I find your mouth has something . . .

Woman   I'm sorry. This is a time for grief for me.

Soldier   I've fought my way through the desert. My tranquillisers were lost. My girl texted to say she's got together with this – sorry – fuckwit. I mean, what's this all about? What is this all about?

Woman   Please, can I go? My mother-in-law is very bad. The shelling, she needs me. I want to –

Soldier   No no no. You sit, you sit, you sit. 9.34 a.m. Interview continues. Describe the day the statue comes down.

Woman   Please, I am worried. My mother-in-law may die. I feel grief.

Soldier   And my, what about my . . . ? We all have . . . The statue comes down.

Woman (*flatly*)   The troops have arrived in the city. My husband and son have died in the bombing. I am told that my mother-in-law is in the hospital. Very critical in the shelling. I am trying to get to the hospital. It is very hard. Troops and insurgents. Many of the roads are blocked. A soldier comes to me: 'Want to be on TV? Want to be on TV?' 'Please, I must find the hospital.' 'Come on, you're a pretty girl, be on TV.' Soldier pushes me with gun into square. Two hundred people have been chosen to go into square. 'You passed the audition,' laughs woman next to me and many people laugh. Maybe this is funny. I'm sorry, I did not find this funny. Soldiers have attached wires and wires to truck to great statue of dictator. There is a rock band. They sing Elton John and Freddie Mercury. I don't believe they are homosexuals. 'I must go to the hospital. I must see my mother-in-law.' Soldier blocks me. 'Square is closed off now. This is freedom. This is democracy. This is history. Stay.' I am pushed back into crowd by soldier's gun. There are many TV crews. We wait for a long time. My mind is so upset. I think my mother-in-law may die and think I never came to her. 'What are we waiting for?' I ask woman in crowd. 'For prime time,' she says. Is this a religious belief?

Soldier   No.

Woman   What is . . . ?

Soldier   It's TV. It's ratings. It's advertisers.

Woman   Thank you. I've wondered. Finally prime time comes – there is a green light to signify the prime time has begun – and the statue comes down.

Soldier   And how did you feel?

Woman   Nothing.

Soldier   Freedom. Democracy. History.

Woman   Yes, we used to talk about those things when my husband lost his job at the university, but actually . . .

Soldier   You're an incredible woman.

Woman   I don't feel anything for these big words.

Soldier   Do you love me?

Woman   I'm sorry?

Soldier   I really want you to love me.

Woman   I've been a widow for five days. Your army . . .

Soldier   I'm in a lot of pain here. I want you to love me. How do I make you fall in love with me?

Woman   My duty is with my mother-in-law.

Soldier   If we were back home, I'd take you to a bar, drink all you can, a film, a Chinese, I'd make love to you very gently. I'd know what to do. But here – how do I make love to you here?

Woman   My husband was laid to rest yesterday. My son will be laid to rest tomorrow.

Soldier   Frigid bitch.

Woman   Please.

Soldier   Sorry, sorry but . . . look at me, I'm a person, I'm a human person, with a heart, I have so much love to give.

Woman   I have a right to respect.

Soldier   I am opening my heart to you and what am I getting?

Woman   I understand that I am being held in the occupied zone but still the international treaties give me the right to respect.

Soldier   Oh yada oh yada /oh yada oh yada dooo.

Woman   If you do not give me that respect, I demand the right –

Soldier   Fuck this, fuck this, fuck. You wrote letters, I bet you, articles all during the dictator years?

Woman   My husband −

Soldier   Exactly, exactly.

Woman   We campaigned.

Soldier   And you were published in the − yes − there was newspaper stuff in my paper? TV documentary crews . . . hidden cameras . . . blah blah.

Woman   The world had to know.

Soldier   Cruel life under the dictator. Freedom. Democracy. You shouted it out? You shouted it out? You shouted it?

Woman   I campaigned.

Soldier   Well, we're here now. History is happening. Freedom. Democracy is happening. Happening. And you won't even − frigid bitch. You don't even feel a little bit of love?

Woman   Thank you.

Soldier   I'm sorry?

Woman (*flatly*)   Thank you for freeing my country. We suffered greatly. We prayed for freedom and democracy. You were brave. You fought your way through the desert. You pulled down the dictator's statue. You made history. You have given us Freedom. Democracy is happening. (*Gets up.*) Now my mother-in-law −

Soldier   Oh no, oh no, oh. 9.39. Interview continues.

Woman   What do you want?

Soldier   Don't play with me.

Woman   According to the protocols −

Soldier   Don't use that stuff on me.

Woman   I am now being held against all the international agreements.

Soldier   The heart is so much bigger. The human heart than any –

Woman   This should be recorded as an illegal –

Soldier   For love, for love. I want you to understand. Don't you understand how hurt I am? How much I need love?

Woman   My husband died easily – a bullet in his head.

Soldier   Every moment you don't love me you're torturing me.

Woman   My son was slower. His spine was crushed by a bomb. There was a pneumonia in the hospital. It was many days.

Soldier   Is there no woman – no woman who can ever just give me the love that I deserve?

Woman   I look around at the city. I look at you now. And I think this is all a dream. Nightmare. I'm walking in peace somewhere else. But this is grief. Everything around me is real. Everything around me is happening. Only I don't feel like this is real because of grief. One day everything will become real again.

Soldier   If you love.

Woman   There will come a day when the numbing is over.

Soldier   Or maybe never, maybe, you know, maybe, maybe . . . my mum . . . cancer blah blah blah . . . I was ten . . . she smoked forty a day so what can you . . . ? But nothing's been real since . . . that bitch fucked off . . . I'm a kid and the bitch fucks off . . .

Woman   Show some respect.

Soldier   She'd have smoked in the fucking coffin if she could . . . She goes . . . she goes . . . We sit by her side till five in the morning and then she goes . . . And nothing is real again. We got a 'happy family'. My dad meets Marion in the garden centre a couple of years later. We're happy. But I want something . . .

Woman   Your mother is resting.

Soldier   But me. But me. Don't want to be – but me? I am walking this earth and still there's nothing. It's all numbness. Nothing's real. Come on. Help me here. Help me. Hold me. Tell me that you love me.

Woman   There is nothing in the international agreements –

Soldier   Oh please – paper, talks – we're people, we're people –

Woman   This interview must be conducted according to protocol.

Soldier   Bitch bitch bitch bitch bitch bitch bitch bitch.

Woman   You could be my son. I would smack him.

Soldier   I could be the man you love.

Woman   I stole the medicine for my son from another child's bed. In war you will do anything. But still my child died. Both children died.

Soldier   I saw you on the TV when the statue came down. We'd occupied the hotel. Found some beer. Turned on the TV. Saw your face and I thought: 'There is something about her, there's something . . . she's got . . . ' And so when I saw you I said, 'Okay, pull her in. I can question her.' You see? You see? But it was stupid. Enjoy the moment. But you're not loving me back so – I can't carry on, just can't. A life without love is . . . I'm going to . . . 9.41 a.m. I have decided that life on this planet is pointless. There is no love in this world. I have decided to shoot my brains out. There will now be the sound of gunfire.

Woman   No.

Soldier   Stand back, please. I don't know what happens.
But I guess – mess.

Woman   No.

Soldier   Maybe it's enough to have seen the most beautiful,
wonderful woman. Maybe that's enough. Maybe to ask for
her love back is too much. Maybe I'm asking for too much.

Woman   Don't be a child. Put the gun away. NO.

Soldier   You gonna hold me?

Woman   I'm gonna hold you.

Soldier   Oh thank you thank you thank you.

She holds him. A pietà: mother and child.

My life has been . . . I bring you Freedom and Democracy.
And now you bring me love.

Woman   I am holding you.

Soldier   9.42 a.m. Operation Enlightenment is complete.
I am being held in the arms of a woman who feels love for
me.

Woman   I am a mother and wife who is grieving. My
mother-in-law is in the hospital.

Soldier   We are each of us broken people but if we reach
out and offer another person love we're . . . That is the future.

Woman   How can I feel love?

Soldier   Of course you feel love.

Woman   It wouldn't be right for me to feel that now.

Soldier   Forget about right. Forget about wrong.

Woman   I am unable to feel that now.

Soldier   So you're saying . . . you're saying?

Woman   Please, I'm holding you. That is enough. That should be enough.

Soldier   I want more. Please. I want more.

Woman   That is enough.

Soldier   Oh no.

Woman   Shhh now, shhh. Rest in my arms.

Soldier   My country is safe. It's a safe, numb place. The people are happy people. Underneath I ache but still I . . . I can go to the supermarket, I can go to the garden centre, I go for a cup of coffee. It's alright. Why did I leave that? Shat my pants fighting in the desert. Saw a man have his head blown off right beside me and that was it – shit in my pants. Did all that because you were crying out for freedom and democracy but now, but now . . . I need to be loved, okay? Is that so wrong, okay? Is that so fucking wrong? And I tell you this, I tell you this –

Woman   Calm yourself.

Soldier   No. I will invade every fucking country in the fucking world, okay? I will fucking invade them all. Got the will, got the firepower and I will fucking do it. They want supermarkets, they want garden centres, they want Xboxes, they want Starbucks. They got it. It's coming. It's coming. It's fucking coming.

Woman   I'm going now.

Soldier   No you don't, bitch, no you don't.

Woman   My mother-in-law –

Soldier   Fuck her fuck her fuck her.

Woman   – will need me . . .

Soldier *fires.*

Soldier   9.43 a.m. I have shot detainee in the foot to prevent her escape.

Woman Oh – bastard.

Soldier Everything is coming to the whole fucking world. See me? I'm bigger than mountains and rivers and seas. My head is big, my arms are big, my dick is big, my feet are big. They are big enough to go anywhere.

Woman Take me to the hospital.

Soldier I will go everywhere. Freedom and Democracy will be everywhere. And somewhere, somewhere, somewhere, somewhere someone will say to me: 'I love you.' Is that too much to ask? Is it that someone should see through all the shit – the shelling, the mortar fire, the landmines, blah – and just see I'm a person looking for love?

Woman I demand to be taken to the hospital under protocol –

Soldier Shut the fuck up.

He fires.

9.43 a.m. I have shot detainee's right kneecap because she, because . . . there was a provocation. You okay?

Woman There's great pain.

Soldier I suppose, yes . . . Detainee reporting pain. Some blood but not to an excessive degree. Do you love me?

Woman Please – the hospital.

Soldier Do you love me?

Woman I have to be seen by a doctor.

Soldier It won't kill you. Do you love me?

Woman Take me to the hospital.

Soldier Say you love me.

Woman I love you.

Soldier Do you mean that?

Woman   Oh please. I love you I love you I love love you
I love you I love you I love love you.

Soldier   Do you mean that? Look me in the eyes and say it.
I have to see you . . . Look me in the eyes. Here.

Holds her head so their eyes meet.

If you can't say it to my eyes it doesn't count.

Woman   . . .

Soldier   Well?

Woman   . . .

Soldier   Well?

Woman   . . .

Soldier   There's nothing there. Fuck. You're dead.
You're . . .

Woman   I am feeling so much pain.

Soldier   Love me. Love me. Love me. Love me. Be my
mum. Be my girl. Be . . . just . . . I don't . . . you can . . .
any . . . shit . . . be . . .

Woman   Oh.

Soldier   9.44 a.m. Detainee has lost consciousness. I have
impure thoughts. I have thoughts of rape and torture. I want
to abuse my position and abuse this woman. I am reporting
what I am feeling. But I am not driven by animal desire. I am
a human being and like all human beings I have a choice.
Rape and torture are only appropriate when dealing with
terror suspects and only with proper medical and legal
supervision. I do not give myself permission to rape and
torture the detainee. I choose, as a human being, not to rape,
torture or abuse the detainee. Bless Freedom. Bless Democracy.
The right choices have been made. Suspect is regaining
consciousness. You alright? You alright? You alright?

Woman   Please?

Soldier   I am the man you love.

Woman   I want to get away from here.

Soldier   I'd earn lots of money. I'd buy you so much stuff. And at night if I was lonely and afraid you'd hold me. Isn't that great? Doesn't that sound great? We'd watch TV. Eat Chinese. Play the Xbox. Go to the garden centre. And we'd make love together very slow and gentle and beautiful. I'd get jealous of the love you give our kiddies but I'd get over it with counselling and we'd be very happy together. There's nothing like the love a woman feels for a man. It's incredible.

Woman   This is your freedom? This is your democracy? How stupid we were. I cheered you through the desert. I called out to you because . . . what a fool I've been. You are just another hell.

Soldier   No. My country, it really is –

Woman   Fuck you.

Soldier   My country's a better place.

Woman   Fuck. May the ghost of my husband and my son and a thousand million angry spirits rise up from the ground and bring their hate to you. May the hospitals and the craters and the battlefields throw up the angry dead and may they find you and may they kill you. The spirit of an angry nation will not rest until you are destroyed. Of this I am sure: your country and your people and your civilisation will burn and be thrown into the flames of Hell for the horror of this day. We will never be together. I want freedom. I want democracy. I don't want this. I don't want you. I want a better world but how can I . . . ? Is every world just a hell? I will go to the hospital.

Soldier   Please. Say: 'I love you.'

Woman   I don't do it.

Soldier   I'll cut out your tongue.

Woman   I don't do it.

Soldier   I'll cut it out.

Woman   I don't do it.

Soldier   Because you can't . . . Oh this is a pointless world with no point and the . . . still in the . . . freedom, democracy, freedom, democracy, freedom, democracy, freedom, democracy.

Woman   Hear me now. Look. In the eyes. Yes? I hate you I hate you I hate you I hate you I –

He cuts out her tongue. She struggles and then passes out.

Soldier   9.47 a.m. I have cut out detainee's tongue. My mission is pointless. Nobody loves me. Now I must choose if I shoot out my brains. Maybe there is love in another place, maybe if we invade again then a woman will say . . . or maybe it is better to shoot now. I wish I had an order from a superior. Please somebody tell me, 'Shoot out your brains' or, 'Son, don't shoot out your brains'. But there is no order from above. The choice is mine. This is democracy. This is what we call democracy. Democracy – I hate you.

Play Eight

Love (But I Won't Do That)

Soldier, **Marion**.

Soldier I'm aching for a fuck.

Marion Don't.

Soldier You don't . . . women . . .

Marion I'm having more coffee. Would you like more coffee? I think maybe some more coffee.

Soldier Last night I really thought we might –

Marion This is Fairtrade, which is important, isn't it?

Soldier You could feel my hands on you, right? That wasn't really sleep?

Marion Even drinking a cup of coffee you can liberate or exploit –

Soldier My finger, you weren't actually sleeping through that?

Marion We must make sure we only deal with the coffee farms where the labourers are treated with dignity, where a minimum wage is –

Soldier You felt me, huh? Come on, you felt me? See this finger – these fingers – these fingers still smell of you so don't tell me? Don't tell me, huh? Huh?

Marion I'm a sound sleeper.

Soldier It's not a bad smell.

Marion I have camomile tea and a herb pillow. I'm right off.

Soldier   You were pretending, you were pretending, come on, come on, just cos I'm in a uniform, just cos I carry a gun, I'm not fucking thick. Don't treat me like I'm fucking stupid, okay? I AM NOT FUCKING STUPID.

Marion   I wish you wouldn't eat sugary snacks. Anger –

Soldier   AAAAGGGGGHHHHHHH!

Marion   So much anger is caused by sugary snacks.

Soldier   Anger anger anger anger is caused by –

Marion   The blood sugar shoots up and then slumps down, a roller coaster of –

Soldier   My dick. My balls. My cock's up for hours, you could see that –

Marion   I was preparing, cooking, making the linguine.

Soldier   All evening you knew.

Marion   I get very lost in handmade pasta. It does taste better.

Soldier   But still you and then you, you you faked sleep? Yes? Yes? Yes?

Marion   Let's not – I've got a busy day – you?

Soldier   You weren't asleep.

Marion   We've got the new boys from the viral marketing team coming in to brief us before the client arrives. Apparently 80 per cent of the spend of this one is going to be viral. Only 20 per cent on the more, on the, the older media.

Soldier   When am I going to get a fuck?

Marion   They think I'm a dinosaur, they really do. When I talk about targeting the spend on TV they just laugh in my face and call out 'Pterodactyl!'

Soldier   I've got to have a fuck.

Marion   I've started to play along. Flap my wings. Caw caw caw. Pterodactyl. Caw caw caw.

Soldier   We're supposed to be, this is supposed to be, this is an . . . alliance.

Marion   I'm supposed to be their boss, but it's important to show you can laugh, yes? And I can laugh, yes? Yes? Yes? Yes? Yes? (*Laughs, then cries.*) Oh I'm sorry, sorry.

Soldier   Hey.

Marion   No I am, I'm really, really . . . oh. (*Cries.*) I'm sorry.

Soldier   Don't . . . let it out.

Marion   There's just been so much to take on board, you know? Everything's moved . . . so fast. And I suppose there's bound to be stress, isn't there?

Soldier   Of course.

Marion   I've tried taking St John's wort and I think that does kind of –

Soldier *kisses* **Marion**.

Soldier   Was that alright?

Marion   Of course. That was lovely.

Soldier   So I'm not just an animal?

Marion   Of course not, no. You're a person.

Soldier   Sometimes you make me feel like an animal.

Marion   I don't mean to. Sorry. Sorry.

Soldier   I'm just here to defend you. The kids. The house. That's what I'm here for.

Marion   I know, and we're all very grateful.

Soldier   I like it here. Pleased when the CO picked out this house for me.

Marion   It's a lovely house.

Soldier   You're a lovely lady.

Marion   Thank you.

Soldier   And I'm . . . ? What do you think about me?

Marion   I think you're a big strong handsome brave soldier fighting for freedom and democracy, all that we believe in.

Soldier   So why . . . ?

Marion   And, if we didn't have you, our world would have ceased to exist long ago and been eaten up by the evil ones.

Soldier   You lock the bathroom door. A piss. A shit.

Marion   You don't want to –

Soldier   A shower. You lock the door. You keep me out . . .

Marion   Well . . .

Soldier   You change behind that door. You take off your day clothes and you come up in that huge great T-shirt –

Marion   It's comfortable.

Soldier   You pull the duvet up to your chin, you cling to the side of the bed –

Marion   I'm sorry.

Soldier   How many times have we made love?

Marion   It's only been three weeks.

Soldier   How many times?

Marion   I don't . . . I'm not counting.

Soldier   I'm counting. I'm counting every minute of every . . . I'm counting it out. Every last. Twice.

Marion   Yes?

Soldier   We've fucked twice.

Marion   I thought more . . .

Soldier   Not counting the failures. One of us has to come, okay? If neither comes then –

Marion   Can I put the bread away now or would you like more toast?

Soldier   Twice in three weeks, what would you call that? What would you say that is?

Marion   I'm going over to rye bread. There's bloating.

Soldier   I would say that is shit that is – that is – yes that is – okay – that is fucking shit, yeah?

Marion   I'm sorry.

Soldier   Allies. Bedfellows. Why are we doing all this unless we fuck?

Marion   I don't know.

Soldier   You've got to – How do I feel, how are you making me feel, have you thought – what do I – ?

Marion   I really don't –

Soldier   Rejected. Hurt. Belittled. Patronised. Humiliated. You lie with your duvet up, your T-shirt on and your – the legs are clamped and that's what you are doing to me –

Marion   That's not what I mean.

Soldier   You know exactly, exactly, exactly, you know exactly what you are doing.

Marion   I don't. NO. NO.

Soldier   Yes yes YES, you are hurting me – here inside – as though I have no feelings – but I have feelings – I have a huge – I have feelings – I – I – I –

Marion   Yes, of course. I'm sorry. I've been a selfish person. I've led a privileged life. I want to learn from you. I am learning from you. Please.

Soldier   I've got a girl back home.

Marion   You never said.

Soldier   Well, now we're . . .

Marion   Of course.

Soldier   She still texts me. I wanna marry her one day. But this is a long war.

Marion   One day.

Soldier   Evil always loses somehow but sometimes can't see . . .

Marion   With guys like you fighting –

Soldier   Thanks.

Marion   I'm right behind you.

Soldier   Here's my girl. (*Photo on mobile phone.*) Bethany, she's called.

Marion   She's very pretty.

Soldier   I know she's fat. She likes all the crap stuff. Cold pizza for breakfast. She doesn't have a Stairmaster like you.

Marion   Everyone's different.

Soldier   But she likes a shag. Every night. Two or three times on a Sunday.

Marion   Gosh.

Soldier   Imagine that – to grab hold of that any time you want to. Really lose yourself in there.

Marion   I need to get the car out of the garage.

Soldier   That's what I'm used to, see? Fuck after fuck after fuck.

Marion   We're going to have to move your stuff so I can get the car out of the garage.

Soldier   When you're used to that much fucking –

Marion   I don't want to be late for the viral boys.

Soldier   And now you – it's physically, emotionally, psychologically – there's a lot of hurt. Do you know that?

Marion   I understand.

Soldier   So do you think you can . . . ?

Marion   I'll do my best.

Soldier   Tonight?

Marion   I'll really try.

Soldier   I want a really good session. And I want it tonight.

Marion   Well, I'll see what I can do, okay?

Soldier   No. Let's not 'see what you can do'. Let's promise.

Marion   I need the car out of the garage.

Soldier   I want a promise. Here. Now. I want you to promise that you will take off your clothes in front of me. No bathroom, no – I'll watch as you get totally, totally naked. You will play with your breasts for a moment, you will cup, you will run, you will trail over your nipples before you offer yourself to me –

Marion   You've thought about this.

Soldier   Three weeks. I will take you. You will not be passive. You will not get fucked. We will fuck together. Together we will fuck for a long time.

Marion   I'm not Bethany.

Soldier   I know that. She's – home. You're –

Marion   I'm older. I'm different.

Soldier   I want to come on your face tonight. That's what I really want. Pull out, climb over you and –

Marion   No.

Soldier   I'm sorry?

Marion   No.

Soldier   You're not going to . . . ?

Marion   I don't like that. That's horrible. Some man –

Soldier   Me –

Marion   – coming on my face. It's too . . . I feel cheap. I'm not a tart. I want some dignity.

Soldier   That's what I'm going to do.

Marion   At least allow me some dignity, okay? I'm a person. I have money. I own a house. I have children in good schools. I own my company. Yes, we need you. Yes, there's a war on. Yes, you're protecting us. Yes yes yes, but for fuck's sake, for fuck's sake, for fuck's . . . give me a little . . . Cum dribbling down my . . . no, please.

Soldier   If it's what I want to do.

Marion   It's not what I want to do.

Soldier   Well, I'm sorry I'm sorry I'm sorry –

Marion   Now can we move your stuff so I can get my car out of –

Soldier   I've been fucking lenient with this, I've played along with this, you know?

Marion   I just have a massive thing about punctuality.

Soldier   Well, let's not pretend, eh? No more fucking pretending? No more pretence. I am sick of this pretence.

Marion   I really want your help.

Soldier   The rules are changing, okay? Okay? If I say strip – you strip, no questions asked. If I say legs open, the legs open – no fucking about. If I say enjoy yourself, you will enjoy yourself. You will come and come and come and come like you have never come before.

Marion I can't.

Soldier You can. You will.

Marion No.

Soldier Oh yes.

Marion What are you? You're brutal, you're cruel, you're clumsy, you bring your boots through the house, your hands are huge and rough as sandpaper, you smell of cigarettes and beer, your erection against my back makes me sick, the smell of your shit in my bathroom lingers for hours –

Soldier All of this, all of this, all of this, all of this, all of this is true.

Marion It's enough that I have you in the house, that I let you in my bed, but now you –

Soldier I will do what I want.

Marion You will take away every last piece of dignity from me.

Soldier I will I will and you will love me for it and you will thank me for it.

Marion No I won't do that fuck off no I won't won't no fuck off.

Soldier Because I am bigger. I am stronger. I have guns. I have an army. I am everything. So if my spunk –

Marion Please. I don't want to do it.

Soldier – over your face makes you feel bad –

Marion I'm grateful for all you – I respect –

Soldier – you live with that, yes? You live with that.

Marion I can't.

Soldier You're sure?

Marion   I . . . Maybe my upbringing . . . some flaw . . . I never smoked with the other girls after lights out so maybe . . . maybe I'm uptight, but still . . . my fault . . . but no.

Soldier   Then this is what will happen. I will talk to my CO today. I will explain that I have been experiencing difficulties with cooperation. This ally wants everything her own fucking way –

Marion   All I –

Soldier   SHUT UP SHUT THE FUCK UP DID I GIVE YOU PERMISSION TO FUCKING SPEAK? NO. SO SHUT – I will explain and he will understand and we will withdraw from this house. I will take my weapons and my mines and my – and I will be reassigned, a house where they want me, a house where –

Marion   I'm sorry.

Soldier   A house where they're not too fucking stuck-up to get their fucking pussy wet.

Marion   No, I like that, it's just –

Soldier   And no defences, no weapons, no soldier, how long you gonna – ? How long you really gonna last before the insurgents . . . ? A couple of days, weeks if you're lucky, month'd be a miracle. You can't fight – your kids can't fight, so . . .

Marion   Don't go.

Soldier   All you can hope for is a good clean bomb to carry you off straight away, nothing too messy –

Marion   Stay, stay, stay, stay, stay, stay, stay –

Soldier   I'm sorry, you what? You what?

Marion   I'm begging you to stay.

Soldier   Say that again.

Marion   Please.

Soldier   This is another picture of Bethany. (*On phone.*)
That's just after I've come over her face.

Marion   . . .

Soldier   How did you think Bethany looks with my cum
over her face?

Marion   . . .

Soldier   I think she looks very beautiful.

Marion   Please. My meeting. I need you to escort me. Your
gun is –

Soldier   You understand the terms? I'm staying on if . . .

Marion   Yes. I understand.

Soldier   And accept? We got to work together on this one.

Marion   I understand and I accept. You are very welcome
here. Thank you for protecting us. Thank you for giving me
your body.

Soldier   And my love. I've got love . . . I know in three
weeks we can't . . . but in time . . . I only really knew Bethany
after the first year.

Marion   You still love her?

Soldier   Always. But I'm here now. Am I brutal with you?

Marion   Sometimes you seem . . .

Soldier   I know I am. I don't mean to be. I suppose that's
war. That's fighting. You don't notice. You get scared. And
then you find yourself doing cruel things.

Marion   It was your regiment shot my husband.

Soldier   You can't always tell who's theirs and who's ours.

Marion   Is that why you asked for my house to protect?

Soldier   He died straight away. I'm a good shot. He was
coming towards me. I took him out. He looked surprised,
then he died – like that.

Marion   His face was still surprised in the morgue.

Soldier   I feel guilt.

Marion   I'm still waiting for my feelings.

Soldier   But you learn in training – friendly fire is an inevitable consequence of war.

Marion   We hadn't had sexual intercourse for years, that side had gone so . . .

Soldier   I'll be gentle with you.

Marion   Thank you.

Soldier   But I have to do it. That's what men . . .

Marion   Of course. I understand. What's in the boxes blocking the garage?

Soldier   Ammunition. Six extra crates arrived last night. You were in the shower.

Marion   Let's move the crates so I can get to the meeting.

Soldier   You missing your husband?

Marion   He was here every minute for twenty years. Now there's nothing. It's very strange. Everything feels wrong.

Soldier   Maybe if I loved you . . .

Marion   Yes.

Soldier   We're going to have to get used to each other cos this war's going on a long time. This is just the beginning.

Marion   I really have to go.

Soldier   Can I do a picture of you with cum on your face tonight?

Marion   I . . .

Soldier   You'll look so beautiful.

Marion   I won't. I'll look old and uncomfortable and . . .

Soldier   You're going to have to learn to trust me. Can you do that? If you want protecting . . .

Marion   I'll learn to do that.

Soldier   Good girl.

Marion   But tonight please start slowly. You can humiliate me later. But tonight – I don't want to feel like a tart tonight, alright?

Soldier   Alright.

Marion   Let's just forget the world and make love tonight – soldier boy.

Soldier   To attention, ma'am.

Marion (*laughs*)   So I see.

Soldier   It's gonna be a good night.

Marion   I'm sure.

Soldier   And in time . . . love –

Marion   Let's wait. Just you – yeah.

Play Nine

The Mikado

Alan, **Peter**.

Alan   Isn't this lovely?

Peter   Yes.

Alan   It's lovely and calm here. Lovely and calm. Don't you think this is lovely and calm?

Peter   It's lovely and calm.

Alan   Would you say this is a Japanese garden?

Peter   The bridge is certainly . . .

Alan   Oh yes.

Peter   A Japanese bridge . . . (*Sings.*) 'Three little maids from school are we –'

Alan   Hah hah. (*Sings.*) 'Come from the ladies' sem-in-ar-y –'

Peter (*sings*)   'Three little maids . . .' (*Speaks.*) Yes, it's a Japanese-style garden.

Alan   Maybe we should . . . maybe . . . ?

Peter   Mmmm?

Alan   Maybe we should introduce some Japanese features into our garden.

Peter   I thought ours was a traditional English-style garden.

Alan   But a splash of Japanese –

Peter   Too complicated. Don't. You complicate . . .

Alan   Yes?

Peter   You don't need to complicate. It's English, there's no need to complicate.

Alan   Alright then. The new bench is alright?

Peter   Of course.

Alan   You don't think the new bench was too complicated?

Peter   I think the new bench is lovely.

Alan   I thought we were agreed, I thought we agreed that day at the garden centre that the bench was right, that the bench was lovely, the right –

Peter   We did. It is. The bench is lovely.

Alan   Well, I like it.

Peter   And so do I.

Alan   Just sitting on the bench smelling all those roses, it's . . .

Peter   Paradise.

Alan   Isn't it, yes?

Peter   It's paradise on the earth.

Alan   I'm glad we're . . .

Peter   So we don't need to add a splash of Japanese to that, do we?

Alan   No. No – you're right.

Peter   Of course I'm right.

Alan   You're always right.

Peter   I'm nearly always right.

Alan   You're nearly always right. (*Pause.*) Glad to have you around.

Peter   Thank you.

Alan   . . . Glad you didn't . . . pop off.

Peter   Ah well . . . not my time, was it? When my time comes . . .

Alan   Indeed.

Peter   When my time comes then I'll 'pop off'.

Alan   . . . I was the Lord High Executioner at school.

Peter   I didn't know that.

Alan   They brought in boys from the junior school for the little maids. I got a kiss out of one of them.

Peter   You never told me.

Alan   This was . . . it was so long ago.

Peter   To think there are still secret little maids after all these years.

Alan   Oh . . . There are millions.

Peter   Stud muffin.

Alan (*laughs*)   Good God. 'Stud muffin'. 'Stud muffin'. What about you? Have you got any secret little maids?

Peter   Secret little maids? Hah. I wish.

Alan   Any secrets at all?

Peter   Any secrets? Far too many secrets.

Alan   Well . . .

Peter   Well . . .

Alan   I spoke to the guy next door.

Peter   Martin?

Alan   With the SUV.

Peter   Martin with the SUV.

Alan   I spoke to Martin with the SUV and Martin told me that they'd just had a valuation. They've just been valued, they've been valued and they can get over seven hundred and fifty thousand pounds.

Peter   I see.

Alan   Well, what do you think?

Peter   What do I think?

Alan   Yes. What do you think?

Peter   I think it's an awful lot of money.

Alan   Isn't it? Isn't it? Isn't it an awful lot of money? To think that prices have just leapt . . . and Martin hasn't even done the work that we've done.

Peter   I didn't do any of the work. You did the work.

Alan   I suppose so.

Peter   I was in the hospital. You did the work.

Alan   I wanted you to have the ground floor en suite in case –

Peter   Ground floor en suite. And here I am walking around.

Alan   But actually the work will have benefited the property a fair bit. If we go for a valuiation.

Peter   Silver linings.

Alan   Silver linings.

Peter   Silver linings.

Alan   Martin's selling up. He's off to the countryside. Said he wants his children to climb trees and pick blackberries while they can. Makes sense, doesn't it?

Peter   I didn't even know he had children.

Alan   Oh yes, Martin has children. Two children.

Peter   You think we'd see the children.

Alan   Martin says the children are on computers while they're here but Martin's sure that in the countryside it'll all be tree climbing and blackberries.

Peter   Let's hope so. They could be the last generation I suppose for whom there's any tree climbing and blackberries.

Alan   What do you mean?

Peter   Global warming.

Alan   Global warming? That's a gloomy thought.

Peter   Sorry.

Alan   Oh well – we'll never know whether the globe warms. We'll be dead.

Peter   Much brighter thought. Much better.

Alan   Will it rain?

Peter   Not for a while. We're alright.

Alan   Such an unstable year. Rain sun snow rain. Random.

Peter   It's going to get more unstable. Floods, like the Bible.

Alan   We'll be alright.

Peter   I don't think gated communities are spared –

Alan   We're on higher ground. We're safe. Whole counties will go before we do.

Peter   That's alright.

Alan   Still be nice to . . .

Peter   Mmmm?

Alan   Sometimes I think . . . I don't know . . . the Dordogne.

Peter   The Dordogne? Do you?

Alan   Yes. The Dordogne. Be lovely down there. We could get – what? – eight hundred and fifty for the house, buy something terrific for a third of that in the Dordogne, lovely nest egg.

Peter   You've been planning. While I was in the hospital.

Alan   I wasn't used to sleeping by myself. I didn't sleep well.

Peter   You should have called.

Alan   The nurse said no calls after ten.

Peter   You should have ignored the nurse. I had sleeping pills.

Alan   I used to lie there and I thought, if he gets well . . .

Peter   I see.

Alan   Dordogne.

Peter   Dordogne. So that's your plan.

Alan   That's my plan.

Peter   But you've done so much work on the garden.

Alan   Yes . . .

Peter   Just when you've got the garden looking so lovely.

Alan   I'll miss it of course, but we'll have a bumper huge garden in the Dordogne. Ponds bridges lilies arbours follies gazebos orchards.

Peter   You'll be busy.

Alan   I'll get a man in. Little old Frenchman.

Peter   You've done so much to the house here –

Alan   Worth it as an investment. But really . . . what do you really think of our place . . . ?

Peter   I think it's fine. I'm fine as we are.

Alan   I did at the . . . We were both keen.

Peter   We were.

Alan   But now . . . a gated community is a little bit . . . antiseptic.

Peter   Which is good for you sometimes. If you're wounded.

Alan   I suppose.

Peter   If you've got a wound, antiseptic is the best thing.

Alan   Yes. Of course. But still.

Peter   I don't want to do all that moving over again after just one year.

Alan   I see, okay.

Peter   Moving's very tiring. Why can't you settle?

Alan   I really want to do it. The Dordogne.

Peter   No.

Alan   I really want us to sell up.

Peter   No.

Alan   I think the Dordogne might be a perfect –

Peter   No.

Alan   I'll sort out the move, you go and stay with Ian and Hilary for a month and I'll do all the –

Peter   No.

Alan   This isn't a whim. I have thought about this. You're healing. You're getting better. You're getting stronger, and in the Dordogne –

Peter   No.

Alan   – would just be the perfect place for –

Peter   Listen. You're wrong. I'm not healing. I'm not getting better. I'm not getting stronger.

Alan   Yes, and if you –

Peter   No, I – I need to be here – I need to be near the hospital – I need to – I'm not going anywhere . . . It's complicated.

Alan   . . . Yes?

Peter   Because it's come back. It's aggressively come back.

Alan   Aggressively . . . ? When . . . ?

Peter   They told me yesterday and –

Alan   Before the garden centre? Before we chose the bench?

Peter   Before the garden centre. Before we chose the bench.

Alan   They told you yesterday that it had aggressively come back and all the time you just went along with the garden bench and everything?

Peter   Yes.

Alan   Don't you think that was an incredibly selfish thing to do?

Peter   Was it?

Alan   Yes, an incredibly selfish thing to do.

Peter   I don't see how.

Alan   But – how could you not . . . ?

Peter   I wanted it to be lovely. I wanted today to be lovely. I wanted everything to be lovely. But actually . . . actually . . .

Alan   Are you frightened?

Peter   I should say I am frightened, yes. Are you frightened?

Alan   I am frightened, I suppose I am, yes, frightened. Do they say – ?

Peter   They never say, of course. They'll never tell you if it's months or whether it goes on and and on and on and on.

Alan   But you – do you want to live?

Peter   Oh yes. I want to live.

Alan   That's the most important thing, isn't it? That you want to live?

Peter   That's an incredibly important thing.

Alan   We'll have to treat it very aggressively.

Peter   Of course.

Alan   Fight back.

Peter   Absolutely. Yes. Fight back.

Alan   We'll fight it. Get right down inside you and take the little fucker on and send him packing. That's the way to do it. Isn't it? Isn't that the way to do it?

Peter   I suppose so, yes. Yes, it is.

Alan   Are you ready for the fight?

Peter   I suppose so. I mean, I'm tired but . . .

Alan   I love you very much.

Peter   Do you know, I wish you had it. I wish you had this cancer too.

Alan   Do you?

Peter   If I'm honest I wish you had it too. I wish I could send it out of my fingers now and pass it on.

Alan   You can't.

Peter   No, this stays inside.

Alan   But you want me to have cancer. What is that? Is that anger?

Peter   I suppose it must be anger.

Alan   Are you angry with me?

Peter   I don't think I'm angry with you. No.

Alan   What cause have I given you to be angry with me? I've loved you. I came to the hospital every day. I didn't sleep. I worked in the garden. I prepared the en-suite bathroom, all because I love you and I want you to live and our future will be . . .

Peter   It's not you.

Alan   I should hope not. I'm not perfect.

Peter   It isn't only you.

Alan   I know I'm not perfect but I am actually a very good person.

Peter   On the train, hospital to home, before the garden centre, I was on that train and I looked around and those people – they all seemed so . . . hideous.

Alan   People can be very ill-mannered on trains.

Peter   They were laughing and talking. The children. The children especially were incredibly hideous.

Alan   No manners.

Peter   And they had their music playing and someone was being kissed and someone was eating and I really wanted to . . . explode.

Alan   Shout at them? Give them hell?

Peter   No. No. Not shout at them. Not give them hell. Not like . . . I'm on the train. They're all so fat and stupid and contented. So fat, so stupid, so contented that I literally wanted to explode – like a bomb – explode. Explode like a bomb. Wasn't that silly?

Alan   So you wanted . . . ?

Peter   I wanted to go BOOM. Go BOOM and carry them all off, drag them down to Hell or something but just – BOOM kill them all like that. BOOM.

Alan   I see. I see. Maybe that's a normal response.

Peter   A normal response? I don't know. Maybe it's a normal response – possibly.

Alan   You've had such a blow. Learning that it's come back.

Peter   I suppose that must be it.

Alan   Learning that it's come back is such a terrible blow, isn't it?

Peter   It is, isn't it? I would have done it. If I could. This . . . thing . . . ticking away inside of me, if I could have detonated it I would have detonated, and I would have killed everybody on the train carriage.

Alan   I think you should talk to somebody about that.

Peter   I'm talking to you about it.

Alan   Yes yes, you are. You're talking to me about it. But maybe somebody else. Somebody who understands.

Peter   There'll be an explanation?

Alan   There's always an explanation.

Peter   Of course. There's always an explanation. I felt the same at the garden centre. I wished I could explode at the garden centre. I wished I could make everybody die at the garden centre.

Alan   You should have told me.

Peter   You were busy. You were choosing the bench.

Alan   We chose the bench together.

Peter   I suppose we did.

Alan   We did. We chose that bench together.

Peter   Of course – we chose that bench together.

Alan   And our home? Did you want to blow up our home? Our garden?

Peter   No. I was calmer then.

Alan   Well – that's something.

Peter   Do you know, I think it might rain. Shall we go back to the car?

Alan   Maybe we should.

Peter   I think maybe we should go back to the car.

Alan   What do you want now?

Peter   It doesn't matter.

Alan   I'd like to know. What do you want now? Are you ticking inside?

Peter   Oh yes.

Alan   I see.

Peter   I am. Just as much – maybe more than – yes I yes it's there tick tick tick.

Alan   And if you could . . . this beautiful garden . . . ?

Peter   This beautiful garden I would consume in flame. I would swallow it in one huge gulp and crunch – destroy.

Alan   The beauty here, the people here –

Peter   The beauty here, the people here would be gone. They would be nothing. All of it would be nothing.

Alan   And me? Our love? All these years –

Peter   – would be nothing too. Because, because this is so much bigger than that.

Alan   I never knew what a selfish person you are.

Peter   Am I?

Alan   You are an incredibly selfish person. And yet still you will expect, you will expect the visits to the hospitals, the sleepless nights, the – you will expect all of this?

Peter   I suppose I will, yes. I will.

Alan   Well, maybe I'll just go off, go off, find some little maid and off we'll go to the Dordogne and I will be selfish. Maybe that's what I'll do.

Peter   Maybe you will.

Alan   You will be so alone. Do you want that?

Peter   No. I don't want that. Do you think you could do that?

Alan   I could.

Peter   I don't think you could ever do that.

Alan   Maybe you're right.

Peter   We'll carry on. We'll sit on the new bench tonight if the rain holds off and we'll carry on.

Alan   Why should we do that?

Peter   Because that's what you do – let's get back to the car – you carry on.

Play Ten

War of the Worlds

A **Chorus***: the people of a city.*

— This is for you. We gather in this square for you. This is dedicated to you. You brave beautiful people. You unbowed children of freedom and democracy. This is our humble tribute to you. From our city to your city. With love.

Sound of a bomb blast.

— You have been bombed. We are sickened.

— We are yes, we are yes, we are really, really . . . sickened.

— When we – the news – we are overcome by – sickened.

— It's morning – I have my shower, I totally and utterly exfoliate, I juice and I put on the news for just a few moments and there it is.

— I know because the children are crying. We have just started to make love, which is unusual for us, when I hear the children crying. Not tantrum, not attention, not . . . a new type of crying like I have never heard before and I rush through into their bedroom, just stop making love straight away and rush through into their bedroom, and the children are there with the television on and you were being bombed. We are sickened.

— You are being bombed. Buildings are falling. The castle, a garden centre, a train, a theatre – they are each – a bomber just blew himself up and – the images are so sickening. And you are all dying and I feel how horrible that must be.

— I see a man on a stretcher. His face is . . . blood. The doctor cuts inside right there in the middle of the street. Cuts into him and manipulates his heart, manually – like – watch – squeeze release squeeze release – kept this man's heart going.

And I, I, I . . . yes – I fall in love with him. I can't see his face, the blood. I can't see his body – covered in some sort of insulated . . . but still there and then I am thinking – I will show you now – I was thinking (*demonstrates*): 'We are one, you and I, we are as one and if, when you come through this, we will meet and we will love each other and lead a very happy life . . .' Of course you, he, that man dies a moment later. They pull the blanket over his face and the doctor runs on to another person who needs him. And I am overcome with grief. Isn't that just the strangest . . . ? I am eaten up with sorrow for a man on a TV channel who had thirty seconds on the screen while I was eating my breakfast. Am I some sort of strange – ?

– No no. We feel as you do. Here's the little girl – see? – the little girl I pick out running away from the blast, running away and she's a little black girl but she's been turned to white by the ash from the blast. See? See? The little girl is running towards the screen and I'm eating my breakfast and I call out to her – let me show you how I call out to her – watch me. (*Demonstrates.*) 'Come to Mummy come come come.' You see? I am actually standing here in my kitchen and I am calling out 'Come to Mummy'. For a second I even feel like she could push through the screen or I could reach through, only a second, an insanity – what an effect those sickening images can have on you.

– I don't think I've ever seen anything so sickening on my TV at breakfast.

– We've never seen such sickening things on our televisions.

– These are the most sickening things ever to be seen on television.

– How can you feel anything but totally and utterly sickened? Do you feel sickened?

– I do, I feel sickened and the children feel . . . I shouldn't let the children watch, the children really shouldn't . . . but none of us can move. Just . . . (*Pause.*) I cry as much as them and then Thomas comes in and we all sit on the bunk bed together, the whole family, and we all watch the kids' little tiny telly and we watch the thousands and thousands of casualties and I see a woman who looks like my mother, she looked so much like my mother, my mother who the cancer carried off so long ago, and this woman actually sends me a message through the television, she sends me a message through the television and she says – this is her message (*demonstrates*): 'I love you. I love you with all my heart, I am so proud of you, my child.' Very simple words, but words Mum never actually said – fair enough, it was eating her up, that illness – Mum never said them, but that illness was eating her up – but now that woman with her body blown apart by the bomb is sending me a message through the telly. So when she dies I cry actually, do you know more – I never cried when Mum died so – Now I cry like . . . I cry like this . . . Watch me crying for you . . . (*Demonstrates.*)

–   You have been bombed. I cannot function, I cannot live, I cannot work or eat or sleep.

–   I go to work. I try to sell and buy and deal and do everything I'm supposed to do – to analyse, to forecast, to initiate, but it's not working because I am so heavy with this grief.

–   This is me making love to my lover until I say: 'No please', and 'Please stop, please pull out of me. This feels so wrong. It feels so wrong to be making love at a time like this – like there is a dead person in the room. I cannot make love when there is so much grief.' He pulls out of me. I'm so lucky because he understands it, he feels it too. My lover feels the grief that I feel. He is such a good lover. I call him three-shot Thomas because . . . well, because. But now. Here we are. See us watching you. Watching the footage over and over. So little footage. Too few cameras for your pain. Over and over but not enough.

–   This is a little graveyard. The children have made this little graveyard in the front room for all of you, for your dead children, and now they spend the time there crying and holding each other. My children cry for you like this – (*Demonstrates.*) I do wonder sometimes, should I pushing them out – out into the sunlight and say, 'Play, be children, for God's sake play', but I can't because we're all feeling, we're all feeling – Thomas says – (Show them please.)

Thomas   I'm selling the company. I might . . . Really thinking about it. Because what's the . . . what's the point of a media production facility after this?

– And I really can see what he means. (Thank you, Thomas.)

– You have been bombed.

– You have been bombed and nothing will ever be the same again.

– You have been bombed and what is the point of anything in our lives? I want to drive to the sea, drive to the beach and just . . . feel.

– Here is your photo that I cut out of the newspaper. There were so many photos of dead people. But you were the one who spoke to me. I don't know why just some . . . Here is your photo and here are the flowers I cut from the . . . Garden flowers for you, and I bring them into the kitchen and then I come in and now I cry and cry and cry and cry and cry until I lie on the floor in the kitchen and now I will, I let out great screams of grief. Watch me as I do this. Watch me as I do this for you. Please see my grief. See it. Watch. Watch. See. (*Acts out this grief.*)

– This is the letter I've written to you. May I . . . ? My letter. 'I'm sorry you had to die. It is so wrong. It is so cruel. I saw you at breakfast on my television. I'm sure other people love you. I hope . . .' (*Long pause.*) I'm sorry I'm . . . (*Long pause.*) 'I hope you have friends and family who love you and who are grieving but I just want you to know that I, a stranger who is not a stranger, loves you with all my heart and my life from now on is dedicated to my grief for you.' I have written my letter and I didn't know what to do with it and now I'm putting it in this envelope just marked – see? – 'TO THE DEAD' and – somebody take it from me please. Take it. Carry this across the waters to the dead.

–   Everyone, please – come here – form a group, that's it, and send a message to our sister city. Is that everyone? Yes? Can we . . . look to the – that's it – and . . . together.

–   YOUR SUFFERING IS OUR SUFFERING. WE NEVER FORGET.

–   And . . . press 'send'.

–   And now here we are. Here we all are. The city. Gathered in the square.

A giant image played on a loop of the other city exploding.

A voice repeats over and over: 'Why are you bombing us?'

Black ribbons are distributed.

Some come forward and lay black flowers before the image.

Everything is videoed.

–   I'm so sorry. I don't know you. But will you hold me and share my grief?

–   Of course I'll hold you. Of course I'll share your grief.

–   Thank you. This feels right, doesn't it? Isn't it right when there's so much pain that we all come together like this and hold each other and share each other's pain?

–   May I cry?

–   Of course of course – let it out – let go – drive it out of you – drive the sadness out for all of us to see. Here – everyone, see – look now – all of you look at this one woman – as I drive the sadness out of her – come grief – come pain – come howl – come – YES!

A huge cry of grief.

–   That's it. Again?

–   Later.

–   Anyone else?

–   For the moment I'm hollow. Please – I need to sit.

–   Oh yes oh yes oh yes this is the right thing to do. Can we all join hands please? Everyone join hands? The whole city? Queer banker trucker mum junkie immigrant second-generation lonely celebrity wheelchair bohemian? Join hands – now. Together.

–   That's it. The right thing to do.

–   Yes. The right thing to do. Oh yes. Look at our city. Look at our city coming together now. All coming together. All of you. No . . . there is no selfishness here. No 'I' right here. So much time we waste on 'I' but here it's all 'we' and how noble that makes us now.

–   No more words. We go beyond words. Only music can express our grief.

Everyone's hands are now joined. Music is listened to. Maybe a montage of images.

–   YOU HAVE BEEN BOMBED. WE ARE SICKENED. WE ARE GRIEVING. WE FEEL PAIN. YOU ARE FAR AWAY FROM US. BUT OUR HEART IS YOUR HEART. YOUR PAIN IS OUR PAIN. YOUR WORLD HAS CHANGED FOREVER. WE LOVE YOU. WE WILL ALWAYS LOVE YOU BECAUSE WE ARE AS ONE WITH YOU FOR EVER.

–   Goodnight. Sleep well. Our city has done the right thing tonight. Sleep, the rest of those who have done the right thing.

–   Tonight I think I will sleep for the first time since you were bombed. I am so much – how can I . . . ? . . . Yes . . . lighter. I'm lighter.

–   Home now. Look at us. Over here. Back home. Shhh. The children are asleep. I took down their graveyard in the living room – see . . . all gone? They didn't object – and now Thomas and I will finally make love on the carpet. This will be the spot. Right . . . here, I think. And it will be the best we have had for many years. He will come inside me. I'll allow it. I love him.

– Now I will tidy up the flat. I'm going to take down your picture. Can I do that? Yes. (*Does so.*) There. Should I have done that? Yes. Now seems the time. It somehow – I don't want to cling. I will always remember you but I won't cling.

– Oh. I . . . Can't see my mother's face. Ever since she died I've seen her face, but now I . . . don't know, somehow she's not there any more. Please . . . let's . . . Show me the book of photos of my mother. (*A book of photos is produced.*) Thank you. Of course. Thank you. Here she is. Here she is on the bench in the garden with the fag in her hand. That's her face. Of course. But (*closes the book*) gone again. (*Closes eyes.*) No. Can't see her. It won't stay. Goodbye, Ma. (*Long pause.*) Bye.

– Coffee. Good morning. Here is your coffee.

– A new day. A new day and it's breakfast here, I have this – look – lovely strong coffee. I'm sitting in a really buzzy spot. Look at me. All of you – *regardez moi*. Attention. It's all buzz right here. I have a buzz job amongst the buzz people and on the way to my bzzz bzzz bzzz office I pop in for a buzzy coffee. Bzzzzzz. And there's the TV – over there – it's on – and you're on the TV and you say to me, this is what you say:

– 'Why did they bomb us? We are the good people. That's what I just can't understand, why would you bomb the – us – the good guys? We are good. We – hey – we shop. We bring up our families. We keep order in our society. Our elected representatives make wise decisions. We have core values: freedom and democracy. The world yearns for our core values. And as quickly as geopolitics allows we are bringing the world our core values – freedom and democracy.'

– And I'm dropping my little gang at the crèche and the TV is playing amongst the struggling hordes of the teeny terrors and suddenly you are on the TV and you speak to me and you say to me, this is what you . . .

–   'My good brother was driving a good bus that morning. A good man doing a good job. But now he is dead. He died on the street in front of our good TV cameras. From my own kitchen, surrounded by my own good family, I watched my own good brother die. My grief runs very deep.'

–   On, I'm looking after my lover in hospital and the TV is on so loud. I move to turn off the TV but suddenly you say straight out to me:

–   'You wanna know who did this? You wanna know who did the bombs? I'll tell you. I'll tell you. The evil ones did this. They looked at us and they saw our goodness and it was a threat to their utter evil. And so they had to do this. They had to bomb us with their evil. Believe me, my friend, evil is strong but if the good ones come together we can fight the evil ones and we will win.'

–   And I move away from my lover in his hospital bed and I move up so close to the television – like this I move – and you look at me from the television and you say:

–   'Evil or good? Right or wrong? The righteous or the wrong? The choice is yours. But the fight is beginning and you must choose. Choose, my friend, choose. God or the Devil. Here it is – good . . . or evil. The battle is beginning. Choose. Decide. With whom will you fight? Choose. Now.'

Pause.

–   Choose.

–   And I'm not quite sure why, but I – Oh, but I wanna –

–   Really? So do I. I –

–   Me too. Breakfast time and I –

–   We, we we, we . . .

All laugh.

  –   Stop that.

  –   Stop. That is not . . .

Hysterical laughter.

Appropriate.

All the **Chorus** *are now laughing hysterically.*

  –   I'm sorry, I'm sorry, I'm sorry but you are so fucking, so . . . (*Laughs.*)

  –   You are so . . . stupid. (*Laughs.*)

  –   You are so . . . vulgar. (*Laughs.*)

  –   You are so . . . naive. (*Laughs.*)

  –   You are so old-fashioned. (*Laughs.*)

  –   You are so crude. (*Laughs.*)

  –   You are fat, ugly, thick, unsophisticated, idiot, idiot. (*Laughs.*)

  –   Freedom democracy good evil God Devil oh my God. (*Laughs.*) Oh my fucking God. (*Laughs.*) What kind of fucking stupid fucking children are you, you – (*Laughs.*)

  –   Ridiculous ridiculous ridiculous. Ridiculous.

  –   Good. Evil. You fucking stupid . . . Phantoms. I piss on you. Piss on you.

  –   FUCKING IDIOTS!

Silence.

  –   Sorry. Please. We're – so . . . Please go now.

Silence.

  –   Oh. How I hate myself. I really . . . totally . . . You were bombed only a few days ago. I am laughing at you. What a wrong person I am. What a monster. Why did I laugh? I'm so sorry. So bad. What I'll do now is . . . I will fold everything.

Everything in the drawers, the cupboards. Fold them up
really really neatly. The socks, the pillowcases, the . . . I'm
folding till the laughter stops. Folding like so. (*Demonstrates.*)
There . . . calm now, Why? Why did I laugh ? Well . . . quite
frankly it's your own fault – you made me laugh at you –
when you – you have – Why did you say such stupid . . . ?
Please don't ever ever *ever* do the battle of good and evil shit
ever ever again, okay? Okay?

–   I want to – please – I want to feel that feeling I had
before. That sad feeling. The one I had for you. So please –
could you – thank you, run again the images of the bomb?
Hello – are you listening? I want the images again. Thank you.

The images are rerun.

Isn't that sickening? They are sickening. That's it. Rerun and
rerun and rerun and rerun and you see – look at me – I'm
going to get that feeling back. Look at me getting that feeling
back. It's coming. It's – are my eyes moist? Anyone? Can you
see tears? (*Pause.*) It's got to come. Please. I want it to come.
I want to cry like I cried before. Just to grieve for you. Where
are the children? Someone call the children. Call to the
children to come and watch the reruns so that we can all cry
like we did before. Build the graveyard again. (*Calls.*) Kids!
Kids! Thomas! Kids! Come here and . . . It's the images, kids.

Silence.

Thomas – where are the . . . ?

I remember now. The children and Thomas are playing
swingball, there's a barbecue – they don't want to – and I
watch and I . . . I'm . . . empty. Sorry . . . can't feel what I felt
for you before. I really want to but I . . . Well, quite frankly
it's your fault. When I see you on that TV spouting that,
that – yes, sorry – shit. You have stopped me feeling what I
felt for you before. I feel – well – nothing. Nothing. Alright –
turn off the images. Off now.

–   Ma on the bench in the garden with the fag in her hand.
What a silly old woman she was. Puff puff puff fag fag fag.

Cheap little bits of wisdom. 'Look after the pennies' . . . 'Do as you would be done by.' God, how I hate that stupid old bitch. The cancer came before I could tell her, but I hate her. How I wish I could have told her face to face: I hate you, Mother. You did nothing for me. Nothing but blight my life. Where are you, witch? Show yourself, Ma. Show yourself. So I can tell you. HATE. Come out. No? (*Pause.*) No.

–   Oh. These are terrible, terrible feelings. I want to . . . I say to my lover: 'Just hold me. Let's just be calm and hold each other and love each other', because I have to feel that here in the middle of the world is some sort of sanity, just a . . . stillness, just a simple love and now – oh thank God – here is my lover . . . my lover. (*Embrace.*) Oh yes, yes, yes, yes, yes, we're okay. Everything's okay. Thank you. Shhhhhhhhhhh.

–   And I want to sleep but you're on my TV, and you're standing in a field of wheat, there's wheat as far as the eye can see and there's just a pickup truck and you and you're saying to me this:

–   'I am an angel. I shine in the pure light of the Lord's radiance. My wing has been torn in the bomb attacks. But I will fight back. It is always the duty of the good ones to fight the evil ones. There must be a war. Let the war begin.'

–   Yes, I suppose we will have to make war on the attackers. These terrible people who can just blow apart a civilisation will have to be attacked. Which I suppose is right. I suppose we'll have to do that. Oh well, I suppose we'll do that. We'll do it. Let's go to war. Okay. War – okay – yes – war war war agreed?

A reluctant, bored show of hands.

Okay. War.

–   On the TV now. The war's begun. Twenty-four/seven coverage. The kids watch it. I'm busy.

–   'You idiot, you fucking idiot. Angel. Broken wing. What kind of, what sort of shit is this? All the years I thought we had the same language but now you're speaking and you're speaking, you're speaking such, such, such, such . . . shit. Angel. Freedom. Democracy. You are − ignorant blind stupid bully and I hate you now − and I − Thank God you were bombed so that I could see how much, the truth will . . . how much I hate you.' (*Pause.*) . . . Oh. I'm scared of myself, that a person, a people, a person, that me, that I, that I could feel, that we all feel − Isn't that awful? Does anyone else feel: thank God you were bombed? (*Long pause.*) Anyone? Anyone at all?

One by one the **Chorus** *all come forward and show their assent with a 'Thank God you were bombed.'*

−   We all feel . . .

−   We all feel such terrible − to you who have been bombed we feel these terrible − sorry sorry sorry sorry − terrible feelings thoughts feelings, but really − honestly that is how we feel.

−   Kids? Kids. Sleepy time. Time to sleep. Sleep.

Sound of bombing.

−   You have been bombed. It's happened again. I see it again.

−   It's on the TV now. Listen. That's the children calling, 'Come on, Mummy, come come come.' They want me to see the bombing. I'll go to take a look in a moment. Just got to take these. Calcium magnesium iron. I've got the blend of fruits just right in this today.

−   You are being bombed. I am busy. I have a meeting with our viral marketing boys at ten. I hear the news but − excuse me − I have to move the car out of the garage.

−   I really want my stomach to feel tight. I really want it to feel like it has not the slightest bit of give in it. This an advanced mat work class. She really pushes you here. I really want to be pushed here. I really want my stomach to a level that it's never been pushed. This really is a great crunch.

Sound of another bomb.

–   You are being bombed again and again. It's everywhere. Everywhere you go. Everywhere on every media outlet we see that you are being bombed again. Again again again again. You are being bombed.

–   You are being bombed. I wake up. You are being bombed. I shower. I exfoliate. I prepare the fruit. You are being bombed. I juice. I turn on the television and you have been bombed again. The worst so far they tell me.

–   You run towards me. In your arms you hold your dead child. Your child is dead in your arms and most of her head has been blown away and you hold your child out to me like so as if to say, 'Oh help me oh help me help me.'

–   And I say – I don't say this in anger. I am calm. But please listen as I say :'You had this coming. Can't you see – you had this coming?

'You with your stupid bullying you had to . . .

'Somebody had to strike back somebody had to . . . '

–   You hold your dead child towards me and I say now: 'I am . . . oh . . . pleased this has happened to you.'

–   I hate you and I am pleased that this has happened to you.

–   That is the most awful, that is the most terrible, that is . . . no . . .

–   I am pleased.

–   Oh my God, oh my God. There is nothing now. We are no longer human. We are . . . we look at this and we . . . please . . . There is nothing of the human being of me now. Or you. No humans left.

Enter **Man** *drenched in blood.*

Man   I am dead by rights. But if you just reach inside. (*Holds up knife.*) Cut through my chest. Cut. Please. Find my

heart. Squeeze. Release. Squeeze. Release. Squeeze. Release.
My heart. If you reach into me I might live for just –

–   I can't.

Man   I'm a hero. You're a coward.

–   A hero. Yes you are. I'm an average, you're a – But
now . . . dead hero. I'm alive.

The **Man** *lies dead.*

–   I never turn on the news now. I never read the newspaper.
There's a war going on. But somehow . . . it's best if I don't
know about it. It does such terrible things. It disturbs my
calm. And I treasure that. My calm. Look at me being calm.
I don't want to hate you. I've worked on that and now I don't
think about you. It was a rather lovely day today I thought.
And I think . . . Yes. I think we could have a rather lovely day
tomorrow. Tomorrow. Lovely.

Play Eleven

Armageddon

Emma, Honor.

Emma   And He watches me.

Honor   And He watches me.

Emma   He watches me as I sit on the bed.

Honor   He watches as I count the numbers on the doors.

Emma   He watches as I look at the minutes on the clock.

Honor   He watches me as I check the buttons on my jacket.

Emma   He watches me as I pull my skirt below my knee.

Honor   He sees the sweat on the back of my neck.

Emma   He sees the redness in my face below the paint.

Honor   And I search inside myself: Should I go back?

Emma   Inside I'm asking: If I'm not here, if I run now to the parking lot and go home –

Honor   Finding a place inside myself where He's not watching.

Emma   There's no place inside yourself where He's not watching.

Honor   But there is no place inside yourself where He is not watching.

Emma   He sees that I am frightened but I can't go back.

Honor   He sees my fear but also . . . He watches as I reach out.

Emma   He watches as I take a taste of liquor from the tiny bottle in the tiny fridge.

Honor   He watches as I knock on the door.

Emma   He watches as I hear the knock on the door.

Honor   He knows the feelings I have for the woman behind the door.

Emma   He knows what I feel for the boy in the corridor.

Honor   And in time He will make my feelings known to me.

Emma   He knows but He doesn't tell me what I feel – that is still a mystery to me.

Honor   Love and hate, lust, disgust, violence, tenderness.

Emma   And in time He will reveal them to us.

Honor   In time I believe He will reveal them to us.

Emma   I must answer the door.

Honor   Why so long answering the door?

Emma   Give me your strength to answer the door.

Honor   Maybe He has led me to the wrong door.

Emma   He sees the trembling in my hands as I reach towards the door.

Honor   Hello? Hello?

Emma   Yes yes, I'm here.

Honor   Her voice is tight.

Emma   He wants to bully me with that voice. The door opens.

Honor   She is older than I remembered. Something to do with the light.

Emma   He looks like a boy there in the light. Maybe He is a boy.

Honor   And He knows that I am thinking of my mother who lived her life for alcohol and cigarettes and men who beat her.

Emma   And He knows that I feel old and He knows that I am suddenly ashamed that maybe there is the smell of liquor on my breath – the tiniest sip from the tiny bottle from the tiny fridge – but still . . . the smell of liquor on my breath.

Honor   And my mother died and she was never saved and I look at her and I ask: 'Can I save you?'

Emma   And I look at this boy and I think: Are you one of the chosen ones? Shall our shining faces see the glory on the day his light shines on the earth and he calls the chosen ones to join him?

Honor   And I say: 'Can I come in?'

Emma   And I say: 'Of course, yes.' And I think I see a camera turn and catch you come into the room.

Honor   From the ceiling in the corridor the camera turns and watches as I step into the room. He is in that camera as he is in all things.

Emma   I want to kiss you. I want to kiss you. I want to kiss you. He sees that and He sees how much I want to kiss you.

Honor   He has seen the dreams I have of you. Your body.

Emma   And He is watching my mouth, the lipstick bleeding into the lines around my lips, the tang of liquor still on my tongue.

Honor   In my dreams you were so much younger.

Emma   I am old and my mouth is ruined and I say, 'Excuse me.'

Honor   And I say, 'Sure.'

Emma   And I step into that tiny bathroom and I rip the cellophane from the tiny toothbrush and I squeeze the tiny toothpaste tube.

Honor   And I sit on the bed and I – hah – I sit on the remote control.

Emma   I jump. I jump at the noise.

Honor   A bomb blast. A bomb tearing through the fabric of that building.

Emma   The noise of the bomb is overwhelming.

Honor   And I call through to the bathroom, 'Sorry sorry.' I call through: 'Sorry.'

Emma   But I can't hear and I call out, 'What? What? What? What?'

Honor   And I find the volume and I turn down the volume of the news of the bomb blast.

Emma   My gums are bleeding from the bristles.

Honor   And I say: 'There's been another blast. In the war. The news is coming in. More of our boys are killed.'

Emma   And He hears my fear, as every day He hears my fear, as every day my fear . . . as every day I watch the TV, more bombs, more of our boys killed, more of our boys fighting in his name.

Honor   And I flip the channels till I find a choir and they are singing of your goodness and I sit and I watch them sing of your goodness.

Emma   My mouth is blood and liquor and toothpaste.

Honor   I want to cry and shout and sing with the beauty of your goodness like I always do. Oh praise you, praise you, praise you.

Emma   My boy is in the war.

Honor   I watch you. He watches you. We watch you step from the bathroom.

Emma   My boy is in the war.

Honor   Yeah?

Emma   'My boy is a fighter for freedom and truth and democracy.' He is speaking through me now.

Honor   Well – hallelujah.

Emma   Hallelujah.

Honor   There's nothing finer than to fight for freedom and truth and democracy.

Emma   It is his fight.

Honor   It is his fight.

Emma   Can I ask you . . . ? Can we pray? Can we pray that my boy is safe? Can we pray that my boy escaped this bomb and that he can continue the fight for freedom and truth and democracy?

Honor   And I say: 'I'd like that.'

Emma   And I say: 'Thank you. It's just a thing I do every time . . .'

Honor   It's what he'd expect.

Emma   It's what he'd expect.

Honor   And I take the Bible from the table beside the bed.

Emma   You look so beautiful lifting the Bible from the table beside the bed.

Honor   And He watches us as we kneel down and He hears us.

Emma   He hears us as we pray for my boy.

Both   O Lord, you have chosen our land to be the land of freedom and democracy. We thank you for that. O Lord, you have cursed our enemy with tyranny and poverty and our enemy has grown envious of our blessed good fortune. And our enemy has attacked our blessed country. And now we bring them freedom and democracy as we bring freedom and democracy throughout this world. Oh, ours is a heavy burden but we carry it with pride. For it is your will. We are the free ones. We are the chosen ones. We glory in thy light and long to join you in thy heavenly kingdom. Hallelujah. Hallelujah. Hallelujah.

Honor   You've been drinking liquor?

Emma   You see the bottle as He saw the bottle.

Honor   This is your liquor?

Emma   There was temptation . . . a little fridge. It was a test. I failed.

Honor   Oh, sister.

Emma   It was the smallest drop. I was frightened. I failed. Will you forgive me?

Honor   It's not for me to forgive.

Emma   I'll wash it away.

Honor   My mother was taken away by liquor. When things got slow at the canning factory, she took to drinking. By the time things were faster at the factory she was too deep in drink to ever work again.

Emma   I don't want to touch any more.

Honor   She would bring men back. She had sexual relations with them. They took many drugs. I was a boy. I was so frightened. I'm going to go now.

Emma   No no no. See. And I pour the liquor down the sink and I call out begone begone begone.

Honor   He saw my fear. And He called to me. He spoke to me as my mother never did.

Emma   He called me later. My body is sullied. It has known many men. I have spent years filling my life with alcohol and drugs and empty relationships. My boy left. We haven't spoken in three years. He said, 'You are no longer next of kin.' I was in the gutter but finally he called to me.

Honor   Does He want us here tonight?

Emma   I don't know. I have asked Him so many times.

Honor   But He doesn't answer.

Emma   He doesn't answer.

Honor   I watch you. At your booth. Taking the calls. Counting through the day.

Emma   I've watched you. Peered over my booth.

Honor   And at service, I see you arrive. I see your hunger for the word.

Emma   I see you. The ministry. There are so many families. And you seem so alone.

Honor   Thank you for agreeing to be here.

Emma   I don't know that I should.

Honor   I don't know. When there's no guidance . . .

Emma   I'm sorry that I'm so old.

Honor   You don't seem old to me.

Emma   You can be honest.

Honor   You seem old to me . . . but still I desire you.

Emma   Oh.

Honor   Yes, I have a great desire for you.

Emma   Surely that must be wrong?

Honor   I suppose it must.

Emma   It's my boy. O Lord. O Lord. It's my boy's face on the TV screen. And I kneel before the TV screen and I hear them tell me: 'Your boy has been killed. Your brave strong beautiful boy who was bringing freedom and democracy to a land where there was no freedom and democracy has been blown away. He gave no next of kin, saying he is all the father and mother that I need.' He is dead. He is dead. My boy is dead.

Honor   I'm so sorry.

Emma   That I should learn like this in this tiny motel room with a huge TV and liquor and blood and toothpaste in my mouth and a boy who I have batted and swayed at when we work at the call centre. This boy I have arranged to meet to do something we dare not name. This is not the way I want this to be.

Honor   I'll die in a just cause. For each of us there is a just cause at the right time.

Emma   There should be tears now. Bring me tears.

Honor   This makes me even more resolved in my cause.

Emma   I want liquor. I want drugs. I want gratification. If only they would fill me up now.

Honor   He is watching you. He is tending you.

Emma   I have been hollowed.

Honor   He forbids you alcohol or drugs or sexual gratification.

Emma   MY BOY IS DEAD! AGGGGGHHHHH! MY BOY IS DEAD!

Honor   Our nation is proud.

Emma   MY BOY!

Honor   A hero. He is with the King. He is at his right hand.

Emma   I WAS HIS MOTHER. I was his terrible terrible mother.

Honor   But more than that he was our nation's, he was our president's, he was our God's.

Emma   Tears. Tears. Tears.

Honor   And now there are tears and she falls to the floor this old woman and for hours she fills the room with her sobs and the TV fills the room and sells us beer and health insurance. And I pray a silent prayer.

Silence.

Emma   Thank you for your prayers.

Honor   Thank you for allowing me to be here. He spoke to me.

Emma   Yes?

Honor   He told me that it is right that I'm here.

Emma   Good.

Honor   This is a moment of huge trial for you.

Emma   And for the world. The good against the evil.

Honor   We'll win through. He is with us. Of course.

Emma   I'm going to lie on the bed. I'm very tired. I'm going to lie and . . .

Honor   Would you like me to read to you? I know a passage I'd like to share with you.

Emma   Yes. No. I'd like you to lie beside me.

Honor   And I lie beside you.

Emma   He sees the boy lying beside the old woman.

Honor   He sees the young man lying beside the old woman. And He knows what is in my heart.

Emma   And the boy's arm moves over the old woman.

Honor   Moves over the old woman.

Emma   And I am comforted. And the game show becomes a comedy show on the TV and the room is filled with laughter.

Honor   We are chosen to join Him in Heaven where we will live for all eternity.

Emma   We are chosen to join Him in Heaven where we will live for all eternity.

Honor   Why do you work at the call centre?

Emma   For the health insurance. I have diabetes. You?

Honor   Health care also. I have a history of depression.

Emma   I'm sorry to hear that.

Honor   So we're both little angels with broken wings?

Emma   How like my son he is.

Honor   And now I move my hand up her body and I slip my hand inside her shirt and I stroke her breast. Do you mind that I do that?

Emma   He sees that hand moving over my breast.

Honor   Do you mind that I do that?

Emma   I don't think it can be altogether the right thing to do.

Honor   I don't think . . . And my mind is filled with images of her body bending and twisting, laying herself open to me, swallowing me, offering . . . and I try to push those pictures so far down, down where He can't see. But He sees that. And I try to burn up her body, burn it away with flame, consume it until it no longer exists but always her body comes back to me.

Emma   How easy it would be to give myself to him now. How easy and how wrong.

Honor   Just to take both our bodies and push them together.

Emma   We are both such weak people.

Honor   If I had a bomb now I would blast us both apart rather than allow any sexual gratification to take place. It's what He'd want.

Emma   The vomit rises in me. The death. The liquor. His touch. I go to the toilet bowl.

Honor   Late-night TV. The images are so unseemly. I find a preacher and a choir.

Emma   My stomach emptied. I rub toothpaste over my teeth and gums.

Honor   Will you look at this ministry? This guy is good.

Emma   How much longer?

Honor   Eh?

Emma   How much longer before the final days when He fills this world with light and He takes up the good to be by His side?

Honor   In our lifetimes.

Emma   You're young. I'm old.

Honor   Very soon. Only a few more years. Do you hate this earth?

Emma   It's His creation. It's beautiful. But still . . .

Honor   It's not the shining glory.

Emma   It's not the shining glory. See my boy.

Honor   My mother was never saved.

Emma   I'm sorry.

Honor   She was a sinner. If you deny salvation . . .

Emma   Will you stay here tonight?

Honor   I can't. There's too much temptation here.

Emma   I understand.

Honor   Your body is full of . . . I wish it were more covered.

Emma   I wish everything in this world were taken away so that there was no temptation.

Honor   As long as we stay strong.

Emma   We'll get there. I want to be with Him so much.

Honor   Me too.

Emma   And the boy goes away and I stroke my breast just once before I lay down on bed and I sleep with the TV on so that a late-night movie becomes my dreams.

Honor   You have tested me.

Emma   You have tested me.

Honor   And I have denied temptation.

Emma   I was not tempted.

Honor   And every day we bring freedom and democracy to this world.

Emma   And the Kingdom of Heaven is oh so very close.

Play Twelve

The Mother

Haley, Male Soldier, Female Soldier.

Haley   You got up early. I don't normally get up this early. This is very early for me.

Female Soldier   Mrs Morrison –

Haley   Really – I'm a lazy cunt, I suppose. Yeah. Real fuckin' lazy. But you know.

Female Soldier   Mrs Morrison –

Haley   They call it clinical depression. But I don't know. Clinical depression? If that makes them feel better.

Male Soldier   Mrs Morrison –

Haley   Bone fucking idle, that's what I'd call it. Bone fucking idle.

Male Soldier   Mrs Morrison –

Haley   That's what I am. Bone fucking bone fucking idle.

Male Soldier   Mrs Morrison –

Haley   I'm a bone fucking bone idle bitch and I need some cunt come along give me a kick up the fucking arse and say, 'Get out the fucking place and look for a fucking job cos there's job's out there for those who can be fucking arsed to look.' That's what I need.

Female Soldier   Mrs Morrison –

Haley   I'm a cunt. There's hard workers and there's lazy cunts. And I'm a cunt.

Female Soldier   Mrs Morrison –

Haley   Does bad language bother you? I thought you being army . . . The army everything's cunt the other, right? I mean when Darren come back he was all . . . Does it bother you? Cunt cunt cunt cunt cunt cunt cunt cunt cunt.

Male Soldier   Mrs Morrison –

Haley   Cig? Go on. I won't tell.

Male Soldier   I give up.

Haley   Good boy. Your mum must be proud of you. Me too.

She lights herself a cigarette. Offers **Female Soldier**.

Haley   Yeah? It's better than a landmine, darling.

Female Soldier *takes cigarette.* **Haley** *lights it.*

Haley   That's it. Few minutes less on this planet, isn't it? Gotta be a plus.

Male Soldier   Mrs Morrison –

Haley   Will you fuck off? We're enjoying a moment of cancer here.

Male Soldier   Mrs Morrison –

Haley   Bet you got a tiny dick. You ever seen his dick? I bet his dick's tiny.

Male Soldier   Mrs Morrison –

Haley   Bet you wouldn't even feel him slip in, would you?

Male Soldier   Mrs Morrison –

Haley   Oh, sorry, are you two together like – ? (*Mimes sex.*) Sorry.

Male Soldier   Mrs Morrison –

Haley   Do you want breakfast? I might have some bread rolls. I don't eat much. The pills they put me on, they, you know . . .

Female Soldier   Mrs Morrison –

Haley   You could do with skipping a few breakfasts, you fat bitch.

Female Soldier   Mrs Morrison –

Haley   You can kick me if you want. Insulting the army. That must be worth a kicking. Come on. Who's first? What is it? He gets me down but then you do the real damage, eh? Is that it? Bet that's it? That's got to be it. Men got a bigger punch but they fight with rules. But women – there's no fucking rules, isn't that right? No fucking rules. I've not had a scrap for a few years now but the girls, they were always the biggest cunts. Come on. You kick me till I'm down and then she can do the real damage. Tear a tit off. Come on, the pair of you. I deserve it. That's what I deserve. Come on. No? Fucking pussy.

Female Soldier   Mrs Morrison –

Haley   I'll get you a roll. Do you want anything in your roll? Bacon? Sausage?

Female Soldier   Mrs Morrison –

Haley   Sausage, bacon, egg?

Female Soldier   Mrs Morrison –

Haley   What's it to be? What you gonna have in your breakfast roll?

Male Soldier   Mrs Morrison –

Haley   I'll do a bit of everything and you can choose later. You watch the breakfast telly while I – there, who wants to push the buttons? – you find the breakfast telly, while I –

Male Soldier   No.

Haley   I'll only be a few minutes.

Male Soldier   No.

Haley   It's no bother. Really. I've got a microwave.

Male Soldier   No.

Haley   No? This is my house, this is my house, I worked thirty years so don't you fucking tell me don't you fucking tell me. You're not occupying my fucking house, alright, so don't you fucking tell me –

Female Soldier   Mrs Morrison –

Haley   Out there you can march into any cunt's house and torture the fuck out of the towelhead cunt but you're not there now, you're here, and while you're here I got rights and this is my house so don't you tell me.

Female Soldier   Mrs Morrison –

Haley   How old are you? How old?

Female Soldier   It doesn't . . . Twenty.

Haley   You?

Male Soldier   Thirty..

Haley (*indicates herself*)   Forty-three. Fucking old. They shouldn't give you this job. Pair of kids.

Male Soldier   Mrs Morrison –

Haley   You don't have to . . . job done. Go and buy yourself a coffee on the high street. You don't need to . . . We can just pretend you did it. I won't tell.

Male Soldier   Mrs Morrison –

Haley   What is it now? Starbucks? Go on – off you go.

Female Soldier   Mrs Morrison –

Haley   You spend half an hour in there, you watch the world go by, you talk about what you saw on telly last night and you go back and you say 'job done'.

Female Soldier   Mrs Morrison –

Haley   But do me a favour, yeah? Don't say I took it well. I never took anything well. Say she took it fucking badly. No, don't say that – say she, she . . . that's it! . . . processed it, say she got it out of her system, she cried and we talked about all the brilliant times she had with Darren. Say: she got out photos from school and holidays, she took us up to his room – which she was looking after lovely – and yes of course there was lots of tears, of course there was, but still she listened and she acknowledged. There was no denial. They hate that, if you're in denial. So – no fucking denial. She didn't take it too bad or too good otherwise they'll up the pills and they're already making me feel like a mong and I don't want that. Say: she took it about right. Can you do that?

Female Soldier   Mrs Morrison –

Haley (*to* **Male Soldier**)   I'm sure you can do that.

Female Soldier   Mrs Morrison –

Haley (*to* **Male Soldier**)   But I'm not so sure about her. She looks a bit fucking thick to me. Am I right – a bit fucking thick?

Male Soldier   Mrs Morrison –

Haley (*to* **Female Soldier**)   That what they call you, 'thick bitch'? bet they do. Thick bitch. Thick bitch. Thick bitch.

Male Soldier   Mrs Morrison –

Haley   No, really, thank you. I'm alright. You've been . . . I'll get myself a roll and egg and I'll watch the breakfast telly.

Male Soldier   Mrs Morrison –

Haley   Are you sitting on my telly thing?

Male Soldier   Mrs Morrison –

Haley   Which of you is sitting on my telly thing?

Male Soldier   Mrs Morrison –

Haley   Don't fucking mess me about. Come in here ruining my day. I do breakfast roll and telly, then go up, get a bit of dinner and my ticket – rollover week, so . . . then home for dinner, a sleep, my quizzes. I like my day so don't you don't . . .

Female Soldier   Mrs Morrison –

Haley   Which of you's got my pointer? One of you's got my pointer? Yeah? Yeah? Come on. Cos when I find out who it is I'm gonna stick your fuckin' teeth so far down your fuckin' throat. Come on, you cunts. Come on, you cunts. I'll have you. I'll fucking have you. Who's first? Or together, yeah? I'll take you both on together.

Female Soldier   Mrs Morrison –

Haley   Alright, you bitch, I warned you –

She goes to hit **Female Soldier** *but is restrained by* **Male Soldier**.

Male Soldier   Mrs Morrison –

Haley   You ain't gonna have tasted fist like this before, thick bitch.

Male Soldier   Mrs Morrison –

Haley   Think you're hard but I'm hard as fuckin' – ow!

Male Soldier *has pulled her arm up behind her back.*

Haley   You're hurting.

Male Soldier   I'm restraining.

Haley   It's hurting, darling. Don't hurt me. Don't. Doctor told me: take it easy. Take it easy, he told me, and he give me the pills.

Female Soldier   Mrs Morrison –

Haley   He's strong, isn't he? I like a strong man. I've always gone for a strong man. My husband was a strong man. Weak heart but a strong man. You're hurting me.

Female Soldier   Mrs Morrison –

Haley   Tell him to stop hurting me. I got rights.

Female Soldier   Mrs Morrison –

Haley   I got rights. I know what you do. I know you lead them around on chains and shit on them. But that's not here. Here we don't do that.

Female Soldier   Mrs Morrison –

Haley   We're human beings here. Are you human beings? No, I don't think you are. I don't think you fucking are.

Female Soldier   Mrs Morrison –

Haley   ANIMALS.

She breaks free and leaps around acting as a monkey.

Oo-oo-oo-oo-oo-oo-oo-oo.

Male Soldier   Mrs Morrison –

Haley *gets down on her hands and knees. She barks over and over.*

Male Soldier   Mrs Morrison –

Haley *howls at the moon.*

Male Soldier   Mrs Morrison –

Haley *bares her teeth and growls at him.*

Male Soldier *gets down and looks her in the face.*

Male Soldier   Mrs Morrison, it is my sad duty to inform you that your son Darren Morrison was –

Haley   No!

She bites his nose. He leaps back.

Male Soldier   Fuck. You bitch, you fucking fucking bitch.

He goes to kick **Haley**. **Female Soldier** *pulls him back.*

Female Soldier   Hey no no NO!

Male Soldier   Fucking mad.

Haley *growls.*

Male Soldier   You're fucking mad.

Haley *growls.*

Male Soldier   See you? You're the worst I've ever seen.
'It was for his country. It was what he would've have wanted.
I wished his nan had lived to see the funeral.' That's what
you're supposed to . . . not . . . I wouldn't put you on pills.
I'd send you down the funny farm.

Female Soldier   Alright.

Haley *yaps.*

Male Soldier   Down the funny farm and chop inside yer
head till you could act normal. You wanna act normal you do.

Female Soldier   You're bleeding.

Male Soldier   Course I'm fucking – (*To* **Haley**.) If you're
infected I'll have you.

Female Soldier   Here.

She gives him a cloth to mop the blood.

Male Soldier   Ooooowww.

Female Soldier   Mrs Morrison, it's our sad duty to inform
you that your son Darren Morrison –

Haley   It's just the words, I don't want you to say the
words.

Female Soldier   I have to.

Haley   Why?

Female Soldier   It's a requirement.

Haley   Big on rules.

Male Soldier (*still bleeding*)   Fuck.

Haley   Sorry, I just . . .

Male Soldier   . . .

Haley   No, I mean it, I do, sorry, not your fault, you got a job to do. I know that. I used to have a job to do. Canning. It was shit but you know . . . We all stunk of ham, we did. You'd be after a shag but that ham'd be right in your skin and the blokes'd be, 'You're a can tart.' Some of 'em didn't mind. Some were picky. But still, you'd always manage to pull something if you waited till chucking-out time, know what I mean. (*To* **Male Soldier**.) Kiss it better?

Male Soldier   Fuck off.

Haley   Come on, I'm a mother, I know how to –

Male Soldier   Oh fuck.

Haley   Let me have a look. That's it, that's it. Oh you poor wounded boy you. What they been doing to you? (*To* **Female Soldier**.) Water.

Female Soldier   We really don't have –

Haley   Bowl of water, TCP, plaster. NOW.

Female Soldier *exits.*

Haley   Look what they done to you. Look what they done to my beautiful boy.

Male Soldier   Mrs Morrison –

Haley   Did they hurt your beautiful face?

Male Soldier   Mrs Morrison –

Haley   Shhh now shhh now shhh. They're jealous of you cos you're so lovely. That's what. Jealous and they hate you. They hate us. Cos we got good lives. We lead good lives. This is a good house, innit? You got a good room. I kept your

posters up. Everything about our good way of life they hate so
they bomb and they shoot and they −

Enter **Female Soldier** *with bowl of water, cloth, TCP, cotton-wool
buds, plaster, towel − all on a tray.*

Haley That's it. We're going to get you better. We are
going to get you totally better. Yeah?

She washes his wound with the cloth and water.

All coming off. All going. Bit of a sting.

Applies TCP.

Brave boy.

Plaster on. **Female Soldier** *out with tray of stuff.*

Haley No more fighting, eh? Yeah? Promise me? You did
your bit and that was good but no more fighting now, eh?
Just stay home for a bit. There's a new quiz on the telly.
You'll like it. You stay home and watch that with me. Or go
out and have a bit of a piss-up with your mates and then
bring us back a curry, we can share that, yeah? Good old
breakfast when you're feeling shit cos of all the drink. You'll
love that. I'll love it. Welcome home.

Female Soldier *comes back in.*

Male Soldier Mrs Morrison, it is my sad duty to inform
you that your son Darren has been killed in action. Darren
was a well-respected and well-liked member of his regiment
who died as he lived fighting bravely for a noble cause. His
CO sends you his most heartfelt condolences at this time of
grief. Darren's belongings will be forwarded to you shortly.
His coffin will bear the regimental flag if you so choose. Our
country, our Queen, freedom and democracy will always be
indebted to Darren for this sacrifice he has made.

Haley   . . . Were those the words?

Male Soldier Yes.

Haley   Not so bad as I thought. You said them lovely. No, really. Really. Really. Really. Lovely.

Male Soldier   Thank you.

Haley   Well – you get practice. How many you do?

Female Soldier   There's further counselling.

Haley   In a day like? What's the record?

Female Soldier   In the home. At a centre. Or groups.

Haley   I'm not a joiner.

Female Soldier   A visitor?

Haley   I don't like people in the house. It throws the day. Who else you seeing today? Let him do the speech, he does it really . . . you do.

Female Soldier   You gonna be alright?

Haley   Course I am. You got kids?

Female Soldier   No.

Haley   Well. In time. You're young.

Female Soldier   I don't want 'em.

Haley   Want? Want don't come in to it. One day and your body's gonna need.

Female Soldier   Oh no.

Male Soldier   We gotta get on.

Haley   Every woman's a mother.

Female Soldier   No.

Haley   Mother. Blessing and a curse. Blessing and a curse. But you're gonna need –

Female Soldier   No, I ain't ever gonna, I'm never gonna. I seen too much to – never bringing a kid into this.

Male Soldier   Come on.

Haley   Course you will.

Female Soldier   No. The world ends with me. No kid. I'm breaking the cycle. It's too much.

Haley   Then what you fighting for?

Female Soldier   I suppose . . . nothing.

Haley   Have a kid, darling. Go on. Find a fella. Doesn't have to be around long. Have a kid. Inside you. Then out you: Mum, Mum.

Female Soldier   No.

Haley   I'll look after you. Babysit. Childminder. I'll support, I'll –

Female Soldier   No no nothing ever no fuck off witch witch –

Male Soldier   Hey hey –

Female Soldier   I ain't mother. Never gonna be mother. Don't wanna – just fight for my country and that's –

Haley   Mummy!

Female Soldier   FUCK OFF.

Male Soldier   Hey.

Haley   Right. Pointer. You put it down and then . . . I spend half my bloody time looking for that pointer. Really, I could go over to the fucking telly, but I get it fixed in me head, right, 'I had the pointer and now I got to find the pointer', which is stupid, isn't it? But then that's me, isn't it? Fucking thick. You going out there again?

Female Soldier   Yeah.

Haley   Good luck. You're a smashing girl. What you got? Boyfriend? Girlfriend?

Female Soldier   If there's anything else we can do . . .

Haley   Ha!

She has found the television remote control.

It's always here. Sometimes right in front of your eyes – you gotta be patient. Right – fuck off the pair of you.

Female Soldier   We can make you breakfast.

Haley   Oh no. No thank you.

Female Soldier   It's not a problem.

Haley   I'm not a breakfast person. Cig'll do me.

Female Soldier   Maybe eating –

Haley   I – don't – want – to – eat.

Female Soldier   Right.

Haley *turns on breakfast television.*

Haley   This one is my favourite cos he's always on the lash the night before, then he's doing his presenting but he fucks up. I like it when they do the fuck-ups. That's my favourite bit. One day he did so many fuck-ups they threatened him with the sack. It was in the paper. But they knew he was popular so they kept him on. He's alright, isn't he? I mean, I would if he was asking. I definitely would. She's a bit of a cow though. She's always in the magazines saying how much she loves her husband but apparently she always fucking around. She loves black cock, apparently. I mean, I can see the appeal but still. She's two-faced. When they do bits on the war I flick to something else cos I don't wanna know but they don't do the war much cos it's all the same really, isn't it. Once one kid's been blown up then what's there to say? It's all just body bags and that's just boring really. They're doing ideas for doing up rooms this week and I like the little poof does that. Think I'll do up my room. Haven't done anything with that in years. Purple's nice and a bit of a furry rug and there's mirrors with beads round which is good. Oh – he's on 8.45 – that's good, I haven't missed him. Oh yes – I like the little poof. He makes me laugh. You gotta laugh.

The **Male Soldier** *and* **Female Soldier** *leave.* **Haley** *carries on watching the TV. For a long time she is emotionless as the TV chatters on but finally emotion comes.*

Play Thirteen

Twilight of the Gods

Susan *and* **Jane** *on either side of a desk.* **Jane** *has a breakfast roll and coffee.*

Susan   Do I get a breakfast?

Jane   You do.

Susan   I heard if I came here I'd get a breakfast.

Jane   You do, Susan, yes, you get a breakfast.

Susan   Do I get my breakfast now?

Jane   No, Susan, you get your breakfast at the end. There will be medical supervision while you eat your breakfast.

Susan   I'm very hungry.

Jane   Alright.

Susan   We've got no food in our zone.

Jane   I see.

Susan   There's nothing . . . We – we get no food, it's really –

Jane   I'm sorry.

Susan   So I think you should put that in your report.

Jane   If you like.

Susan   Yes I do yes I do yes – you write it down, you write it down and you put it in your report – my zone has no food.

Jane   Thank you, Susan, I will.

Susan   Do it now.

Jane   I'm sorry?

Susan   Let me see you do it now. Write it down. There is no food in my zone.

Jane   Alright alright, if that's what you want I'll . . . (*Writes.*)
Food supplies unsatisfactory in –

Susan   No no no, there is no food. There's nothing. There's
starvation. There's –

Jane   Susan feels there's no food in Zone Eight.

Susan   I know that. I don't – I know.

Jane   It's gone in.

Susan   You've got to let them know what's happening in –

Jane   I've noted the food situation, okay? The food situation
has been noted.

Susan   Malnutrition. Starvation. Gastro . . . We're being
taken away. Death in the –

Jane   Susan, I have noted, I have noted, I have noted the
food situation. Can we move on from the food situation?

Susan   If you like.

Jane   I do. How was the bus – ?

Susan   Can I have some of your roll?

Jane   My? Oh –

Susan   Sorry – just I haven't . . . It's been weeks since . . .

Jane   Of course. Yes. You –

Susan   I don't want to beg. I don't want to be a beggar like
this. I used to be an important person. I taught in the
university. I was respected by my students. I wasn't this
pathetic – I'm not this pathetic – But I'm just so –

She goes to grab the roll but **Jane** *moves it away.*

Jane   Susan – I'd rather you didn't actually, I'd rather you
left that roll alone. Now I've brought you here because I want
you to help me. I'm writing a report and I want your help.

Susan   I don't like being thin. I don't like having these bones sticking out of me.

Jane   Susan.

Susan   But you – what do they bring into your side? Is it all special provisions for your side? Is that it?

Jane   No, it's just –

Susan   Look at you, you're fat, you're enormous, you huge great – and still and still you've got wobbling – and you sit there with breakfast you –

Jane   We are trying to get food to the zones.

Susan   To the victor the spoils, to the vanquished fucking fucking malnutrition, yes yes yes?

Jane   Susan, Susan – we want to bring you food, there is food, we are trying to bring food through – There is a world out there that cares and wants you to have food – it's important. Do you really believe the world is so bad?

Susan   No.

Jane   Good, no, the world is – only the insurgents stop us getting the food through, do you see? We try but we're attacked and we – It is not us. We are doing our best. But when there are destructive forces in your own people then –

Susan *grabs the roll and bites.*

Jane   Give me that. Give me that. Give me.

She grabs the remainder of the roll and returns it to the desk.

Susan *chokes.*

Jane   You see? You see? That's what happens. That's what happens. You see. If you just, just –

Susan *chokes.*

Jane   Here. Sip a bit of this.

Susan *grabs the coffee.*

Jane   Very, very carefully. Just a little sip otherwise it makes it worse. That's it, Susan. You're doing really well. You're doing well. I'm so proud of you. It's very important you – slowly, okay? You chew very very slowly.

Susan *chews slowly.*

Jane   We've had reports. People without food for too long, they suddenly get food and the food, the food, the food actually kills them, so could you just . . .

Susan   Okay.

Jane   We've got a report to write and we don't want you dying, do we? Eh? Eh? No, we don't.

Susan   No – we don't.

Jane   See . . . this report here. Man went off to the desert for six months. He got caught by the insurgents, freed himself. He made his way back to the city and found his wife living in a hole in the ground. She was a little shrunken creature. She hadn't eaten for months. And he was overwhelmed to see this woman – they'd both been civil servants – reduced to this . . . husk. So he went out and he bribed a soldier. Gave the soldier the last bit of money he had and he got this lovely red apple and he rushed back to his wife and he handed her the apple. And of course she fell upon it – it was food, but it killed her. Her body was so unused . . . It's all in here. Loved her. Gave her an apple. Hanged himself from a tree. See? All in the report. So you see – when I deny you things, when I say no, it's not because I'm some bitch who – I'm just trying to – do you see? We are learning, Susan. Mistakes have been made but we're learning from them.

Susan   Can I have some more coffee?

Jane   I'm not sure. I really don't know what the medical situation is with coffee.

Susan We get water but actually all you taste is the sterilising tablets.

Jane I'm sorry. I'll note that.

Susan I really dream about coffee. I used to have coffee in the mornings. I'd leave the house early and drive across town to the university but I'd stop on the way for coffee and a breakfast roll. I miss that.

Jane I'm not sure. Caffeine is such a powerful drug.

Susan Tyranny was bad. I wrote articles. I protested. I did what I could. But every morning I had coffee and a breakfast roll.

Jane Susan – I'd really rather you didn't have coffee without proper supervision.

Susan If you think that's best.

Jane I do, yes. I think that's best.

Susan That's your privilege, isn't it?

Jane I'm just trying to be kind.

Susan That's your privilege. You occupy. You decide who gets the coffee and when they get it.

Jane This really isn't some big political –

Susan You say – pull the thin bitch in to help me write the report and the soldiers pull the thin bitch in.

Jane I hope they were friendly. They did make clear this was voluntary?

Susan Well – here I am and now you can do what you want with me because the power is all yours.

Jane I really want to work with you.

Susan I really want some more coffee.

Jane I just want to do what's best.

Susan   Let me have some coffee.

Jane   That's why I came here – because I want the best for your country.

Susan   I won't drink the whole cup.

Jane   I saw how it was before on the television – the abuse of human rights and now the war, and I just wanted to be here to do the right thing.

Susan   Let me try a few sips – see if it's alright. It's not bread. It's not an apple.

Jane   Well . . .

Susan   We'll be very careful.

Jane   Well, alright.

Susan *takes a few sips of the coffee.*

Susan   Very good. Good coffee.

Jane   I think that's enough.

Susan   Very . . . Reminds me of civilisation, of having a civilisation, of normal things, of happy times.

Jane   Except it wasn't really . . . it wasn't such a civilisation . . .

Susan   No.

Jane   There was no democracy. No freedom. No human rights. There was massive infringement –

Susan   I know, but still . . .

Jane   You're in transition, Susan, you're a society in transition.

Susan   I miss the coffee.

Jane   Everything's going to get so much better.

Susan   Do you think so?

Jane   Twenty years' time you'll be leading the world –
social and economic and freedom.

Susan   Can I have some more coffee?

Jane   I'd rather you didn't.

Susan   I see.

Jane   Just until we can be sure the caffeine – there's no ill
effects?

Susan   No.

Jane   Well, that's good. Good. Well, if you'll help me with
the report, you're going to get a supervised breakfast
afterwards. A specially prepared purée, eaten under medical
supervision. So that we don't risk killing you. We have learnt.
We've progressed. How to move people on to food –

Susan   This isn't me, you know – this bony bitch grabbing
at food.

Jane   I'm sure it isn't.

Susan   I was always big. I loved food. I loved to cook. I'd
cook all weekend and then I'd have friends over from the
university and we'd feast on a huge fish and lots of dishes and
talk –

Jane   This was under the old regime?

Susan   You'd be careful what you talked about, but food –
you could eat till your stomach swelled. I loved that.

Jane   It'll happen again. Once everything's settled down.

Susan   But now – one bite of bread and I'm choking.

Jane   I know I'm privileged, Susan, I know that I – I've
been very lucky all my life.

Susan   I'm not judging you.

Jane   Alright.

Susan   You're being very good to me. I appreciate it. You're doing a good job.

Jane   Thank you.

Susan   I expect you miss your home.

Jane   Let's get on with the report.

Susan   Everyone would rather be in their own country, wouldn't they?

Jane   Sooner we do this, the sooner you get your breakfast.

Susan   Who have you got at home? Husband? Little boy?

Jane   I'm going to push on with the report. How was your bus journey?

Susan   I expect you're a very good mother.

Jane   Susan – let's move on with the report.

Susan   If you like.

Jane   How was your bus journey?

Susan   Why are we doing this?

Jane   Susan.

Susan   What is the point of the questions?

Jane   The point – the point –

Susan   Yes, yes.

Jane   Susan, I can still withhold your breakfast if I find you uncooperative.

Susan   I'm sorry, I'm sorry, I don't want to – no – I need to eat – but please, I'm an intelligent – I was once an intelligent woman. I have the kind of mind that asks questions. I don't want it to, sometimes I wish . . . I fought my father to go to the university. Sometimes I wish I was more . . . pliant. But I always – why? Why? Why? You see? I'm sorry. But if I can just understand what the report . . .

Jane Alright alright. It's because . . . I suppose . . . I
suppose it's because we've intervened, we've intervened in,
we were impelled to intervene in, because of the terrible
things that were happening in your country – human rights,
et cetera – we felt impelled to intervene and now we – me – I
and my colleagues – we want to find out how you think we're
doing, okay? Since we've intervened, since the dictator's
statue toppled, how do you feel things are going? We want to
listen. Listen and get a picture. Alright?

Susan You're a mother, aren't you?

Jane I'm . . . look . . . I'm a foreign power. I'm bringing
order. I'm bringing freedom and democracy, I . . .

Susan My little boy's seven. He's called Dan. Before the
invasion he used to play on a bicycle with stabilisers on the
street with his friends. I've been living in the cellar with him
for the last six months. Sometimes we enjoy ourselves. I make
up stories. He makes up stories. The Little Devil. That's a
character we made up. The Little Devil who – His friend with
the broken wing –

Jane How was your bus journey today? Any suspected
bombs or bombers or other alarming incidents?

Susan No.

Jane Good, good. And how were the checkpoint guards?

Susan How do you mean?

Jane Were they helpful slash polite slash efficient?

Susan One of them squeezed my bottom, which was –

Jane I'm sorry. I'll note that. Sexual harassment.

Susan He was a boy. I shouted at him. We understood
each other.

Jane It's important that we keep a record of sexual
harassment cases. But otherwise – ?

Susan   Otherwise fine.

Jane   Did you find your bus journey satisfactory?

Susan   Yes.

She grabs the rest of the bread roll and starts gulping it down.

Jane   Susan, no Susan no Susan, stop that.

Susan (*mouth full*)   You have no idea, the hunger. The total, when you feel so hungry you –

Jane   Susan, stop that now. You must. That man. Apple. Hanging from a tree. Susan.

Susan (*mouth full*)   Food. Food. Food.

Jane   You fucking – I will not kill someone – I did not – you grabbed that food – I came here – freedom – choice – democracy – human rights – our core values.

Susan (*mouth full*)   Food. Food. Food.

Jane   This is not why I came here. A better world. You grabbing grabbing – Oh Susan, what have you done.

Susan *begins to choke.*

Jane   Susan – I gave you every warning. I – I want to kick you now, you know that? Kick your stupid – I brought you freedom, you bitch –

Susan *collapses on the floor, choking and fighting for breath. This continues during:*

Jane   I brought you your freedom. We fought our way through the desert to bring you our core values and now you can't even, you can't even – you grab like you've never seen – oh fuck. What is the point? Shit. I look at the world. Look at it. It's such a terrible place. So much terrible oppression. Women in veils. Women with their clitoris cut off. Young men brainwashed. People branded with hot irons for speaking the truth. No elections. Rigged elections. I see all this. And what am I supposed to do? Stand by? I've got everything. I've got so much. I've got freedom, I've got democracy. I've got so many human rights. Am I supposed to just stand by when the world is in darkness? No. I have to intervene. I have to. So why does it get messy? Why does it always get so fucking messy?

She takes a waste bin from behind the desk.

Susan, I'm now going to induce vomiting, do you understand? I'll induce vomiting but please in here – okay? Let's keep this orderly, alright? Alright.

Jane *pushes her fingers down* **Susan**'s *throat.* **Susan** *vomits into the bin.*

Jane   That's it, Susan – all up, get it all up, you'll feel better for that.

Eventually, **Susan** *slumps back and* **Jane** *feeds her coffee, cradling her.*

Jane   That's it, Susan, yes yes. Here we go. Susan – keep your eyes open. Just keep your eyes open – focus on me, Susan, try to focus on me. Try to look at me. Try to look at me. Open your eyes, Susan. Open your eyes. Susan, listen to my voice. Listen to my voice. Listen. Susan, I don't have a partner, a husband, I don't have a child. Susan, I have the most appalling taste in men. Susan, I pick men who hang around for a few months, I pick useless men with useless jobs, with pretend jobs, men who I support and then move on, they graze and then they move on. Susan, I think about having a child but that moment's going now, Susan, that's a little window that's closing – listen to my voice, listen to my voice – so the window's closing and I probably won't have a child, but I know people with children so . . . My flat is so lovely, Susan, I'm really making my flat the most lovely place. I love magazines with really beautiful interiors in them and that's what my flat is like, like a magazine interior. and one day I think it will be in a magazine interior. I really think that one day. One day you'll get a new university so beautiful all chrome and glass and so much inward investment and you and your students will be able to speak freely just like our students speak freely. Susan, that's really going to be fabulous. I'm very optimistic, Susan, because everything is working out – the plans are in place, the infrastructure, the investment, the – freedom and democracy, freedom and democracy.

Susan's *eyes close.*

Jane   Open your eyes, Susan, open your eyes. Susan, Susan – open your eyes.

Play Fourteen

Paradise Lost

Liz, Maria.

Liz I couldn't sleep. It's been several nights now and I . . .
my sleep is rather special to me . . . I think it is, isn't it? . . .
I think sleep is really rather special . . . such a healing thing . . .
I totally believe in eight hours . . . I'm a great believer in . . .
and so I've really been rather disturbed . . . you see . . . I
thought for several nights it was a fox, an urban fox . . . then
I thought, yes, an urban fox in some sort of pain, always at
the same time, the same pain the same time seems . . . I
thought: really I ought to be out in the garden looking for the
fox but really . . . really I wouldn't know what to do for a fox,
so I tried to block out the fox . . . I have earplugs, sleeping
pills and a CD of the waves which often . . . But then after a
week or so I thought maybe it's cats. I've never had cats so . . .
I mean I don't know much about the sound of cats but . . .
I think the female cat does make a terrible . . . Isn't it strange
how in the natural world the female of the species makes a
sound of great pain when she is being made love to? . . . I've
always thought that was very strange . . . you would have
thought . . . So I thought leave it, leave it, leave it, leave it,
leave it . . . it's a lady cat and she's having the time of her life.
Lives. (*Laughs.*) Lives . . . but I suppose actually, you know . . .
I have a great problem being honest with myself. I never tell
myself the truth . . . which is why I suppose nothing's ever
worked out on the relationship . . . I have terrible troubles
with self-deception . . . but a couple of nights ago . . . the
scream, the scream comes, and I said to myself if you're
honest . . . if you're honest with yourself . . . just be honest
with yourself . . . you know where that scream's coming from,
you've always known where that scream's coming from. That
scream is coming from the flat downstairs. That terrible

scream in the middle of the night is coming from the flat downstairs. Is it you screaming? Is it?

Maria   . . .

Liz   I haven't been down before because I didn't want to invade your privacy . . . privacy is so important, I know . . . and . . . but you are keeping me awake . . . I'm Liz by the way . . . I know we've never actually . . . You always look very busy so I never want to . . . anyway, I'm Liz. I'm Liz. I'm Liz. And I know you're Maria because I've seen it on the letters in the hallway. Sorry. I'm not a snoop. But you can't help noticing. You notice the names when you're looking for your post, so I know you're Maria. Is it you, Maria, screaming in the night? Is it? Because I've never noticed any other . . . and it's certainly a female scream and it's certainly happening down here so I think . . . I think . . . I think it is you, Maria, screaming out in the night. If it's not, tell me now and I'll . . . Listen, Maria, I don't want to invade your privacy any longer, I've invaded your privacy for long enough so I'll . . .

She makes to go, comes back.

I work for an airline, Maria. I work very unusual shifts. I whizz all over the globe at very strange times of the day. So my sleep is terribly important. It's terribly important. The airline are very strict about – us girls have to look a certain way and if I've been up all night because you've been screaming then . . . do you see? Do you see? Could you just give it a rest because my sleep patterns are disturbed enough without . . . ? Is it a fella? I'm not a prude . . . I do know what goes on . . . I mean, if you're into that side of things then fine, fine . . . You hit him, let him hit you . . . we're all consenting adults . . . Who knows, maybe I'd go there with the right fella . . . but at two in the morning . . . two in the morning when I have to be in the airport at six . . . great screams at two in the morning . . . that's not on . . . This is such a terrible conversion . . . they charge you, you pay over the odds, such a terrible conversion . . . I'm sure you can hear me take a piss in the night. I know you hear me take a piss in the night. I try to make my way around the flat as quietly as possible after eleven . . . eleven o'clock is my rule, so I'd be grateful if you . . . Yes, Maria, yes? Yes? Yes? Just you and whatever fellas or whatever you have in here, just as long as . . . Can you tell them that? You tell them that, Maria, yeah? Please, Maria, please.

Maria *sobs.*

Liz   Does he beat you, Maria? Is he abusive? Is that what it is? Are you in an abusive relationship? So many women are in abusive relationships. I've been lucky I've never . . . but so many men . . . so many men . . . they think they love women but actually, actually they hate women, don't they? I think to a certain extent almost all men hate women. I really do. Well, what you have to do, Maria, is tell him: no more, out, the door is barred. And if he won't listen then maybe you'll have to go into a refuge for a while, maybe that would be best . . . maybe if you looked online . . . there are places of refuge for battered women . . . Don't cry, Maria, don't cry, there are plenty of places of refuge for battered women. Is he here now, Maria? Is he here now? Is he?

Maria *sobs, shakes head.*

Liz   Then you stop all the tears, you get into bed, you stop crying and you get some sleep. In the morning you change the locks and if there's any more bother from him – into a shelter for battered women you go, you see? Yes. Now – goodnight, goodni – good morning. I have an incredibly early flight so good morning and let's both try to get some sl –

Maria (*grabs* **Liz**)   No.

Liz   Don't do that, Maria, that's a silly thing to do. No, Maria, no, I don't want you to do that. I don't like you doing that. Will you stop doing that, Maria? That's not a nice thing to do. Let go of me, Maria. Let go of me. Let go OF ME!

A struggle before she gets **Maria** *off.* **Maria** *sobs.*

Liz   I'm sorry, Maria, but I don't want to get involved in
your life. I just can't get involved. It's too much for me to
get involved in. I won't get involved. No. I have such a busy
life. Many, many, many countries I can't possibly . . . I just
can't . . . you have to take responsibility for yourself, Maria . . .
you have to take responsibility for your own life . . . Sooner or
later we all take responsibility for our own lives . . . that's it,
isn't it? You share a lovely building like this and you try to be
pleasant, you try not to disturb, you smile if you pass on the . . .
But at the end of the day you take responsibility for your
own life.

Maria *seems calmer.*

Liz   There we are. Good girl. That's better now. That's
much better now. I'm going now. I'm going to my bed. And
I . . . Please, I don't ever want any more screams in the night,
I don't ever want to be woken in the night, I don't ever want
to come down here again – You've got a lovely place but I
don't ever want to come down here again. Goodnight.

Maria *pulls up her sleeve.*

Liz   What's that, Maria? What's that?

Maria *comes closer.*

Liz   Is that a burn? Have you burnt yourself? That's a nasty
burn you've got there. Did he do that? I think you should go
into a refuge if he did that. Are you harming yourself, Maria,
is that it? Do you hate yourself, Maria? Is there a lot of self-
hatred? Are you applying a hot iron to your arm and
screaming in pain? I wish you wouldn't do that . . . I wish . . .
This is . . . you smell of . . . this place smells . . . I wondered . . .
But actually this place stinks of burning flesh. Oh dear,
Maria. Oh dear . . . oh. You bathe that, yes, you make sure
you bathe that before you go to bed. Bathe it and bandage.
Bathe and a bandage and try to get to sleep. Then you go to
the hospital in the morning. They'll sort you out. Everything
will get sorted out at the hospital.

She turns to go. **Maria** *tugs at her.*

Liz   Maria, no, please please please, I know something awful is going on here . . . I know that . . . I know . . . but I honestly, I honestly, I honestly . . . oh please, Maria, I honestly can't get involved.

Maria *falls to her knees.*

Liz   No, don't do that. That's terribly undignified. That's silly. That's just silly. That's not doing anybody any good. You're not doing anybody any good by . . . Come on, Maria, come on . . . Oh . . . listen, another time, maybe we can talk, maybe we can . . . but tonight, this morning . . . I'm just so tired, just this morning I'm just so tired and I . . .

Enter **Gary** *and* **Brian**.

Liz   What are you doing here?

Gary   Taking care of Maria.

Brian   That's right. We're taking care of Maria.

Liz   Who are you?

Gary   It doesn't matter.

Liz   I'd like to know.

Brian   He's right. It really doesn't matter. It really doesn't matter.

Gary   How's she doing? How are you doing, Maria?

Liz   I'd like to know who you are.

Brian   Just doing our job. That's all we're . . . doing our job.

Gary   Come on, Maria, up you come, you remember me, you remember me, don't you? Hello, Maria. You remember me. And you remember my partner.

Liz   What is your job? I'm sorry. I'd like to know what your job is.

Gary   Well, here we are, Maria, we're back. Both of us back.

Brian   We're both back to see you.

Gary   Did you expect to see that? Did you? Did you expect to see both of us back so soon?

Liz   I still don't understand . . .

Gary   It's alright, we can handle the situation. We'll handle the situation from now on. Where should you be now?

Liz   Well . . .

Brian   Where would you like to be?

Liz   Upstairs in my bed. In my bed in my flat. In my bed in my flat with a CD of the waves playing.

Gary   Then that's what you do, that's what you do, Liz. You go back to your flat upstairs and listen to a CD of the waves playing.

Liz   You know my name.

Brian   There's been post in the hallway, Liz. We haven't been snooping, but when there's been post in the hallway . . .

Liz   Of course . . . of course . . . I see . . . I see.

Gary   How are you doing there, Maria? How's your memory? How's your memory tonight? Your memory any better tonight?

Brian   Go on then, Liz. Go on. Bed. Waves. Go on. No need to get involved here – nothing for you to get involved in here.

Liz   Of course.

Gary   I think your memory is gonna be much better tonight, Maria.

Brian   You look tired, Liz.

Liz   Do I?

Brian   A bit . . . haggard. You get those waves on before you get too haggard.

Liz   Alright.

Brian   Goodnight, Liz.

Gary   Night.

Liz   Goodnight.

She starts to go.

Gary   Hello there, Maria. What are you going to tell us? What would you like to tell us tonight? Are you going to tell us anything tonight? Come on, Maria.

Brian   Come on.

Maria *screams.* **Brian** *covers her mouth.*

Gary   Maria, shhh shhh shhh.

Liz   Do you know anything about the burns?

Gary   I'm sorry?

Liz   There's a burn . . . a . . . branding . . . on the arm . . . just above the . . . see?

Gary   No.

Liz   Sorry?

Gary   I don't see that.

Liz   Yes, look it's here, it's here . . . here there's a . . . you see?

Gary   I'm sorry, no . . .

Liz   But you must see –

Gary   Liz, Liz, Liz . . . I learnt . . . I learnt . . . I learnt a long time ago . . . we are all disgusting, we're disgusting people . . . We're not even people, we're –

Liz   I think she's in pain.

Gary   We are each of us so horrible, so horrible . . . there's nothing . . . no animal, no devil . . . not the Devil himself . . . We are all so horrible.

Liz   I thought maybe you could take her to the hospital or something or something she –

Brian   She wants us to get involved. Won't get involved herself. But wants us to –

Gary   Listen, listen, listen, LISTEN, I'm speaking, I'm speaking. We're all so disgusting. There is nothing about us that is not . . . Hell. I'm disgusting. I disgust myself. The things I do are . . . the things I do are so disgusting. But we have to . . . I have a wife, I have children, there's a mortgage, we . . . you know, visit the garden centre, eat linguine . . . I'm a normal guy, you know, at the end of the day I pay my mortgage and I'm a normal guy so . . . I have to carry on. I have thought – hang yourself. Of course . . . at times . . . hang yourself from a tree . . . but when you go down and there's a perfectly ordinary wife and perfectly ordinary kids and you're . . . oooh . . . drinking coffee then . . . you have to carry on. Because that's what you do. That's what you do. You carry on. And if you're going to carry on you can't, you can't let it, can't let it . . . So this arm, this arm . . . No. I look at this arm and . . . no. I see no burn.

Liz   But surely you – she's –

Gary   No.

Liz   Somebody has branded her.

Gary   No no no no no no no no. There's nothing there. You don't see anything. There's nothing to see. Otherwise how are you going to . . . ? You have to live with yourself and that's hard enough to do without seeing . . .

Brian   Come on now, Liz, it's getting – Liz, come on, time you were in bed.

Liz   Maria – would you like me to stay? If you'd . . . if you really want me to I'll stay.

Brian   I don't think that will be –

Maria (*nods*)   Mmmm.

Liz   She wants me to stay. So if you don't mind, if you don't mind, I'm going to stay . . .

Gary   There'll be nothing to see, Liz. There's never anything to see.

Liz   I'm sure, but still . . .

Brian   We're just doing our job.

Gary   We're not bad men. We're not evil. We're no worse than . . . There's lots and lots of, so many men like us . . . Yes, we're disgusting, yes, the – Yes, I wish – The world isn't perfect, I wish the world was perfect. I'm disgusting. I feel guilty. I hate myself.

Brian   We have to do our job.

Maria *screams.*

Brian   No, don't, Maria, no don't, no –

He slaps her hard about the face.

Liz   No. No. No. I – please – I don't want you to do that.

Brian   That's a horrible noise, Maria. Maria – what a terrible noise.

Maria *screams.* **Brian** *punches her in the nose.*

Liz   No, that's – now that is – just you – stop now – stop, stop. She's bleeding, she's bleeding, she's bleeding. Come on, Maria. It's alright. I'm here, I'm here. Liz from upstairs. Liz. Look at me, Maria. You must have seen my post in the hallway. Liz from upstairs who works for the airline. Come on, Maria.

Gary   Look, I know this is upsetting, Liz. It's upsetting for all of us. So if you'd rather go upstairs –

Liz   No.

Brian   I think you better go upstairs, Liz. Go on, Liz.

Liz   No, I'm – Maria wants me – no!

Brian   Alright.

He starts to unpack a tool bag.

Liz   What's all that?

Brian   Tools of the job.

Liz   I see.

Gary   Just recognised . . . Not under ordinary circumstances . . . but under extraordinary circumstances . . . Under extraordinary circumstances . . . The tools of the job. If we lived in ordinary times then, lovely – lovely times – all Monteverdi and linguine – lovely – but we don't, we live in extraordinary –

Liz   The bombs.

Gary   Exactly, thank you thank you thank you, the bombs. They're bombing us. They hate us and they're bombing us and our freedom and our democracy so, so . . .

Brian   Extraordinary measures.

Gary   Extraordinary measures.

Brian *takes a hammer and breaks one of* **Maria***'s knees. She screams.*

Liz   No, don't, she's a person, she's a person, she's . . . No, don't do that . . . you musn't do that.

Gary   Have you lost anybody in the bombs, Liz?

Liz   Please, she –

Gary   Who have you lost?

Liz   The attack on the hospital. My friend was . . . Her boyfriend was in the hospital . . . sleeping by the bed . . . most nights by the bed . . . most nights . . . because she loved that man so, too, so much . . . and then the guy, the bomber, the kid, bomber kid, walks in one day, walks in one day, walks in and out they go, out they go, out they . . . The kid burns them all to Hell.

Gary We've all lost somebody. We're all hurting. Does Brian seem brutal to you?

Liz He . . . yes . . . very brutal.

Brian I know I am. I hate that. I'm sorry.

Gary He is. Brutal. I'm brutal. You're brutal.

Liz No.

Gary Liz, you're just as . . . We're all brutal and we're all hurting inside. Brutal and hurting, that's us.

Brian *swings the hammer at* **Maria***'s other knee. Screams.*

Liz Stop it please stop it please no that's enough now you've gone far enough now stop stop stop.

Gary Liz, do you know Maria, do you know anything about Maria, do you know who she is?

Liz I've . . . I've seen her post . . . I've smiled . . . we've never spoken but . . . I've . . . She's been here a year so you . . .

Gary Maria hates you, Liz. Maria hates everything about you. Everything about your way of life. Maria would like to bomb you. Maria is planning to bomb you. She's planning and she . . . she's been training and scheming and consulting and . . . The hospital guy, she knew the guy who took out your friend? That was Maria's son. And Maria loved that boy and she sent him away to a training camp and he learned how to blow himself up and take your friend with him.

Liz Ridiculous. No, you're . . . a fantasy.

Brian All true. Every word . . . She doesn't believe in justice and freedom and democracy, she . . . And now we want names from her.

Liz Rubbish. Rubbish. Rubbish.

Gary Ask her if you like. Go on. Ask Maria.

Liz   I will. Alright. Yes. I will. Is this true? Is this true what he's saying?

Maria   . . .

Liz   Maria? Please, you're a normal, you –

Maria   Fuck you. Fuck you and fuck your world.

Liz   Maria – don't. No.

Maria   Your smug arrogant world that shits on the rest. That takes everything from the world and shits it back on us. I hate everything about your world and I will burn it in flames if I can. I will take you with me, neighbour.

Liz   Have they done this to you? Has your mind – ?

Maria   I am sane. You are mad. I am good. You will be destroyed. Destruction is coming so soon.

Liz   You stupid fucking –

Brian (*gives her the hammer*)   Go on, Liz, have a bash. Have a bash.

Liz   I . . . I . . . Yes. (*Takes the hammer.*) Oh, that's heavy.

Gary   It's kinder. More humane. Cracks with a single blow.

Liz (*to* **Maria**)   My friend. Such a great woman. So loving, blown away, you tore her away.

Maria   We're all lovely, Liz, but she was part of your world. She was a part as you are a part and so she deserved to die.

Liz   FUCK YOU. FUCK YOU.

Gary   Bash her, Liz. Bash her. She'd do you if she had the chance.

Liz   Yes yes yes yes yes yes yes yes yes yes yes yes.

Liz *swings the hammer at* **Maria**'s *head.* **Maria** *screams.* **Maria** *stops the hammer in mid-air.*

Gary   Not gonna do it, Liz?

Liz   Thank you. But no. I don't want to get involved, thank you.

She hands the hammer back

I really don't want to get involved. I'm just not the sort of person who . . .

Brian   You go to bed, Liz. Put the waves on and get into bed.

Liz   I will – thank you. I will because sleep's so important, isn't it? Eight hours is so . . . so . . . yes . . .

Brian   Off you go. And we'll try to keep the noise down.

Liz   Would you? I'd be really grateful. Thank you.

Brian   Not long now. Not long now and she'll snap.

Liz   Alright. Alright. Alright. Goodnight.

Brian   Alright, Liz. Goodnight, goodnight.

Gary   Goodnight. Liz?

Liz   Yes?

Gary   We're doing a good job

Liz   Oh yes. I'm sure you are.

She goes.

Gary   Now then, Maria – where were we?

Play Fifteen

The Odyssey

A chorus of **Soldiers**.

—   We are leaving you now.

—   Our planes are waiting, the convoy is prepared and we are going.

—   Goodbye.

—   I don't think . . . I'm sorry but I don't think you've ever engaged with us as people. But we are. People. I know I am. I'm a person.

—   We are each and every one of us a person.

—   Maybe you don't have such a sense of that, maybe your society is more . . . maybe your society is different in some fundamental . . .

—   My little boy has grown up. He has a girlfriend. He messaged me. My little boy with a girlfriend. It's quite incredible.

—   My wife tells me she's been faithful all this time. Every night she messages me: 'I love you, I pray for you, I am faithful to you.' She tells me that so I suppose it must be true but . . . she works in a call centre. There's lots of kids. Young kids. Young boys who are there for a few months making a little money taking the calls. The sight of an older woman. The challenge. I hope they've been kind to her. I love her very much. We love each other very much. But temptation. She's very weak.

—   There's a garden bench I want to sit on. Very simple. Sit on the bench in the garden. So simple. But when there's been shelling and bombing . . .

–   Maybe you can't imagine this, but there is no shelling and bombing in our cities. Our cities are beautiful places. Beautiful shops. Leisure facilities. People who move about in freedom, every day making the democratic choices that shape their future.

–   Doesn't that seem incredible? I can hardly believe it myself. It's been so long, I can hardly believe it myself.

–   But it's true. It's true. It's true. I remember the . . . oh, the power and the thrill and the beauty of the . . . choice. We have so much choice. Who will provide my electricity? Who will deliver my groceries? Which cinema shall I go to? There is a choice at home. I long to be back.

–   You haven't known that yet but you will one day.

–   What will be ours in twenty-four hours will be yours in . . . there's no easy path . . . but Hope and Belief and Love will take you there as they surely must take everyone there.

–   You will get there. Everyone gets there.

–   Oh, the path is long but please believe, believe, believe.

–   Our pilots are testing their engines. They are in radio contact with air control. We will be leaving very soon.

–   The welcome that we will have back home. My wife will welcome me and we will make love as we haven't done since the first few happy months of our marriage.

–   My boy will call to me: 'Come and play on the Xbox, come and play on the Xbox!' And we'll sit together and play for days on end.

–   We will be heroes. We will be thanked and saluted. We will be rewarded. So few are prepared to dedicate themselves to the battle for freedom and democracy –

–   Freedom and democracy –

–   Freedom and democracy –

—   — as we have dedicated ourselves to the battle for freedom and democracy.

—   But our core values are everything because they are humanity's core values.

—   Do you see that now? Do you see it? Oh, please don't tell us our time has been wasted.

—   Surely our time hasn't been wasted? Only when I look at you . . .

—   When I look at you, you seem so beaten and so . . . You seem like a little husk. Like there's no person there at all.

—   Sometimes you look at me with dead eyes and I think I read, I, I, I . . . maybe . . . project, I project hate in your eyes. I used to see an analyst when I was . . . back home. I would drive across the city very early before the day had begun and I'd see a little Jew and he told me I had a tendency to project so maybe — do you hate me? Do you hate me? Please don't . . . it would very . . . hurtful if you hated me.

—   We've had tough times together, you and I. Let's be honest. You've bombed us. We've fought back. Tough times. There's been crossfire. The civilian casualties of war. It's been horrible. But that's all ending now.

—   It's all ending. We'll soon be on our way.

—   And you have to begin. You have to rebuild.

—   Of course there's a struggle — yes. There's nothing on a plate. But we journeyed before you. Several hundred years ago we discovered the path out of tyranny and hatred and darkness — we moved into the light and now you too can move into the light.

—   The fight was harder for us — there was no path to follow — but for you there's a path to follow — so follow, follow, follow — and all will be well.

–   There will be inward investment, there will be
international recognition, there will be the freedom and light
I know you crave.

–   Tomorrow my husband and I will barbecue a fish, we'll
play swingball, Martin and his kids will come round.
Tomorrow will be a normal day.

–   This has been a hell for us, this place. If you could see the
beauty of the place I come from and this . . . The tribal . . .
the anger, turmoil . . . This is something that will stay in my
head for a long time. I don't want to offend, but when I
dream about you they won't be good dreams. I will dream of
a mission to a city where I carried the torch of freedom but all
the people of the city wanted to do was burn me and blow me
apart and destroy the torch of freedom.

–   Not all the people. No. You are good people.

–   Of course – you are a good people.

–   But the evil people here . . .

–   You have been misled so many of you by evil people. We
have called out to you but too often evil has called out louder.

–   The convoys are ready, the air is clear. So close to
goodbye.

–   Goodbye.

–   Goodbye.

Waving, music.

–   This our last gift to you. Our final gift.

The **Dictator** *is brought in.*

–   We never thought we'd find him but with Hope and
Determination anything is possible.

–   The scum.

–   You scum.

–   The lowest scum of them all.

–   A statement.

Dictator   What a sorry man I am. You saw me for thirty
years as a big man, the biggest man, but I'm not. I was
greedy. I took your money and land. I grew so big. I saw you
as my children. I wanted to love you all. But I abused you. I
led you to a nightmare. I pray for punishment.

PUNISHMENT!

My wife and sons are dead. I shot them when the city was
invaded. I wanted to protect them. I said to them, 'This is the
act of a kind man', as I pulled the trigger. But of course it
wasn't kind. It was an act of cruelty, as all my acts have been
acts of cruelty. I pray for punishment. I was a coward. I
couldn't shoot myself. So I ran and hid in a hole in the
ground. Punishment, please.

PUNISHMENT!

But these last few months I've been in a hole in the ground.
I have had no food and now my stomach has grown so unused
to food that if I were to eat food it might kill me. I pray to the
great powers of freedom and democracy – punish me.

PUNISHMENT!

I'm a pathetic weak creature. My evil was great. I did not
believe in democracy. I did not believe in freedom. I did not
believe in choice. I did not believe in human rights. I did not
trade our oil. I did not develop our economy in the way it
should have been developed. Punish me as I should be
punished.

PUNISHMENT!

Shoot me or stab me or electrocute me and hang me or throw
me from a high place. There are so many ways. I know them
all. I have used them all. You must . . .

PUNISHMENT!

I will never see the future that you will see. In twenty years' time, you will be a fat people, shopping with joy, eating with joy, smiling at your elected representatives, smiling as your children debate freely at the university, trading with the world, a world of delights – of leisure activities and entertainments. Truly I do not deserve to see such a world.

PUNISHMENT!

I go to a hell now, the greatest hell where the darkest men in history tear at each like dogs for all eternity. Am I frightened? Yes, I am frightened. I am a weak, cruel man – of course I am frightened. But this is the right, this is right, this is the only thing to do.

PUNISHMENT!

The **Dictator** *kneels.*

– Goodbye.

He is kicked to death by the **Chorus***. Throughout –*

Dictator   Thank you. Thank you. Thank you.

He dies. The male members of the **Chorus** *urinate over the corpse. Once this is done, the female members apply make-up to his face.*

– Goodbye.

– Goodbye.

– Goodbye.

– How I long for civilisation.

– How I long for . . . ? Do you know what I long for? Breakfast. My coffee at breakfast.

– Oh yes.

– A really good cup of coffee. And a little pastry or – if I'm watching my figure – no little pastry. But always coffee.

– Oh yes. And to say to the man in the pastry shop, 'Lovely weather' or 'Planning a holiday?' or 'How are the kids?'

because that's what civilisation means. At the end of the day, that's what makes us civilised. Those little words as he sells me a pastry and I buy a pastry.

—   It is time to heal in my family. My little boy has been troubled. At first he was drawing pictures of people with no heads. Why? We couldn't tell. Then just one person. The soldier with no head. And then he told us the soldier with no head was coming into his room. He wet the bed. This is what war does to a child. My child. But now I'm going to play with him and there'll be theme parks and we'll go to the biggest toy warehouse and I'll say, 'Anything, anything you want', and we'll drive home and there will be food and love. It must be possible to get over this war. I believe it must. If I didn't believe in healing, well, I wouldn't . . . I have to believe in healing.

—   It was an empty relationship with my wife. I see that now. Oh, we talked all the time about the price of our house and booking for the theatre and, and, and politics and so on. But actually somehow very empty. That's all changing now. So much love from now – from now everything is love.

—   Ah, the plane is ready.

—   Finally we're going home.

—   We're seeing home.

—   At last. At last. At last. Home.

—   STOP! THE BATTLE IS NOT OVER YET. STOP! THE BATTLE STILL RAGES!

—   No.

—   STOP! ANOTHER COUNTRY. ANOTHER COUNTRY WHICH IS THE CRADLE OF HATE. ANOTHER COUNTRY WHICH WILL DESTROY THE CIVILISED WORLD.

—   No, please.

–   STOP! ANOTHER COUNTRY WHERE THERE IS
NO FREEDOM TO SPEAK, NO DEMOCRACY, A
PLACE OF TORTURE AND FEAR.

–   I want to go home please. I miss my wife so much please.

–   STOP! ANOTHER COUNTRY WHICH BREAKS
EVERY INTERNATIONAL AGREEMENT. ANOTHER
COUNTRY TO WHOM FAIR WARNING WAS GIVEN.

–   My son has a girlfriend. He's messaged me. Please, I must
see my son's girlfriend at least please.

–   THIS IS THE NEXT WAR. THIS IS THE NEXT
INVASION. YOU WILL NOT RETURN HOME. YOU
WILL INVADE. STAND BY TO INVADE.

–   Please, we are so tired, please we have to stop, please.
Look. We have lived these last few years with bombs and mines.
We lost track of who was an enemy and who was a friend. We
are so lonely. We miss our families. We miss . . . so stupid but
we miss all the tiny things about our lives, things . . . gardens,
coffee, friends, a DVD with a child. We can't go on without
these things.

–   Yes of course we believe in yes – all the core values –
freedom, democracy, yes – but we can't . . . ?

–   How long is this going on? How long?

–   The world's a strange place to us. A map frightens me.
A globe frightens me. I don't know these places. I only know
home. I want to be home.

–   How many places in the world? How many places where
they don't live as we live?

–   How many places where they don't have our core values?

–   Are there dozens of countries, scores of countries,
hundreds of countries that we have to invade?

–   We should know. We should be told. Please. Tell us. How many countries? How many invasions? How long will this war go on?

–   Tell us tell us tell us tell us.

–   Will this war go on and on and on and on and on and on and on? I'm too weary, too . . .

–   We are all too weary.

–   Of course our beliefs are unshaken, yes of course our core values, but still –

–   To sleep to sleep to sleep –

–   Just to let the world run its course – would it be so wrong to let the world run its course?

–   We have to sleep.

Enter a small **Boy**.

Boy   I am proud of my town. I am proud of my family. I am proud of my teachers. We live a happy life. I am happy. I am learning the core values – freedom and democracy. I think they are very good.

I write to a boy in another town far away. He writes to me. He says he is sad. His father said the wrong things. Now his father has been tortured. His brain has been damaged. He can't talk to his son. He sits and looks at the wall and sometimes he cries.

My friend says: 'Who will put an end to all this suffering?'

I say: 'We should put an end to all this suffering.'

Rise up, rise up, rise up, rise up – the battle is just beginning. We are the good people and we have to bring good to the world.

You are leaving this country. You are saying goodbye. It is scarred but it will heal. Now another country calls you and then another country and then another country and then another country.

The struggle is long. The struggle is hard. But that is the future. I am the future. I'm calling you. Wake up and hear the call.

−   Please tell my wife that I love her very much. I know our marriage was often hollow but somewhere in there was love and in time . . . we would have found love. But now . . . I can't face this burden. This burden is too great. It's not that I don't believe in our core values. Of course I believe in our core values. But I can't . . . I'll take my own life. I'll leave now to take my own life. (*Leaves.*)

−   I'm ready. I know the fight is long but it must be fought if there is to be good in this world. How I envy the comfortable world of coffee and pastry but sometimes freedom and democracy demand a greater sacrifice.

−   How I long for those innocent days, innocent happy days when I thought a few years of war, a few years of war to bring freedom and democracy to a world that was hungry for freedom and democracy. How naive I was. How stupid. I'll never see my boy again. I'll never see his girlfriend. Of course I won't. Because this battle goes on for ever. Take me there. I'm ready to fight again.

−   Our plane is ready. Our battle goes on. The world will have freedom and democracy.

−   Goodbye.

−   Goodbye.

Boy   That's right. That's good. It's the good thing to do. Goodbye.

Play Sixteen

Birth of a Nation

A team of **Artist-Facilitators**.

– Your city is in ruins.

– We're being honest about – we're not trying to hide that. Your city is . . .

– A civilisation. An old civilisation is shattered.

– Eggs have been broken.

– Exactly. Exactly. Eggs have been broken. When I got off the plane, when I looked around, when I saw, I thought to myself: eggs have been broken here.

– I was met at the airport. We drove past a pile of rubble. I asked my driver: 'What's that?' And he started to cry. He cried and he said that was the university. 'That was our university. I taught in that university. For years – my students came and I encouraged them to do their very best. And now that is just brick and dust and crater.' That man, that driver, he was broken, as that building was broken.

– Everywhere it's the same, the same everywhere – craters and dust and shattered brick.

– I've never seen anything like it. You follow at home. I keep abreast on the TV but when you see it –

– Devastating.

– Shattered city.

– Shattered city and a shattered people.

– So many dead people. So many people dead because the food supplies haven't reached them. So many people dead because the food supplies have reached them and they've fallen on the food and – months of hunger – their stomachs erupt and they die. They die and they litter the streets.

–   Have you ever seen a seen a city with every building shattered and the people shattered and the dead littering the streets?

–   I never have.

–   Nor I.

–   Nor I.

–   Nor I. And I hope, I hope, I hope, I hope to God, it's something I never see again. I'm looking out from my hotel window, I'm twisting the cap on a little tiny bottle of spirits (why am I drinking? why am I . . . ?) and I'm asking: Shit, did we do this, did we cause all this – did we bring about this – did we we we we we we we – did we wreak all this devastation?

–   And the answer is . . . Yes yes yes yes yes. Yes the West came here, yes the Western powers came here, yes the Western alliance came here, and yes our bombs, our shells, our landmines, our soldiers, our – yes. Yes. Yes.

–   Yes and no.

–   Yes and no?

–   Yes and no, because your insurgents, your interfactional, your tribes, your – maybe even if we hadn't, maybe if we –

–   This was a powder keg.

–   A powder keg, exactly. Exactly. Exactly. Exactly so – a powder keg.

–   A powder keg that we – oh, what a mess. What a mess. What a bloody fucking horrible mess.

–   What a terrible horrible fucking horrible mess these last few years have been.

–   Fucking horrible.

–   Fucking horrible. I marched against right from the –

–   We all marched against it –

–   We all – yes – we all marched against it – right from the beginning we marched against it, we marched against this war. We filled the streets, we called out to stop this bloody war but still our representatives –

–   Our so-called elected so-called representatives –

–   – still our so-called elected so-called democratically elected so-called representatives still they went ahead and pursued their horrible bloody little war.

–   Butchers.

–   Butchers.

–   Butchers.

–   And now look what they've done to your city, to your beautiful . . . once-beautiful city.

–   I've been looking you up, I looked you up and – wow! – what a culture you used to have, what a culture, what an amazing culture you used to have. Before we had a culture, before we . . . when we were sitting in mud huts in the rain, you were, you were – you had your own stories, beautiful huge really long epic stories, your alphabet, sculpting, dancing – you really – you had a culture here thousands of years ago.

–   Thousands of years ago you were here asking: What is life all about? What's it all about and how should the good life be lived? What is a good life? Why do we strive for meaning on this planet? You were asking all these wonderful questions in your beautiful alphabet while we were: grunt.

–   Grunt. Hunt buffalo.

–   Hunt. Skin buffalo.

–   Hunt. Eat buffalo.

–   Yes yes yes, you were so so so far ahead of us, but now . . .

–   But now . . .

–   But now . . .

–   What a horrible sight to see a world blown apart like this, but still –

–   But still –

–   But still –

–   The army's gone now, the army's withdrawing, the army's just . . . Only the peacekeeping force remaining so . . . Calm is returning.

–   Calm is here.

–   Here is calm. Here is . . . a time to rebuild, a time to heal, a time to . . . regroup, rebuild, heal . . . a new forward.

–   A time to move forward.

–   Move forward. Which is why, which is why, that's why we're here. Hello.

–   Hello.

–   Hello. Hi. Hi. Hi.

–   Hi. We're artists. We're a group of – that's what we all do – we're all artists.

–   I'm a painter. I paint.

–   I'm a writer. I write.

–   I'm a dancer. I dance.

–   And I . . . I do a sort of art performance installation sort of bonkers thing.

–   Oh yes, oh yes. And what we do is, what we do, we come to a place like this, a place like this where there's been the most terrible pain and horror and there's . . . We come to a place where everyone's been hurting and we start the healing process by working through, by working with art.

–   We'd like to work with you. Work with you. With art.

–   No, listen, okay, no listen, right, bear with us, okay? Just bear with us, alright? This works, alright? This works. This totally works. We know what we're doing.

–   We've just come from the most horrendous civil war, the most terrible . . . The country was divided in two, neighbour against neighbour, brother against sister, a husband turning on his own wife and stabbing her in the night – and we spent months there and eventually if you . . . people tell stories, people, they paint, they come together . . . they perform together . . . And eventually if you really work at it, if people really listen, if people then eventually . . . peace does return. Peace does come back. People aren't naturally animals. People don't naturally tear at each other like animals. People naturally rub along. If you allow them to, they rub along. And that's what we do, through art, we allow them to rub along.

–   I was a miner. I was born a miner. There'd been mines in my region for centuries. Every man in my family had gone down the mine for as long as anyone could remember. Every morning, you got up at six and you marched with all the other men and you reached the pithead and you put a helmet on and you collected your pick and you were lowered into the shaft and sixteen hours later you came home. And some men were – excuse me – cunts and beat their wives and got drunk and some men were sober and went to chapel and played in the band or sang in the choir on a Sunday. And that was life. For hundreds of years that was life. Then one day, we came through the town to find a sign: 'Pit closed'. Pit closed. Pit closed. Every pit in our region closed. Every pit in, every job practically in our region gone overnight. What a blow. You just . . . your world is gone. We did fight. Of course we fought. The union. But . . . the bosses, government, big business and big government – so much stronger than the people, so much stronger than a few thousand miners. But also stronger because I think – can I be honest, can I be totally honest here?

–   Please.

–   Please.

–   Please.

–   I think in our hearts we knew – I've never said this
before – we knew, yes, we were fighting for a community, a
way of life, the dignity of blah, yes – but we were fighting for
the right to be shut away in the dark, shut down in the pit and
have the coal on our lungs and the right to die an early death
and that was . . .

–   I marched alongside you then. I was only a student, but
we skipped our studies and we jumped in a car and we drove
down to your region and we marched alongside you: 'Keep
the mine open, keep the mine open.'

–   And thanks for that, I am grateful for that, but still you . . .
protesting for – the right for that terrible hacking death was . . .
in our gut, we knew that . . . we knew what a pointless fight
that was, but still when the pit closed, when the jobs finished.
So many people . . .

–   Suicide? Heroin? Depression?

–   Yes yes yes. Suicide heroin depression. You look at the
places, the places where there's everything, where there's jobs
and life and money and your world is – so quickly your world
becomes suicide heroin depression.

–   For me it was abuse. The terrible abuse I'd suffered as a
child. My father had . . . I couldn't see any way of moving
forward but . . .

–   All I could hope for was that the mine would open again.
How stupid was that? I mean, how fucking stupid was that?
That was fucking stupid. Wasn't it?

–   Was it?

–   Oh yes. That was totally fucking stupid. The mine wasn't
going to open, really I shouldn't even want it to open – in a
sane world – but still, when you can't see a way forward . . .

–   Heal through Art. I saw the sign at the hospital. I'd had
no help from the doctor. I'd practically screamed at him: 'My
father fucking raped me you cunt help me help me help help
me I'm in pain all day long. I'm in pain all day long', but he'd
done nothing about it and then I saw the sign: 'Heal Through
Art'. And I thought, Why not? Why not? I was at my lowest
ebb. And so I went to the meeting and there was the paints
and there was Lynne and Lynne just said: 'Use the paints, use
the paints and let it all out, let it all out however you will.'
And I did. I let it out. I let it out.

–   A dance workshop. I was . . . I was just . . . I thought it
was stupid. I was pissed up at home – that's all I'd do those
days – get pissed up from tins and wank with videos – piss
and a wank – when Hannah came round and said we're
doing a dance workshop. And I was like, fuck off fuck off.

–   We found . . . black people and white people, there was so
much distrust, so much history, just to be in a room together,
and when John asked me to pair up with this guy and write a
play together – a short little play – I was like, 'Oh my God, I
can't believe this is happening, our skin is different colours
and here we are sitting down and writing this little play
together.' I mean – I wouldn't have shared a bus with this guy
and here we are writing a play together.

–   My father. His face. His penis. The blood pouring from
me. Over and over again I painted it, over and over again,
and Lynne didn't comment, Lynne didn't – she was brilliant,
Lynne was brilliant – Lynne was just like: 'Keep going.
Wonderful. Be brave. Keep going.'

–   But eventually something . . . I think maybe the fact that
Hannah was German and the German girls on the video
were always the filthiest girls – something made me go to
Hannah's dance workshop. And fuck me – there was loads of
my mates from the mine.

–   I suppose you know . . . socialism was so important to me,
Marxism was . . . I was a Marxist . . . That was . . . that was
my yardstick and then when that all, that sort of imploded . . .

then suddenly I was sort of cast into darkness . . . It was one of those real, you know, 'Father Father why have you forsaken me?' moments. And without Marxism this world was suddenly a pretty fucking pointless fucking place, you know. And so what I was looking for, I suppose, what I was looking for was a form in which I could express that sense of . . . I don't know . . . that essential formlessness, the weightlessness, the dizzying lack of gravity in a state of fallen . . . And that's when I discovered the whole performance art installation bonkers sort of thing, you know, and that really seemed to, seemed to, seemed to give meaning to the lack of meaning – if that makes any sense.

– And it wasn't dance, like – it wasn't ballet, okay? It wasn't tutus and all that shit. It was taking the gestures, the bodies, the gestures and the bodies of ordinary men and women and creating a whole new language from that, a language of theatre, which we . . . And now people come, they come from miles, they drive from the financial towns and the centres of government and commerce and they come to our old mining region and they stay in the new fabulous hotels and they eat in the new fabulous restaurants and the new fabulous hotels and they watch us dance, they watch the fabulous pieces of dance theatre that Hannah has created. And now our region has a new life. Mining wasn't us. That was our definition. But actually that was our prison and now . . .

– I'm not in this to sell my work. Am I a Vermeer? Am I a Manet? Am I a Bacon? I don't know. I don't know and I don't care. This is about me. This is about me healing. And I have, I have healed. I acknowledge what happened in the past. I acknowledge what was done to that poor little frightened little child – to me – I acknowledge that and now I . . . any time I feel bad about myself – out come the paints and splosh! The healing begins. And now I've started to – one week Lynne said: 'I can't make it next week, and will you lead the group?' And I was – ooooh! But actually, you know actually, you know actually, you know I loved it and I still love it. I'm still loving it to this day.

−   Extraordinary plays I've seen written all over the world.
I bring people together in clusters − bring enemies together
to write dialogue and we're creating − Oh it's wonderful, it's
wonderful, it's wonderful, I love it, I love, I love, I love, I love,
I love it.

−   There's so much work to do here. There is so much pain
to heal. There is so much anger that is burning brightly.

−   We acknowledge that.

−   We see that. We really do.

−   But you must sign up for the dance or the writing or the
painting or the performance installation workshops.

−   You must.

−   You must.

−   You must do it.

−   Look, I don't want to be heavy-handed about this, but you
have to . . . You want inward investment? You want tourism?
You want civilisation? You want freedom and democracy ?
You want all − and if this war hasn't been about . . . then what
has it been about? − you want all that then let some culture
in, sign up for some culture, embrace some culture, let some
culture into the ruins of this shattered city − your city lives.

−   Look − why?

−   Why aren't you painting?

−   Why aren't you dancing?

−   Writing.

−   Art performance installation bonkers thing.

−   Come on, you bastards, you fucking ungrateful, you
fucking −

−   This is art, you bastards, this is art, this is fucking art,
everybody likes art, everybody wants art, so make some
fucking art.

—   Wouldn't it be great? Wouldn't it be great? Wouldn't it be great in a few years' time if this was a city of culture, if this city had a festival like . . . other cities have festivals, decent cities have festivals, cities with . . . opera and art and theatre and jugglers and sponsors and beer tents and – it's like a rebirth, these places are reborn, with the arts these places are reborn.

—   As we want you to be reborn.

—   As we want you to be reborn.

—   With a wonderful festival of all the wonderful arts your city can be reborn.

—   Your city will be reborn.

—   Because we want – and you want it – your city will be reborn.

—   Who's coming forward? Who's coming forward? Let's have some come forward so that the healing can begin.

—   The healing power of art can begin.

A **Blind Woman** *is brought forward.*

—   Our first artist.

—   Our first artist.

—   Hurrah!

—   Hurrah!

—   Hurrah!

—   Tell us your story – please tell us of your pain and struggle so the art can be made and the healing can begin.

The **Blind Woman** *opens her mouth. Blood pours out.*

—   The woman has no tongue.

—   This woman has lost her tongue and she has lost her eyes.

—   It has been a hard war.

–   It has been a bitter war.

–   There is a terrible price to pay to win freedom and democracy.

The **Blind Woman** *grunts, holds out a photo, gesticulates.*

–   This woman has lost her family. She has no family. She has no eyes and no tongue and no family. We can only imagine how deeply your pain must run.

–   But still you can paint. Here. (*Gives her a brush.*)

–   But still you can write. Here. (*Gives her a pen.*)

–   Still you can dance the dance of the gestures of the people. (*Her body is moved.*)

–   Join me in an installation. Come come come.

–   It's beginning. You see – it's beginning. The darkness is ending, the darkness is ending and light and civilisation and democracy and art are moving forward – once again they are moving forward, once again –

The **Blind Woman** *screams, throws pen and brush away.*

–   That's it, be brave. Express. Create. Be bold.

The **Blind Woman** *screams.*

–   It's happening, it's happening, it's happening.

The **Blind Woman** *convulses, her body in spasms.*

–   Oh yes dance dance dance.

The **Blind Woman** *spasms, the* **Chorus** *applaud, lights fade to black.*

Epilogue

Paradise Regained

Night. Heat. A luxurious open-plan penthouse flat – we can see the living and kitchen areas and a balcony from which a panorama of a gleaming modern city can be viewed. **Tom** *and* **Matt***, both about fifty.* **Tom** *is thin, dirty, wearing bloodied rags.* **Matt** *is in expensive contemporary smart casual clothing.*

Tom   Kiss me.

Matt   I can't.

Tom   I'm disgusting?

Matt   No.

Tom   So?

Matt   It's difficult.

Tom   We kissed so deeply then, we kissed so –

Matt   Then? Then was . . .

Tom   Yes?

Matt   Then was decades. You were –

Tom   You're fat now. And grey and –

Matt   Yes, I'm fat and grey and you're –

Tom   You're rich.

Matt   Well . . .

Tom   Oh yes. This place. Look at that. What's that?

Matt   It's art.

Tom   It's an original work of art, I would say. Is this artist a friend?

Matt   . . .

Tom   I never had – we never had original works of art, did we?

Matt   No.

Tom   Clipped a few pictures from a magazine in a frame and – kiss me.

Matt   No.

Tom   Look at this city. Look at that.

Matt   It's been a long time.

Tom   It's been decades.

Matt   It's been decades. Things move on. There's been inward investment. There's been a new infrastructure.

Tom   You still teaching at the university?

Matt   I consult. I have a consultancy. We consult globally. On global reconstruction after periods of conflict.

Tom   I see.

Matt   I fly around and we . . . advise on the . . . I try to pass on what we've learned.

Tom   Is that an opera house?

Matt   Yes.

Tom   Hah!

Matt   That's an opera house and that's the financial district and that's a mixture of public and – all mixed up together, private and public housing.

Tom   Our old city –

Matt   – has found, we've found, we've found our, our feet. We've moved on.

Tom   I can see that.

Matt   You should be pleased.

Tom   Should I ?

Matt   Are you pleased?

Tom   Well –

Matt   You've been dead, you've been gone, you've been – twenty years you've been gone – What are we what are we / supposed to –

Tom   Well, I'm sorry I'm sorry I'm sorry I'm sorry. I'm sorry I died. I'm sorry about that. I'm sorry about the landmine. I'm sorry some cunt left the landmine. And I'm sorry I stepped on the landmine and I'm sorry I –

Matt   No no no hey hey hey hey hey hey –

Tom   I'm sorry the landmine didn't carry me clean away. I'm sorry it was weeks in the hospital. Me screaming like a bitch and you weeping and the . . . For all these things I am deeply sorry.

Matt   Please. No.

Tom   And my death was horrible. Pain. I should have said kind things to you. But I didn't. I said cruel things to you and I'm sorry for that.

Matt   It doesn't matter.

Tom   You were the only person I ever loved in the world but in that shitty bombed-out hospital with the morphine running out and the . . . I should have said I love you but I said the most horrible –

Matt   That's okay. Everything's okay. But still –

Tom   I love you. Kiss me.

Matt   Yes.

They kiss.

Tom   Wasn't so bad, was it?

Matt   Course not.

Tom   So . . . you whizz about then?

Matt   Oh yes, lots of whizzing about. The world's smaller, but there's conflicts and they need −

Tom   Of course.

Matt   So I do what I can . . . seminars, workshops. Helping facilitate −

Tom   Hah!

Matt   It's important to −

Tom   Of course of course of course.

Matt   It wasn't easy for −

Tom   Yes?

Matt   It wasn't easy for me, for me, for us.

Tom   Of course.

Matt   Grief is −

Tom   It took me three weeks of pain and infection and delirium before I shook off this −

Matt   Yeah yeah yeah three weeks to die. Three weeks to −

Tom   Second by second −

Matt   Release to paradiseheavenlimbohellwhat? Something?

Tom   Something.

Matt   But we but we but we −

Tom   Please don't even −

Matt   This city was − it carried on − their side shelling, bombing, sniping, our side shelling, bombing, sni − Year after year after − You had it fucking lucky you had it fucking lucky you had it fucking lucky −

Tom   Oh yeah oh yeah oh yeah oh yeah.

Matt   To die was fucking – to die in the first attacks – not to see year after – oh yeah oh yeah oh yeah.

Tom   I like the colours in here.

Matt   Fuck off.

Tom   No really. The colours are perfect. The furniture, the – great curtains. I never knew you had such exquisite taste.

Matt   Well . . .

Tom   Who would have thought you had such good taste?

Matt   Well . . .

Tom   I was the one who taught you everything when we met, wasn't I? I was the one who –

Matt   Yes, you were.

Tom   Which wines and cheeses and – My holiday home – foreign literature – You were like a sponge – a gannet –

Matt   Yes.

Tom   A sponge, a gannet, gannetting it all up.

Matt   I was yes, absolutely totally.

Tom   I made you.

Matt   I was younger, I was –

Tom   Made you and now look at you – a facilitator with a collection of . . . It's actually not too bad a piece, this one –

Picks up pot.

Matt   Made by a refugee.

Tom   Well really? Mmm?

Matt   I give money to an organisation that works with refugees in –

Tom   But actually a rather good piece.

Matt   I think so.

Tom   And so do I.

Matt   The world is getting better. On the whole. Things have moved forward. We might have got sucked back into darkness. But human beings, we have . . . we've moved things forward.

Tom   I want to sleep with you tonight.

Matt   No.

Tom   Not sexually, just in a –

Matt   No.

Tom   But affectionately. Six years, we'd still be together now –

Matt   No.

Tom   No?

Matt   Twenty years? Twenty years and a dead man in my bed? Oh no oh no oh no.

Tom   Do I feel dead? Do I look dead? Do I – ?

Matt   No no no no, you're not – oh go oh go oh go. I'm sorry. But my life is perfect now. My life now is so perfect. I crawled through the city in the months after you went, clawing for a piece of bread, fighting for medicines, I clawed and I fought like an animal and I am not going back to – to – to – no.

Tom   I love you.

Matt   Well –

Tom   I love you and I want to be in our bed beside you.

Matt   Our bed was burnt. I burnt our bed to stay warm when the power ran out.

Tom   Your bed.

Matt   My bed is a beautiful – it's an ethical – ethically produced sustainable thing of beauty and I won't –

Tom   Fuck you.

Matt   My bedroom is a great source of calm and stillness in a world of insanity and I will not allow –

Tom   Fuck it – after all we shared.

Matt   We never – but sorry – no.

Distant music throughout.

Tom   What's that . . . ?

Matt   An orchestra on the dock. The Dock Development.

Tom   Ah yes. So I see.

Matt   We're a city of culture.

Tom   Wonderful.

Matt   It's all part of a process of renewal. Jobs, democracy, investment, freedom. All returning.

Tom   We did a lot of protesting for all this, didn't we?

Matt   Didn't we?

Tom   That dictator was –

Matt   Still have nightmares about – he's cracking my thumbs. They pissed on his corpse in the market place.

Tom   Really? Really? Wonderful!

Matt   Yes . . . Wonderful.

Tom   What is that . . . ?

Matt   It's Handel.

Tom   Of course yes. Handel. Dance?

Matt   Hah.

They dance.

Tom   That's it yes, yes. Look at your waist. Look at all that.

Matt   What would you rather . . . ?

Tom   Just saying . . .

Matt   Still starving? Is that what you prefer?

Tom   No course not, no, still I –

They dance for a while happily, then fireworks off and throughout.

Tom   Oh shit aggghhhhh!

Matt   No –

Tom   Attack attack attack under attack.

Matt   No.

Tom   The shelters, where are the shelters?

Matt   Listen –

Tom   Please deliver us from the attackers, their side, our side – aggghhhhh!

Matt   Listen no hey hey. Listen sssh. Hey. It's fireworks. That's fireworks. (*Laughs.*) Fireworks. (*Laughs more.*) Fireworks. War's over. War's finished. And in our city of culture we have fireworks.

Tom   Oh.

Matt   A whole generation now never seen a mine, a bomb, a – Only fireworks.

Tom   I've shat myself.

Matt   Oh.

Tom   Fear – you . . .

Matt   Here – shower and –

Tom   I'm sorry. In your perfect flat, in your perfect world, it must be an awful thing –

Matt   No no.

Tom   But I still . . . I haven't moved on. The sound still –

Matt   Of course.

Tom   I'm disgusting, but –

Matt   Please.

Tom   To lose my bowels is –

Matt   The shower's new this year. Fantastic shower. Whoosh. You just – you can have new, my clothes.

Tom   Yes?

Matt   You can have some of my clothes and we'll throw these away and –

Tom   Yes?

Matt   Yes.

Tom   Thank you. Your clothes'll hang off me.

Matt   Listen, if you don't want –

Tom   I do. I do. I do.

Matt *exits, re-enters.*

Matt   Shower's on. So just you –

Tom   They don't stop, do they? (*Fireworks, which are still going off.*)

Matt   We've . . . our economy has really thrived so I suppose . . . we treat ourselves to fireworks. It brings the city together.

Tom   Lovely.

Exit **Tom** *to bathroom.* **Matt** *fetches a bin bag. Exits to bathroom.*

Matt (*off*)   Old clothes in here. In the incinerator later.

He crosses, goes into the bedroom, comes out with a selection of expensive clothes which he lays out neatly. The fireworks finish. Handel finishes. Only the sound of the shower.

(*Calls.*) There we are. That's lovely and calm now, isn't it? Lovely. Everyone will be going to bed soon. It's such a happy place now, this city. Wish you'd lived to make it through . . . wish you . . . sometimes used to of course wish I died . . . wish I'd been taken with you . . . Love . . . grief . . . guilt . . . but actually . . . one of us survived . . . the luck of the draw and here I am . . . I survived. I survived. I survived. And yes, I'm fat and I'm rich and I'm − But I'm doing my bit. Doing my . . .

Without thinking, he's made a sort of person from the clothes: a jumper, underpants, chinos, socks, shoes. All laid out like a person. The shower is switched off.

There's more democracy, there's more freedom, there's . . . It was horrible. But it was in the end worthwhile. Yes.

Enter, from the opposite side of the stage as from the front door, **Adam**, *twenty, very good looking.*

Adam   Wasn't it hot today? Wasn't it just so fucking hot today? I have been so fucking hot. Wooh.

He takes off his clothes and goes to open the fridge. Stands in front of it.

Better. Better.

He takes a bottle of cold beer from the fridge and runs it over his body.

Do I look like an advert?

Matt   Maybe.

Adam   Or a porn star? Advert porn star sort of thing?

Matt   Maybe.

Adam   I wish. I wish. Look at this body. Ugly thing. I wish porn star.

Matt   How were your studies?

Adam   Studies?

Matt   Studies yes, studies.

Adam   I went to the beach.

Matt   Why am I paying . . . ?

Adam   It's not hot like this every day. University's always there.

Matt   I'm not paying –

Adam   Hey. Relax. I'll pass. Everyone passes. It's impossible to fail. That's why I picked that course. No one has ever failed that course. Play with my nipples.

Matt   Don't.

Adam   Just having fun.

Matt   You're late.

Adam   Did some coke round Dan and Toby's, played on the Xbox. I texted you.

Matt   I didn't –

Adam   You never switch that phone on.

Matt   I forget.

Adam   Old dog, new tricks.

Matt   Well, maybe.

Adam   Heat makes you so fucking horny, doesn't it? This guy – seventy or something – was wanking at me on the beach.

Matt   What did you do?

Adam   Teased him a bit. Showed a bit of crack.

Matt   I wish you –

Adam   Hey, I'm all yours. Daddy mine.

Adam *throws his arms around* **Matt** *and kisses him.* **Tom** *enters, towelling himself from the shower.*

Tom   Hello. I'm Tom.

Adam   I know. That's cool.

Tom   Tom? Yeah?

Adam   Tom. Yeah. I know you're Tom.

Tom   How do you feel? Angry? Surprised? Shocked? How do you feel seeing me?

Adam   Not much.

Tom   You've seen pictures of me right? You know I –

Adam   History doesn't bother me. My pecs are sharper today. Swimming.

Tom   So you're fine about . . .

Adam   Sun. A few lines. A beer. What's to stress?

Matt   Here's clothes. You can . . .

Tom   Thanks.

Adam   I'm going to lie on the bed and have a wank. Heat. Tug tug tug.

Exit **Adam**.

Tom   Congratulations.

Matt   Please – put these on.

Tom   No, I mean – congratulations. (*He starts to put the clothes on.*) Quite a catch.

Matt   We're happy together.

Tom   Of course you are.

Matt   We're really, really happy. He doesn't . . .

Tom   Yes?

Matt   He doesn't define me. He doesn't try to tell me who I am.

Tom   Yes?

Matt   You were an awful bully. You always told me what I thought. Go on this march. Protest about that. Sell these newspapers.

Tom   There was a dictator who –

Matt   Until really I didn't know what I thought because I had you in my ear all day long.

Tom   Well –

Matt   All day long, carping. Carping criticising ordering bullying.

Tom   Well –

Matt   Oh yes, you really were an awful bully. Most of the time I sort of hated you.

Tom   Oh.

Matt   Oh yes, most of the time there was as much hate as there was love there, you see?

Tom   And this boy?

Matt   It's much easier with him.

Tom   Well, no surprise.

Matt   Listen, he wasn't . . . When he was born, not even born until there was just a peacekeeping force remaining. He's a child of freedom and, and, and democracy.

Tom   The dullness . . .

Matt   Serenity. He's serene.

Tom   Empty.

Matt   Yes, maybe okay maybe yes, dull and empty and okay maybe yes. But I would rather any day . . .

Tom   The shoes fit well.

Matt   Long time I thought: life was pain and struggle and if there wasn't pain and struggle then you weren't . . . I wasn't alive . . . but now I . . . I'm okay with the emptiness. Yes. The emptiness is better. Yes.

Tom   How do I look?

Matt   Better. Much better. Civilised.

Tom   Good. Good.

Adam *crosses to shower.*

Adam   That's better. Much better out than in. As long as I imagine someone's watching I can always crank it out fast.

He goes. Shower on.

Matt   I'm going to cook supper now. If you want to – please – share some food with us, and then . . .

Tom   Alright.

Matt   And then I'd like you to move on. If you sit and eat with us, you'll go and you won't ever come back?

Tom   Do you ever think about the past?

Matt   Not very often, no. I'm new, the city's new, Adam wasn't even born, so . . . the past doesn't figure very large for us. I'm going to chop, so . . .

He moves to the kitchen area, starts to prepare a stir-fry. **Tom** *finds the remote, switches on the TV.*

Matt   Just a stir-fry. I'm dieting, so . . .

Tom   Oh look, an invasion . . . they're invading.

Matt   Yes, of course.

Tom   The world's a better place?

Matt   But not perfect. Not . . . it's getting . . .

Tom   Everything the same. Look at that, the same as twenty years ago.

Matt   No no no.

Tom   Your city's shiny but they –

Matt   – were given fair warning. They . . . We have to . . . Human rights, democracy, dictators who –

Tom   Agh.

Matt   We have to do something. Can't stand by and so – after due warning and – I support the invasion, I actually – There has to come a point where we – Enough is enough and it's our . . . burden to sort out the mess.

Tom   Soldier with his head blown off. Civilian on a landmine.

Matt   War is horrible. War is terrible. War is the last resort. But –

Tom   What's that?

Matt   Chilli oil okay?

Tom   And in you'll go to facilitate the healing.

Matt   Yes, I will.

Tom   What's your price?

Matt   Fuck off oh fuck you off. Yes. Life on this planet is shitty and messy but if you cling on, cling on and pull hard you move forward.

Tom   Progress?

Matt   Progress.

Tom   Well, I suppose that's right.

Shower turns off. **Adam** *enters, wearing a bathrobe.*

Adam   That's good. Pure now.

Matt   Tom's eating with us.

Adam   Cool. Whatever. Is that a new war?

Tom   Yes.

Adam   Wars are . . . samey, aren't they? I'll switch over. Here.

He switches to MTV.

Won't be long till food.

Tom   I won't stay. I'm going.

Matt   Oh. Will I see you again?

Tom   Oh no. No you won't.

Matt   Oh. Goodbye.

Tom   Goodbye.

Matt   Kiss?

Tom   Inappropriate.

Matt   Inappropriate.

Tom   Enjoy happiness.

Matt   Thank you. I will. You look much better in those clothes.

Tom   Well . . . good.

Exit **Tom**.

Adam   What shall we do tomorrow?

Matt   I don't know.

Adam   I want new stuff for the gym and some new games and there's a new juice bar.

Matt   Okay.

Adam   And then we can go to the beach and there's an all-nighter at the Docklands we can go to. I can score some k and e and then we can . . .

Matt   Brilliant. Brilliant.

Adam   I love you.

Matt   I know you do.

Adam   You're so much fun.

Matt   Thank you. Thanks. Are you ready to eat?

Appendix

Yesterday an Incident Occurred

Although originally written as part of the play cycle, Yesterday an Incident Occurred *was substantially adapted for BBC Radio 3.*

Sound of the live audience coming into the hall.

A   Good evening.

B   Tonight a nation gathers. Hurrah!

C   Tonight some of you are here with us in person. Hello – people.

A   Good. Good. Welcome to you. Welcome to this great hall. The hall where our city's democracy swings into action. Take your seats.

B   Some of you are not here with us but in your homes. In the homes you own and care for. And you are joining us on transistor and broadband and Freeview and laptop. Welcome and hurrah!

A   And you are listening not only here but around the world. Hurrah! For just as our freedom and our democracy spreads throughout the globe bringing peace and prosperity, so does our broadcasting spread throughout the globe, bringing peace and prosperity wherever it goes. For wherever transistor and podcast and broadband go, so there will justice surely follow.

A/B/C   Hurrah! Hurrah! Hurrah!

C   Now some of you may not own property, some of you may have done nothing but the most meagre shopping this weekend – you may have envied the rest of us our trip to the garden centre and thought: if only I owned a garden, if only I could buy a bench. But we are inclusive and you, the poor and downtrodden and lonely and illiterate, can join us here. No group, however much they are in a minority, is excluded here. Always room at the back in a multimedia democratic broadcasting environment. Hurrah! Any people here want to – ? Ah. Here's a person. A man in a yellow tie. Hello.

One (*pushes forward*)   Me. Me. I'm here. I'm here because . . . well, because . . . I live in this city and I think it's a lovely city Not just the shops of course – although the shops are lovely, we have lovely shops. But also we have lovely culture. We are a city of culture. And we're proud of that. And there's a choice of culture, a great deal of choice of – an overwhelming choice of culture. Later I may look at some culture. Maybe I'll take in the Vermeer. There's fireworks promised in the park tonight and – wonderful! – next week a whole week of Monteverdi. That's a sure sign you're in a lovely city of culture when they play Monteverdi. So why not join us here any time in our city of culture? I'm here for the announcement the – I support the authorities – justice and democracy – freedom and light – / a choice of broadcast media in a digital –

C   Good, good. To your seat. Please.

One (*retreats*)   I believe I believe. / Justice and democracy.

C   Yes. You're a person. We are people. Here are people. Hurrah! Hurrah for you!

B   And so. Our nation gathers together here because now we, the speakers, have an important announcement to make. So . . . settle please – audience with us here, settle.

Take out noise of live audience arriving.

Audience around the nation, globe – settle. Thank you. Good evening. We have an announcement. To make.

A   We do. An announcement. About civilisation and barbarity.

B   An announcement. About innocence and guilt.

C   An announcement. About the normal and the unforgivable.

B   About the ordinary citizen and the part that he, she, that you can and must play in keeping our society free from the forces of barbarity and terror.

A   You here with us – and you with your meal or your child or your washing in your home – you must join us now at this time of crisis in stopping the terror in our society.

C   Do you agree with us?

B   Please agree with us. Do you agree with us?

One   I agree with you.

C   Who's that? Oh. Man in the yellow tie. You agree with us? You all agree with us?

One   Totally.

C   Good. Good. Good.

B   That's important. Because yesterday, you see, yesterday an incident occurred.

C   Yesterday an incident occurred of a violent nature.

B   Yesterday a . . .

A   CCTV footage of the incident is available to you at home. It's available as a video download now. Click your mouse now on 'brutal attack' for the video download. You can follow the horrific CCTV footage. Are you doing that? Please do that now. Click now.

We now hear the footage running on plasma screens in the hall.

B   Meanwhile here we are showing yesterday's brutal attack to our invited audience. We are showing the brutal attack now to the people with us here on our plasma screens. They are horrific images. The people here are – How do you feel about these horrible images? Let's go to . . . Anyone? Man in the yellow tie?

One   I'm nervous and and . . . revolted.

B   Nervous and revolted by these sickening images?

One Nervous and revolted by these sickening images. As your listeners at homes will be nervous and revolted –

B – if they download now.

A If your computer does not have the correct software (why?) or if poverty or disability exclude you from viewing the podcast vid clip download, here's an audio description – inclusion, inclusion, inclusion, democracy, democracy, democracy – of the incident that occurred yesterday. Someone describe . . .

C But please – a warning – it's a violent and sickening incident. Totally sickening. Who will describe what's happening on the screen?

One Me.

C Again? – Man in the yellow tie. Very well. Describe. What do you see?

One The incident takes place in the shopping centre. The shopping centre where every normal man and woman goes every day to do the thing that the human animal does most naturally, to shop. It's a bright day. And here's a man – see him? – a man . . .

C He's called Alan and he's with his wife and she's called Marion. Very much in love. Thirty years married but very much in love. See that on the footage which the security forces have made public? Alan turns to Marion and he says – the cameras picked this up – sound right up please . . .

Alan (*very muffled*) I love you.

One 'I love you. I love you. I love you.' We should all remember that. Alan is reaching out to buy a purple sweater.

C He and Marion have talked about it all week and now they feel, now is the time for a purple sweater.

One Alan lets go of Marion's devoted hand for a moment to open the door of the shop where the purple sweaters are sold and . . . we switch cameras, and they are inside the shop.

C   This is the only reassuring thing in this otherwise disturbing footage.

One   Oh yes. To know we are watched always is our only comfort in this world.

New muffled acoustic: the shop, muzak.

But now as Alan reaches for the purple sweater a man leaps from the crowd – a stranger, an unprovoked . . . just leaps and throws Alan to the ground.

We hear all this on the very bad CCTV mike.

The man is tearing at Alan and kicking him. Marion is trying to pull him off.

Marion (*muffled*)   No no off off help.

One   And now the attacker is screaming – well . . .

C   Listen hard, see if you can make out the words.

Attacker (*very, very muffled, almost impossible to make out*)   I hate you. I hate everything about your world. I hate it.

C   Almost impossible to make out the words, yes? But we used lip-readers and sound engineers – took off the bottom, fiddled with the top – and we reconstructed a text. And here's what we believe the attacker was saying when he leapt from the crowd and attacked – totally unprovoked – attacked Alan. Here's – please, man in the yellow tie.

One   'I hate you. I hate everything about your world. I hate it.'

C   'I hate you. I hate everything about your world. I hate it.' Chilling words. A horrible attack. The video clip ends.

Silence. Pause.

A   How does that make you feel? You here with us? You at home? How does yesterday's terrible incident make you feel? That unprovoked attack on Alan.

B   Were you affected by the podcast, the video screens or
the audio decription? If you were, seek professional help and
appropriate medication today. Or call us now and share your
feelings, call or text or email us now to tell us what you feel.
We want to know. We're a democratic broadcaster in a
multimedia enviroment. We all have feelings. Feelings are
everything. And in this democracy your feelings are
everything. How do you feel? The lines are open now.

C   Let's ask somebody here with us in the live audience –
let's ask them how they feel about that sickening disgusting
attack. Yes – you – how do you feel about the attack? Man
in the yellow tie.

One   Well . . . Sickened. Disgusted. Angry.

C   Angry?

One   Yeah, angry, angry, and, and, very very sad. I want to
say: they are cancer. These attackers. They are the scumming
cancer dregs. That's what I want to say. And we shouldn't
have to take it. We shouldn't – the ordinary men and women.
Terror – random, violent, horrible, random, pointless attacks.
There is a war on. Abroad. At home. Right here. No one is
safe. If people can just leap from the crowd – they leap and
they assault another human being and they just batter him.
Batter him to death. It's quite horrible.

A   Well, thank you, let's –

One   I don't remember this from childhood. Did people just
leap from the crowd and batter you to death when I was a
child? I don't think so, I don't think so. Oh no. But there are
normal things.

A   Thank you, if we –

One   There's still normality. Oh yes. I had a lovely day
yesterday. Yesterday I walked by the river. It was a beautiful
day. I watched some planes overhead. Some of our brave
boys and girls practising for the battle ahead, and I thought:
This is perfect, this is lovely, this is the most perfect day of my

life. And I – I remember now – I ate linguine in the evening.
Oh yes, linguine – Sorry I don't want to . . .

A   Please – your contributions are valuable. You are an ideal
figure to pick from the crowd.

One   Alright. I just wanna . . . yeah . . . I just wanna say:
Most of us are ordinary. And let's not forget that. Let's not
forget to celebrate the wonderful, ordinary men and women.
The backbone. The backbone should be celebrated. We
should be celebrating the men and women who get up in the
morning, get up, drink their coffee for breakfast, then do their
bit – do their bit to generate wealth for the ordinary families
that make up this society. And tonight those families will be
sitting down and sharing some lovely meals together after
another normal day. Not this terrorist, cancer, scum, dregs.
We hear enough about the terrorist, cancer, scum, dregs.
Let's hear more about the ordinary men and women.

A/B/C   Hurrah! Hurrah! Hurrah!

Applause.

B   Let's go – we've got a reporter at the hospital – let's go
over to the hospital.

One   Oh yes. How's Alan doing after yesterday's sickening
disgusting unprovoked attack that has left us all feeling angry
and sad?

Reporter (*busy hospital acoustic*)   Alan's in a bad way. Alan's
in a very bad way. Marion is by his bed. Doctors are
describing his condition as critical. A lung has been
punctured. There's bleeding on the brain. Will Alan pull
through after yesterday's sickening disgusting unprovoked
attack that has left us all feeling angry and sad? Those are the
words on everyone's lips here: 'Can Alan pull through?'
(*Commotion, flashbulbs.*) I can see Marion – there's Marion –
Marion, can Alan pull through?

Marion (*slightly off mike*)   All we can do is hope and pray. He's a civilised, decent . . . he's my rock. And the scum who did this, this scum will . . .

The line goes down.

B   We've lost them. We'll get them back.

C   Let's hope – he's a civilised, decent, normal human being – let's hope Alan pulls through.

B   Wait. My producer's passed me a note. He's been caught – a man we believe to be the attacker has been caught. If you here look now at the plasma screens – or you at home, a ten-second clip is available now as a download if you text CANCER SCUM straight away – the footage, the footage of the face of, the face that we're already calling the face of evil. What would you like us to do with this man?

A   What would you like us to do with this attacker? Call us.

B   Press your red button now. It's on your remote at home.

A   What do you think should happen to the face of evil?

C   Maybe we should remind ourselves of his words as reconstructed by our experts. Maybe someone can read them – erm – yes – you read them again, man in the yellow tie.

One (*reads*)   'I hate you. I hate everything about your world. I hate it.'

C   Chilling words. A terrible attack. The face of evil. And now – we believe – apprehended.

B   Man in the yellow tie. What would you do to the face of evil?

One   Kill him.

B   Really? Kill him? Really?

One   Oh yes – really kill him.

A   Kill him? Yes? Yes? Yes?

B   And the red buttons have been pressed. A nation has spoken. Democracy. What are the results?

C   Well . . . red buttons have been pressed and then – oh democracy and justice – the overwhelming majority of you joining us from home and overseas agree. Just listen to these voices from a selection of callers.

Callers (*montage*)   Kill him. Kill him. Kill him. Kill him. Kill him.

B   Listen. We would like to kill him. We really would like to. But there is justice. There are systems. Checks and balances. The liberals. You understand.

A   We will kill him if we . . . We only believe it was this man – his face, you see, is partially obscured? Run the CCTV . . .

Muffled noise of the CCTV footage.

The angle, his face isn't entirely clear – you see? You see? Thank you. End the CCTV footage.

CCTV footage ends.

B   So – we need a witness.

C   Yes. A witness is needed.

B   Yesterday an incident took place of a violent nature and a witness is needed.

A   We are here today to announce to you the nation –

B   A proud nation of multimedia choices in a democratic age –

C   We are here to announce to you that a witness is needed. Yesterday an incident occurred. We have caught the probable attacker. And we want to kill him. You want to kill him. But – please – we need a witness.

A   Is that witness you? Is it you, man or woman, sat here with us tonight in the audience? Did you witness yesterday's brutal attack? If you did you must come forward.

Pause.

B   Come on. Someone saw the attack.

C   Or was it you listening on your couch or bed or in your garage at home? Was it you – yes, you at home there with your transistor by your bed or laptop in the study – or you with your stereo in the car? Did you witness yesterday's attack? If you did – come forward.

A   Step forward. Call the helplines. Press the red button. Make yourself known to the authorities. Please.

C   'I am a witness.' Those are all the words you need. You will be treated fairly.

B   But remember this. It is your responsibility. Because you have, oh yes, not just rights but responsibilities in this shining land of democracy.

C   Come forward.

B   Come forward.

A   Come forward now.

Pause.

No? No? No? NO! NOBODY?

B   Listen, we don't want to get heavy – sorry sorry sorry – but it is an offence, it is an offence to witness a violent assault and not report it to the authorities. COME FORWARD.

C   Or . . . you will be punished. PUNISHED. Remember remember remember that it is a punishable offence to witness a brutal attack and not come forward.

Pause.

A   Alright, alright. You were given your warning. One of you is a witness. We know that. The outcome of this broadcast is inevitable because we know that one of you witnessed the attack, has not come forward and must be punished. Someone listening at home – or in maybe you, our live audience – one of you is that witness. So here's what we're going to do. We are currently assessing your level of guilt. You here in the audience. But also you at home. We have so much information. There is CCTV footage, there is search-engine usage, there is credit- and debit-card purchasing, there is travel-card use. We are using all this data and so much more and you will be graded on a scale of innocence to guilt, clean to dirt, health to cancerous scum. The information is in the computer. The computer is grading the reports. Now. Sit back and let the computer find the guilty. Run the computer.

One   Alright. Stop. Enough. Enough. Please stop. Listen. Listen. Listen. Listen. It's me. I'm the witness. The man in the yellow tie. I witnessed the brutal attack. Alan. The purple jumper. I didn't come forward.

C   You? Really? Man in the yellow tie?

B   Yes – man in the yellow tie. You scum.

One   Yes. I am. I am scum. Yesterday an incident took place and I watched the incident. I watched the incident. Yesterday. I witnessed and then I walked away. That was me. I witnessed an incident and I did not come forward, I did not confess, I . . . I knew the rules but still I did not come forward. Why did I do that? Why? I don't know. I remember that taking place but – how to say this? – I remember it happening to another person, another city, another time. An incident occurred and I was a witness and yet – somehow – not a witness. I was there but somehow . . .

B   So . . . you are guilty?

One   Am I guilty? I . . . Yes. I'm utterly guilty.

C   Don't just sit there with the ordinary men and women. Stand up. Step out of the crowd.

One   I am a guilty one. That's what drew me here tonight. I was drawn here tonight because I am guilty scum and I seek punishment.

C   Bring him forward. Come forward. Scum. What should we do with guilty people like you, I wonder? Well?

One   How would you punish me? Well –

C   I'd like to know what you think, listener to a democratic broadcaster in a multimedia age. Text or email us now.

One   What should the punishment be for me?

C   Oh! The first emails and texts are arriving already. They're coming in thick and fast. You've been emailing and texting us in vast numbers to tell us what to do with guilty people who witness and don't come forward.

A   I'm looking through the pile (*massive paper rustle*) and 'Kill the cancer scum' comes the cry. What do you think of that, eh, man in the yellow tie?

One   It's . . . appropriate. Totally, yes. Hang and disembowel. Please.

C   Exactly. Appropriate. Something has to be done. Something. Yesterday's was just the latest in a string of unprovoked barbaric attacks.

One   And ever since these unprovoked sickening attacks began it was clear that new measures would be needed. New times, new crimes, new measures. Harsher times crush forgiveness and demand punishment.

A   New punishments that take account of the new terrible age we live in.

One   Please. Punish me. Kill me. Give me satisfaction. I beg the nation.

B   I'm getting a message from my producer. Oh! – interesting – a committee has been meeting to consider the new forms of punishment needed in this new age of terror. Fantastic news. Have we got a link? Does anyone know?

C   Have we? Can anyone . . . ? Yes Yes. We have we have. We've got a link. A little shaky down the line but basically . . .

B   Great. Let's join them. Then let's join them now. Let's join the committee live as they decide how to punish those like you who witness an attack and don't come forward.

New acoustic. A committee meeting.

Chair   A range of options to punish the rotten eggs in a democractic and humane society. To punish those who witness the attacks, who witness the attacks but do not come forward. And after questioning witnesses and balancing investment and projected incomes, we have concluded that branding – branding is the way ahead. Now if you look at the video screen you'll see an example of a branding. Can we have the video screen?

Off, on the video: the sound of chatter between guards and a prisoner.

Thank you. There will be branding you with an iron. If found guilty the accused will be – At the moment it's illegal of course. But this is a branding that took place in a – shall we say? – sympathetic – yes – a sympathetic neighbouring country whose laws are more . . . they are more . . . clarified than our own. Now if you look you can see . . . The iron will be heated to 250 degrees centigrade prior to the branding. And then . . .

Murmurs of approval.

So if you watch now you will see – yes – here is the branding. Watch the screen to see an example of a perfect branding.

From the screen, the muffled struggle of the prisoner, the guards calling 'Hold him down' and then finally the sizzle of the flesh.

Murmurs from the committee.

And there you have it. The perfect branding. It is necessary to do these things if we are to live in a civilised society. A society where rights are matched by responsibilities. I am convinced – convinced – that all decent citizens will join us in welcoming the branding of those who do not come forward.

Questioner   Mr Chairman, a question – will there be scarring?

Chair   Oh yes. Just here. Just above the right elbow. A livid scar will remain just above the right elbow for life.

Murmurs of on the whole approval but some discomfort.

In the report, a third of the study group actually – oh, bit of a surprise – thanked us for the branding.

Murmurs.

I would like to propose we pass this recommendation straight away to our elected representatives. A recommendation to make branding legal. Are we agreed? A show of hands.

All   Agreed!

Chair   Excellent. The bill will go before our elected representatives straight away. The emergency powers.

The link ends.

B   Well – there we have it, branding. Branding. How do you feel about that, man in the yellow tie?

One   I think it's brilliant.

B   Let's link up with Marion. Marion is the wife of the man who was assaulted yesterday outside the coffee shop in the city centre. Marion's on a link from the bedside of her critically ill husband. Good evening, Marion. You've got a message for the man in the yellow tie and for the world.

Marion (*link, hospital acoustic*)   I have.

A   Will you read it to us, Marion? Would you like to do that?

Marion   I certainly would.

Judge   Then – please . . .

Marion   'Please punish this man who witnessed and did not report this terrible assault upon my husband. He is my rock. I have been married to him for twenty years and in all that time he has been a rock. He has never done anything but good in this world. He loves life and treasures everything about the freedom and democracy we enjoy. This morning, as I brought him a cup of coffee, to his bedside in the hospital, he held out his hand to me and said the words: "I love you." This is my hope. In all the middle of so much evil, love will always continue. I know I've spoken to my elected representative and asked her to ensure the new branding measure is passed without delay and I hope anyone listening to this will do the same. Freedom must triumph. Democracy must triumph. I want these rotten eggs branded. I say it on my website, I'm blogging it to the world, and please I'm sending this message to listeners at home and abroad, on digital and broadband: brand them, brand them, brand them.'

A   Thank you, Marion. A very clear voice. An admirably clear voice. You see, man in the yellow tie?

One   Yes. Yes. It's the voice of the people and it's righteously raised in anger. Hurrah!

A/B/C   Hurrah! Hurrah! Hurrah!

One   Can I ask that you say a prayer here with me? And you listening at home, please join me. Stop what you're doing. Stop and get down on your knees. A prayer – doesn't matter if you're not religious – can I ask that you join me? A prayer that the voice of the people be heard in the house of our elected representatives and that my branding be made legal.

Murmurs of agreement.

Let us pray. O Lord, I thank you for your normal world. I thank you for the normal men and normal women who move about this normal city. I thank you for the normal cultural and normal leisure activities I enjoy on this normal day. Blessed be the normal coffee I drink.

Response   Blessed be the coffee that we drink.

One   Blessed be the normal breakfast roll I break and enjoy each morning.

Response   Blessed be our breakfast roll.

One   Blessed be my Vermeer and Monteverdi, the jugglers and the comedians, the *Bacchae* of Euripides and the wonderful drama – the drama I enjoy on film, on television, theatre and the radios that inhabit thy earth. Give me this day an excellent rate of interest. Blessed be this loyalty card. In mall and in retail outlet, online and instore. And cursed be the . . . the the . . . oh . . . the . . . Cursed be the rotten eggs such as me, those who witness the attacks and do not come forward. Curse them as you once cursed Lucifer and the rebel army as you threw them into Hell. O Lord, send wisdom to our elected representatives. Send our elected representatives the wisdom to pass this legislation. This legislation which will allow those here to brand me.

Response   Brand him.

One   Brand me for ever and evermore. Amen.

All   Hallelujah. Amen.

One   It will come, it must come, that day must surely come. When I shall be branded. Then there will be justice and music and dancing and champagne. And oh, how happy our world will be. A blessed place. A good place. A calm place. A happy place. It's so close. It's just a, a, a – a breath. Yes. It's just a breath away.

B   Thank you, man in the yellow tie. Please, we have to brand people. We have to. It's the only option. It's the only option under the circumstances. You listening at home: who is your representative? Who are they? Will you be calling them, texting them, emailing them – today? Do it today – you must, you must, you must, you must, you must. Democracy is there for you to make use of. Make use of democracy. Let's hear what the backbone has to say. We may lose it, we may lose it. Don't take it for granted. If you don't text or email now and call out for branding, democracy may wither away. Just wither away. And die. Democracy will be dead. It's up to you in the live audience and you at home. Do you love democracy? Or do you hate democracy? Which is it going to be? Contact your representative now. Just text the words BRAND HIM now.

C   Look – look – look at the screens.

Sound of a debate on a TV screen and under.

Reporter   Hello. I'm at the House of Representatives. It's starting. Our elected representatives are meeting. A special meeting of the House of Representatives has been called in the light of yesterday's attack. The engine of democracy has swung into action. They're debating a bill to allow branding to take place.

B   But will the branding be in public? Will it be carried on prime time?

Reporter   Well, I understand there's an advertising lobby for it to be carried on prime time. Will it be a ticketed event? The Culture Minister says yes. Will medical and legal supervision be thorough? Or even excessive? Or maybe the liberals will, maybe they'll chip away with their 'amendments'.

B   As is their right.

Reporter   As is their right. In a democracy. Let's wait and see, shall we? Let's wait and see. But democracy is taking its course. Democracy and freedom and hope and truth.

TV screen off.

A   Let's question this man in the yellow tie. And who knows, maybe by the time the trial is finished the law for branding will be in place?

One   I sincerely hope so. We must punish wrongdoers. I'm a wrongdoer. I must be branded.

A   I'm not sure if I've got the stomach for it. Wielding an iron. Flesh.

B   Nor I.

C   Nor I.

A   You see, I've planned a day of relaxing activities. I've planned a day of incredibly soothing activities. This is . . . I love this city. It's a wonderful city. It's bristling with culture. There's comedy and opera and jugglers and – ooh – oratoria. And it's my belief we should – what's the . . . ? – revel! We should revel in that. Yes? Yes? Yes? Maybe I won't brand.

B   I think, at heart, we're liberals.

C   I am – oh yes – at heart – a liberal.

One   Oh no. Not after everything – no no no. You must brand me. You must. The iron here –

A   It's barbaric.

One   It's right. Do you believe in cameras?

A   Of course I –

One   There were of course cameras yesterday when the incident occurred. CCTV. And it will assist us to finally confirm that I witnessed the assault and failed to come forward. I've always supported the cameras. I would visit garden centres. I would wake to the smell of coffee and croissants prepared by the girl and I would say to my beautiful wife – I have a beautiful wife – 'I think a visit to the garden centre this morning.' And would I mind if a camera was watching? Would I object to observation and analysis? Clearly not. Clearly not. I would have a camera in my car, a camera in the petrol station, a camera in the quiet corner where I chose my garden bench if I could. And I would have them there happily, I would . . . I would . . .

A   Embrace?

One   Embrace them. Because here in my heart of hearts, here in my soul, in my gut, in my head, I am guilty, I am evil,

I am scum, I am cancer, oh, I am cancer scum. I must be watched by the normal people. Because you are the normal people and you must watch and identify and crush and then – oh, how we'll . . . The time is coming, it's coming now, when us scum will be wiped away and only you the backbone will be left. Oh yes. Hallelujah!

A/B/C   Hallelujah!

One   O Lord O Lord O my God my Father my God thy world will be cleansed. It shall, it shall, it shall. Just as thy Heaven was made free from the sinful ones, just as you cast Lucifer down, so shall this city, our country, our empire be clean, clean, clean, clean. So shall I be branded.

One *begins to sob.*

C   That's it, that's it. Act normally. I'm a liberal, I believe everyone should act normally. Smile or frown or . . . cry. Yes, you can cry if you want to. Sob. Whatever you feel is appropriate. That's it. I empathise.

One   What?

C   I'm feeling what you're –

One   You musn't. Look at the CCTV footage. I'll describe.

Muffled sound of footage.

I'll tell you what I see. I see a man who . . . it is myself. Yes. It's me – scum – and I'm . . . A cup of coffee arrives. I drink the coffee. I have a pastry. I read a listings magazine. I suppose I'm considering, yes, considering the possibilities for cultural, for cultural or for leisure activities in this great city. And now I go into a shop because I want to buy a yellow tie. It's my birthday and . . . Now . . . a member of the public steps forward, steps forward out of his – it's a man – steps forward and – oh – strikes one of the shoppers about the head. And now that poor innocent shopper falls to the floor. And the man – the attacker, the face of evil – is kicking him in a frenzy of, kicking him . . . bones are broken, there is severe bruising, bleeding. The skull is fractured. Another man steps forward from the crowd and tries to pull the attacker off. But the attacker is frenzied. He's lost his mind. He is overcome with anger and he pours it into the poor broken body of that poor shopper.

A   You are watching and listening?

One   Yes. I am. 'I hate you. Everything about you. Your world.' I hear that clearly. So, please, you mustn't feel anything for me.

C   I'll do my best.

B   We're getting news – we've got some news. On the link.

A   Then – feed it through,

Reporter (*hospital acoustic*)   Bad bad bad bad tragic bad news. Sorry to say – that. I'm with Marion and a family friend –

Friend   Hello.

Reporter   – and . . . please tell us, Marion.

Marion   I . . . I . . . I can't . . .

Friend   I'm a family friend. I'll say it for you, Marion. Marion's husband has just died.

Reporter   Really?

Friend   Really. His internal injuries. Very severe internal injuries. Injuries sustained during the brutal assault yesterday in . . . I'm sorry, Marion, I can't, a moment . . . I . . . Oh my Lord. (*Sobs.*)

Marion   What is it? Come on, come on.

Friend   I spent – one summer – I never told you, Marion, but one summer . . .

Marion   Yes?

Friend   We were lovers that summer. Before you – Marion . . . We spent the summer on a boat drifting across a lake making love under the moon and stars. We read Shakespeare.

The Winter's Tale. It was so beautiful. We had such a bond.
Oh, this is hurting me very very very very deeply.
Medication, counselling, what do I do?

A   How do you feel about that? I ask the accused with us
here.

One   ... I'm incredibly saddened by the unnecessary death
of a fellow human being. I am almost inconsolable. Words
cannot express the grief that any of us feel for that man's
death. Please give me the very harshest punishment.

Marion (*hospital*)   Please, I – Can you still hear me?

A   We can hear you, Marion. On digital and terrestrial.

Marion   I'd like to make a further statement.

A   Of course – please.

Marion   I'd like to say . . . Fuck the bastards. Fuck them.
Fuck them. Round them up. Round them all up and take
them up to the castle and tie them to a stake and burn them,
burn them, burn them. Please, everyone at home – round
them up and burn them.

Friend   I support you, Marion. I'm feeling what you're
feeling and you're speaking for me.

Marion   Please help the authorities. Please put pressure on
your elected representatives. Let none of us sleep till we've
beaten down every last door and burnt every last piece of
scum flesh.

One   Yes! Yes! Yes! Burn me!

A   Thank you, Marion. You see? You see, the eloquence of
the ordinary man or woman when impelled to act is
incredible.

C   Oh yes. Yes. We're all incredible, wonderful people,
apart from the rotten eggs.

B   Look at the screens – there's news on the screens – news
news news.

C   Turn up the sound.

Reporter (*TV acoustic, huge excitement in background*)   Oh yes! Yes! Yes! It's been passed. It's gone through on a fair majority. The bill has been passed. Our elected representatives say we can now brand people who witness the attacks and don't come forward. Fireworks and champagne. Champagne and fireworks.

The whole courtroom goes wild with excitement.

One   Oh, that is good news.

A   Oh my God, oh my God, oh my God.

One   That's marvellous. That is – oh yes! Hurrah hurrah hurrah! You three must punish me. Brand me!

A   I feel ill. Fear. Revulsion.

One   What does Marion say on the link? Get Marion on the link. Marion, are you there?

Marion (*hospital acoustic*)   That is fan-fucking-tastic. That is . . . Democracy and truth democracy and truth democracy and truth democracy and truth democracy and truth democracy and truth democracy and truth. We can brand the rotten eggs!

Crowd (*at hospital*)   Democracy and truth.

Marion   Fireworks and champagne.

Crowd   Champagne and fireworks.

In the distance we can hear bells ringing, cheering, fireworks.

A   Did we come to power to carry through this awful burden of branding?

One   Please. Let me speak. People of this great city – the people of this great city of trade and industry and commerce – we are celebrating. We are celebrating that a wise decision has been made. I am to be branded. My faith is restored . . . sometimes you think . . . you think . . . democracy is failing . . .

You think . . . I don't know . . . it's not working . . . why this vote, this cross on this box? Why? Sometimes you can't . . . until something comes along, something, and hope is, trust and hope and – God bless democracy – hope and trust are reborn. Give me some some champagne, hurrah hurrah hurrah!

Pause.

Who will brand me? You?

A   . . . I can't.

One   You?

B   . . . I can't.

One   You . . . ? Please . . . Justice must be done.

C   Alright. I'll do it.

One   You can now brand anyone who witnessed yesterday's incident but does not come forward. Under medical and legal supervision, an iron heated to an exact temperature of 250 degrees centigrade will be applied to the right arm just here until a permanent mark is left. Do you understand what you must do?

C   I understand.

One   Heat the iron. I'm ready. Begin my punishment.

C   I'm starting to heat the iron.

An initial sizzle.

B   Stop, stop. We're getting a . . . There have been some amendments.

A   Oh. The liberals. Thank God. The plasma screens.

Unease in the courtroom.

Reporter   Some amendments were made during the passing of the bill in the interests of a humane society.

A   As we surely are.

Reporter   The branding will take place only in courtrooms such as this one. TV crews and commercial radio stations will have to bid for a franchise to broadcast. And calls for burning at the stake at the castle have been, as they say, 'kicked into the long grass'.

One   Not as harsh as I hoped but . . . Oh well, still . . . a victory for democracy and humanity. Oh . . . Yes yes. Democracy and humanity. Democracy and humanity. Our core values. Once again they shine through in every act of our enlightened society. Please, is the iron heated?

C   The iron is being heated.

One   Let the iron be heated faster.

A   But . . . You understand? Branding will hurt. We won't pretend –

One   Oh yes. I will be a pariah for – ooh – decades.

B   But listen, listen, there'll be forgiveness. Somewhere. There's always kind, liberal, kind, forgiving, liberal, kind people who will forgive. There's always refuge from the mob. There's kindness in the world. There's always liberals.

One   I don't want the liberals. Horrible.

A   Your branding will be humane. So different from our enemies. In our enemies' countries, people are dragged kicking and screaming into public places and they are branded without proper medical or legal supervision. Revolting. My stomach is turning. Turning. There – in the heart of that evil empire – people are burnt frequently at the stake. Ugh. Ugh. Their only crime? Their only crime? What is their only crime? Their only crime – It's . . . Oh yes.

C   The iron is nearly hot enough.

A   Their only crime – thank you – their only crime is to stand up and say: 'I am a person. I am my own distinct person. I have my own personality and my own thoughts.' And for this, these people are burnt. Disgusting. Disgusting.

Disgusting. How they yearn for freedom and light and choice, democratic choice, for rights and responsibilities. How they yearn and how we, many of them, take them for granted.

B   The iron has now reached 250 degrees.

C   Bring the guilty one forward for punishment.

One   I come forward and thank this audience, the city, the listeners, the nation for my punishment.

Footsteps as he is brought forward.

A historical moment. This is history. I am the first person – correction – the first rotten egg to be branded since the passing of the new legislation. It is happening in front of the audience here and at home.

C   Do you have words, do you have things that you would like to say to that audience?

One   I do.

C   Well, my friend, now is your moment, now is the moment, now is your time, so . . . speak.

One   I . . . I am a rotten egg. I know that now. The mark will be here on my arm for all of you to see. Like a broken wing. Please despise me, please hate me, please brand me. That is your right – and your responsibility. I will be for ever recognisable to the rest of you. You go to a beach or a cocktail party or a – You sit out there in the shopping centre drinking your coffee and eating your pastry and I will be recognisable to the rest of you. There he goes – there he goes, the scumming, cancer, rotten dregs, the stinking out the barrel the . . . How I wish I could lead a normal life. Paint watercolours. Go fly fishing. Teach my daughter Spanish. Talk online with my friend in Southern Australia. But this will never happen. I am evil and I have been banished from Paradise for ever. This is justice and I embrace it. I did not come forward. I witnessed a violent incident in the shopping centre and yet I did not come forward. Why didn't I . . . ? For one reason and one reason alone. I am a bad person. There is no point trying to understand me. There is no point giving me money. I am bad bad bad bad bad. Please assist the authorities. Please report violent incidents. Please come forward.

I would like 'Fireworks' by Handel for my branding.

A   Oh yes. Handel. There should be Handel for the branding. Let there be Handel. Offer your arm for the branding.

One   I offer my arm for the branding.

A   Now. Now. Handel, speak for us. Handel, give us thy spirit as we celebrate this moment of history. Let us celebrate this branding.

Handel plays on disc, swelling.

One   Hurrah for the normal!

Crowd   Hurrah for the normal, the normal, the normal!

One   Let the branding begin.

B   Let the branding begin.

A   Brand him.

The sizzle of the iron on flesh. **One** *screams.*

One   Agghhhh. God bless the – agghh – cameras. God bless our elected – uuugh – representatives. Democracy and truth and history and freedom and . . . and . . . and . . . democracy and history and truth and – aaaaaghhhhhh!

The Handel ends.

A   Doctor, what's happened?

Doctor   He's lost consciousness – it's to be expected after a branding.

A   Then take him out. Remove the rotten egg.

Groans as **One** *is carried from the courtroom.*

A   Time for us all to go home. Back to your normal homes. Democracy has done its work. Justice has been done.

The courtroom starts to clear.

A (*to* **Usher**)   Democracy and humanity. Our core values.

B   Oh yes. Once again they shine through in every act of our enlightened society.

C   Do you know what I'm going to do now?

B   No. I don't know.

C   What I'm going to right now. Right now I'm going to have a great cup of coffee.

A   Ah yes. A great cup of coffee.

B   I think it's going to be a rather fabulous day.

C   Oh yes. For most of us it's going to be a fabulous day. But for the guilty ones there's always branding. (*Suddenly close to us.*) Are you a guilty one? Do you know a guilty one? You listening at home or in the car? Is there guilt?

B   We ask you this. Please help the authorities.

C   Please come forward. It's easy to make yourself known and to be identified in a multimedia democratic broadcasting environment. It's important if we are to end these troubled times. That we end these series of unprovoked attacks.

A   End them. And let freedom and democracy and justice shine forth across the globe. For ever and evermore.

A/B/C   Hurrah hurrah hurrah!

A   Goodnight.

Over There

for Fundi, with love

Over There was first performed at the Royal Court Jerwood Theatre Downstairs, Sloane Square, London, on 2 March 2009, and at the Schaubühne am Lehniner Platz, Berlin, on 23 March 2009. The cast was as follows:

Karl/Carly   Luke Treadaway
Franz   Harry Treadaway

Directed by   Ramin Gray and Mark Ravenhill
Designer   Johannes Schütz
Lighting Designer   Matt Drury
Sound Designer   Alex Caplen
Original Music   Harry Treadaway and Luke Treadaway

Characters

Karl
Franz

Punctuation

When the text is in bold type **like this** the characters are speaking at the same time.

When the text is in parentheses (like this) the characters are speaking to an offstage character.

Punctuation like this

. . .

means the scene has skipped forward a few minutes.

When you see this / it is the cue for the next person to speak, creating overlapping dialogue.

Thanks

Thank you to all those in Berlin I interviewed while researching the play: Irma Zwernemann, Gertraud Tietz, Nico Felden, Lilly Henze, Dr Peter Becker, Sabine Ratsch, Liselotte Kubitza, Ludwig Bodemann, Richard Graf zu Eulenburg

The interviews were organised by Nicole Nikutowski.

Thanks to Dominic, Diane, Ramin and Ruth at the Royal Court, and Thomas, Tobias, Marius, Maja and Jens at the Schaubühne.

Prologue

California. The present.

Carly Where you from?

Franz Germany.

Carly In Europe? No way.

Franz Germany in Europe. Yes.

Carly My family's Polish. Gdansk. I'll go visit. One day. When I'm an old lady. You? Bet you one day you're gonna want to –

Franz No. Never. Germany's dead. I'm gonna stay right here in California until the day I die.

Carly . . . You wanna come home with me? Most days when the diner's shut I sit down and roll myself a joint and let go. You want to let go with me?

Franz Sure. That'd be good.

Carly Here, you roll for me while I finish off. I like your face. We'll have beers, music, joint and then we'll . . . well, then we'll see.

Franz Let's see.

Carly Hi. I'm Carly.

Franz Oh.

Carly Now you're supposed to say 'That's a pretty name'.

Franz Okay. That's a **pretty name**.

Carly There. That wasn't so difficult was it?

One

East Berlin, 1986.

a.

Franz   I'm sorry. There was a woman in front of me. There was something wrong. They held her for hours. She got so upset and she was crying and screaming and swearing and I had to wait and it was . . . I'm sorry.

Karl   Hello Franzl.

Franz   Hello Karli.

Karl   Did you bring the chocolate?

Franz   Let's go for a **beer.**

b.

Karl   And I would turn the TV aerial and I sometimes I thought I saw you in the programmes – like you were winning a car or something or on the news you'd be like a terrorist.

Franz   A terrorist. Hah! Great.

Karl   Or you'd be an actor in a soap opera only of course it wasn't ever you. And then Papa would come back and he would be: What the fuck do you think you're doing **turning the aerial West. We don't turn the aerial West in this house. Turn it right back again** . . . How did you do that?

Franz   Do what?

Karl   Do that. Yes. That. That's it. That.

Franz   Oh my . . . That's weird, that's strange. I didn't plan it. It just . . .

Karl   Happened? Like that?

Franz   Happened. **Like that.** Yes. There have been times . . . all these years when you weren't there when I saw things,

felt things that I thought were your stuff but I didn't think
hah! We'd **say the same things at the same time**. Hah!
I liked it. I know so much about you.

c.

Franz   It was very hot. It was summer. Aug – No, early
September. Because it felt like you were in . . . it was a . . . it
was . . . there was a lake . . . a forest . . . huge trees . . . the air
was so clear . . . **summer camp**?

Karl   Young Pioneers.

Franz   I saw that place so clear, like I was there. And you
were watching her for a week. I felt it like this – mmm –
tension.

Karl   Yes.

Franz   In my stomach for a week I could feel it like you
were **watching** her all the time but not **talking**.

Karl   Exactly **yes** exactly.

Franz   But then finally you . . . late . . . and she led you
down this it was a corridor something –

Karl   It was a doorway. Doorway of the shower house.

Franz   There was **rain**. Really heavy.

Karl   Really **heavy**.

Franz   And you got mud on your knees your belly your arse.

Karl   Hah! I did. **Mud up my arse.**

Franz   And you were **really** you know, droopy **because**
but finally she you know **worked** you into –

Karl   Took time –

Franz   Worked you and then but once you'd actually
entered her finally then –

Karl   It was my first time.

Franz   When you came . . . I came.

Karl   . . . Really?

Franz   Yes. Came. Which was so . . . I was watching TV with Mama and all this was so clear like I felt myself going into her and when you **came I came.**

Karl   That's brilliant.

Franz   Sitting there with Mama with jizz in my pants. What do you know about me?

d.

Karl   And you would say to Mama: Everything is wrong with our world. **This decadent this bloated this smug and yes I would kidnap a child I would blow up a banker I would tear the facade of this sham world away.**

Franz   Hah! I did. I was a fucking pain.

Karl   And Mama would cry and: **So what you rather? Would you rather be over there?** And you'd say: **Well maybe I would.**

Franz   I was a little shit. You know too much about me.

. . .

Karl   And then in a bar she told you that she was having your child.

Franz   You know about that?

Karl   You only met her two months ago at the party with the smell of marijuana. That's the first time I felt her in your –

Franz   That was the first time. It was. You know everything.

Karl And now she's **pregnant**. Yes? And in that bar you really it really felt like you were going to hit her, strike her in the jaw. I'm twenty-two you bitch twenty-two and I don't want to be a **father** and why didn't – use **something** – I just assumed you were going to – because there's no way I – only thought I'd see you a **few weeks** and now . . .

Franz But I didn't.

Karl I know.

Franz I would never hit a . . . You know that?

Karl Of course not. You held her and said I **love** you.

Franz I did. Yes. I love you.

e.

Franz This was a good idea. When shall we do it again? How about next month?

Karl Next month would be great.

Franz Let's say four weeks today . . . Of course I'll have to check the baby coming and everything I . . .

Karl Of course you will, of course. Will you see Mama?

Franz Tomorrow.

Karl Will you tell Mama that Karli says hello?

Franz Listen I actually I . . . Well I actually I . . . **didn't tell Mama that we were meeting**. I'm sorry.

Karl I see.

Franz She wouldn't have wanted . . . she wouldn't want me to come over here . . . she doesn't think anyone should come over, she . . . it's . . . it's just her strange . . . she still hates everything to do with over here.

Karl Of course. But her son –

Franz   She's not very well. The doctor there's been tests. She –

Karl   What do they – ?

Franz   Cancer. Mama has cancer so –

Karl   I see.

Franz   Which could be totally – if we hit it aggressively we may . . .

Karl   I want to see her.

Franz   I'm sure.

Karl   Twenty years and I still smell her, I still –

Franz   I have to go. The queue at the checkpoint's long.

Karl   Let's swap passports.

Franz   What?

Karl   You take mine. You stay East. Just a few days. I'll take yours. I'll see Mama.

Franz   Impossible.

Karl   Nobody will know. A few days I'll get a visa back here you can go home.

Franz   I don't want to do that.

Karl   We're twins. You like that. We can pass for each other. I'll give you the keys to my apartment. It's not so bad over here. It'll be an adventure. Step through the mirror. Welcome to the East.

Franz   No.

Karl   No?

Franz   I've got a job, a girlfriend, there's –

Karl   She's my mother too, my mother is dying and you won't even let me –

Franz   She'll get she might get better she –

Karl   It's my right to step through that wall.

Franz   You stayed here with Papa. You don't know her any more.

Karl   A child always knows its mother.

Franz   I'm sorry maybe it's me I'm a coward what if you went over there and didn't come back? If I was stuck over here. I couldn't stand that.

Karl   Why did you come here?

Franz   You're my brother. It was natural.

Karl   Track me down? Write the letters? An adventure? Take a look? 'What if it had been me? Just imagine. Just imagine if Mama had left me behind. What if – oh horrible – if I had to live in the East. Just one day and back to my fat girlfriend and my fat life.'

Franz   I've got a kid on the way. I wanted to –

Karl   Don't miss the checkpoint Franz. Back to the West.

Franz   I'll write on Monday.

Karl   You don't want to get stuck over here do you?

Franz   Shall I write?

Karl   I don't think so.

Two

West Berlin, 1988.

a.

Franz   How did you get here?

Karl   I got a travel pass.

Franz   Why didn't you tell me?

Karl   I heard from Ursula that Mama was really bad. I got a letter from the hospital. Ursula helped me. And so I got a travel pass. How's Mama?

Franz   You should have told me you wanted to come over here. I would have helped you.

Karl   Are you sure about that?

Franz   Of course I would.

Karl   I'm not sure I like it over here. It's flashy loud. We have better hospitals in the East.

Franz   They've looked after Mama very well here.

Karl   She would have got much better care back home.

Franz   This is our home.

Karl   Where's her ward?

Franz   Listen –

Karl   You're not going to stop me seeing her now I've come over here?

Franz   She's – . . . Mama died an hour ago. At three thirty more or less she . . . it was really such a combination of things the cancer was so widely but in the end it was her heart that couldn't that's what they're going to put on the death certificate heart failure it was her heart.

Karl   Oh.

Franz I was with her when she . . .

Karl Oh. Wouldn't it have been good don't you think if she could have had both her twins with her at the moment of death? She would have got better care at home. In our hospitals we –

Franz Communism kills cancer? Well, clever communism.

Karl She shouldn't have left. This would never have happened if she stayed at home.

Franz She had a good life. It was a dignified death. I was with her.

Karl I should have been there. Did she mention me? You know. At the end.

Franz They fill you with morphine. She was in a dream.

Karl Did she say my name?

Franz I don't – She mumbled. Sounds. Nothing I understood.

Karl I don't like it here. The West is strange. I'm going home.

Franz I thought about you. I was holding her hand. Three o'clock or so. And I thought: I bet he knows this. Bet he's feeling this as I'm . . .

Karl Well. No. Not a fucking thing.

Franz I thought my twin would –

Karl You're a very sentimental person aren't you?

Franz Let's go back to mine. I'll show you my place. I'd like to show you where I live. Will you come? I'll feed you.

Karl I've only got a few hours.

Franz Please.

b.

Franz   I'd like to see Papa.

Karl   That's not possible.

Franz   If I get a day pass, come East, we could take him for a meal. I'll pay. Will you tell him Mama died?

Karl   He doesn't like me to talk about her. He says it was her choice to come West. And he hated her. And she brought you up over here and so – he says – he couldn't bear to see you.

Franz   Still. I'd like to see him.

Karl   It's never going to happen. Papa is still totally he is still totally our workers' democracy our workers' democracy the finest country in the world. He says, he does – I'm sorry – say you're not his son any more.

Franz   How was the chicken?

Karl   Good. I say open your eye Papa surely you can see –

Franz   There's some more.

Karl   Surely you can see –

Franz   Would you like some more chicken? A sausage?

Karl   But he's still – this is the best way of life.

Franz   He's a man of his time.

Karl   Things are changing. But he hates that. He won't survive without communism.

Franz   Life over here isn't so great. I don't like my job. My relationship's lousy. I split up with the mother of my child. At first it was argue fuck argue fuck. Now it's just argue argue still no fuck argue. I see my boy five days a month.

Karl   That's how it is with relationships. Everything's temporary.

Franz   I'd like you to meet him sometime. Uncle Karl.

Karl   Then you'll have to bring him East won't you?

Franz   If I opened some wine would you drink it with me?

Karl   Of course I would.

Franz *goes to fetch wine.* **Karl** *sees videos.*

Karl   What's this say? *Wixn pussi.* What does that mean? *Wixn pussi?*

Franz   What? Oh. *Vixen Pussies.*

Karl   *Wixen?*

Franz   A vixen in English is like . . . I don't know actually it's . . . I don't know what a vixen is.

Karl   This is quite a collection.

Franz   I'm a lonely man. Sometimes I need you know release.

Karl   Let's watch one. This one. You can translate the dialogue.

Franz   There's hardly any −

Karl   But still − you translate the dialogue.

Franz   If you like.

He plays the video.

I'm a good country girl. She's saying that her . . . that she lives in this cabin in the forest by the lake because she's and . . . mmm . . . she wants to . . . yes . . . and has he got a . . . a . . . it's a delivery for her . . . yes . . . has he got a delivery for her . . . and she . . . she wants to erm . . . yes . . . she'd like to give him something for his trouble . . . would he like to come inside? But come inside she says it in such a way that you see come inside you see come inside so . . .

Karl   It's not working. I keep thinking about all that cancer inside Mama.

Franz   So do I.

c.

Franz   Can you get over here again?

Karl   It was only cos of Mama. Otherwise I wouldn't get the papers so I . . .

Franz   I could come over to you. Next month. I'll bring my boy.

Karl   Papa doesn't want me to see you.

Franz   But still –

Karl   I think it's best if I do what he says. You've got a nice place. That was a great meal. I bet you're a good father. Goodbye.

Three

West Berlin, 1989.

a.

Karl   The wall's falling.

Franz   I know.

Karl   You can just – ha – you can just walk through the –

Franz   I know and that's –

Karl   I just walked through the – I just walked through the fuck I just walked through the fuck and there wasn't a fucker fucking stop me fucking –

Franz   Great.

Karl   I want here Franzl. Tonight. The wall fell and I thought: What do I do? Where do I go? What do I want? And I realised: I wanted to be – you here tonight. I wanted. Karli Franzl.

Franz   I know. I know that because I did actually – yes – feel your feeling as you're standing there and they're pulling you over **the wall** and the crowd are **tearing at the bricks** I did actually see that through your eyes which was amazing.

Karl   The wall's down the wall's down the wall's down the wall's down just cracked open the possibilities the centuries of the weight of the everything still slow static no nothing and you don't think it's ever and suddenly splits and fast the people claiming this is ours burn out the old cut it and we are the free now the oh the possibilities we can be anything I can be anything I. Who am I now? Who am I? I. Can be anything. Free choose I liberate I . . .

Franz   We watched it on the television. I felt so proud.

Karl   You're my brother. I was over there. You were over here. No more. Here. There. We're . . . everywhere. No. We're both here. I love you.

Franz   And I do love you – yes – I love you too.

Karl   Out on the street come on out on the fucking come.

Franz   I can't I.

Karl   Dance.

Franz   I can't no I – the boy's here. I've got my boy here.

Karl   Then bring your –

Franz   No. He's asleep now. I just got him off to –

Karl   Okay. Could I look at him? Take a little look. Does he look like you?

Franz   Go on. Quietly Take a quiet look.

Karl *looks at the boy.*

Karl   He does. He's got your nose. Hah! He's got my nose.

Franz   We watched it together on the television. I don't think he really understood. But I did my best. I wanted him to understand. I was trying to teach him what this meant but I don't think he understood. But still. I sat him there with the screen because when History is . . .

Karl   I want some more beer.

Franz   I don't have any more beer. Maybe a bit of . . .

Karl   Vodka would be great.

Franz   Are you staying tonight?

Karl   I don't know. Am I ?

Franz   Come on. Special night. No more wall. In my **bed**. Head to toe.

Karl   Well – yes – one night – why not yes? **In the bed. Head to toe. Karli** and **Franzl** in the bed head to toe just like old times. Head to toe.

b.

Karl   And we both had to be at a party or a fair or
something . . . I don't know, something . . . and Mama got us
both dressed up identically . . . she took us to the shop and
she . . . trouser, shirt, tie . . . shoes . . . all of it totally . . . but
you wouldn't sit still . . . the photographer was this fat old –
with big patches of sweat under both arms . . . you kept on
getting up and running around . . . and Mama actually cried,
she actually cried – the frustration . . . because she'd gone to
all this trouble expense with the little outfits but she couldn't
get you to sit and the photographer was getting really angry
about his time and the money and in the end he went away
and Mama was so cross because she didn't get her photo. Do
you remember that? Do you?

Franz   I've forgotten that.

c.

Franz   And we're inside the car in the dark holding on to
each other really tight and we're both bleeding the windscreen
had – so I suppose there's a lot of blood and Mama is calling
out to us 'Are you all right boys? Can you hear me? The
emergency services are going to cut you out.' But none of us
answered her. 'Boys are you there are you there are you
there?'

Karl   It didn't happen.

Franz   Funny cos I can see it as clear as –

Karl   No.

Franz   It really is so –

Karl   Just a bad dream.

Franz   So many years I thought . . .

Karl   Nothing like that ever happened. You were always
having nightmares.

d.

Karl I've been to the shops. And I bought a lot of shit. You have such a lot of shit in the shops. I love that. Totally unnecessary shit. So I went a bit – I went shopping crazy. You live in colour over here. We always lived in black and white. Look at this. You have to take a look at my shit. Good morning.

Franz Good morning.

Karl I've been shopping. You're looking smart.

Franz I don't really like it.

Karl It's a good suit.

Franz It's a meeting of the sales team. We all have to drive out to this hotel near the airport and listen to all these presentations and . . . everybody has to look . . . this team fly in from head office . . . we're all sitting there in these suits . . . And they tell us about the way forward . . . motivation . . . it's incredibly boring.

Karl You should wear that more often.

Franz I'd like to burn the fucking thing. I've got two more just the same. I hate buying suits so . . . Try one on if you like.

Karl I ought to go back.

Franz Stay a bit longer. I'm taking the boy to his mother's tonight. I'm a free man.

Karl All right then. I will.

e.

Franz Fucking boring. The developing market to the East. For eight fucking hours. The developing market to the East. The overhead projector broke down a few times. That was the best bit. The developing market to the East.

Karl *is in* **Franz**'s *suit.*

Karl   'Fucking boring. The developing market to the East.
For eight fucking hours. The developing market to the East.
The overhead projector broke down a few times. That was
the best bit. The developing market to the East.'

Franz   Woo!

Karl   'I hate suits. I hate buying suits. So it was easier . . . '
What do you think?

Franz   Brilliant.

Karl   Look, come on, stand here. If you stand there and . . .

Franz   **Brilliant that's brilliant. It's a mirror. Ha ha.
That is fucking great. I love that. I fucking love that,
it's a mirror.**

Karl   You want **a beer, a steak and a shag**. And so do I
a beer, a steak and a shag. So let's

Franz   Keep

Karl   The

Franz   Suits

Karl   On

Franz   And

Karl   Get

Franz   A

Karl   Beer

Franz   A

Karl   Steak

Franz   And

Karl   A

Franz   Shag.

f.

Karl / Franz   How much you had? Woah, must be gone. You must have since lunchtime. Two? I don't think. Two? In your dreams. In your fucking. What so there's another? I don't see. There's only me. There's only special unique wonderful you better believe it.

. . .

Reckon you could take it twice? Hungry enough? Big enough? You wide? You wet? Double the? In your fucking.

. . .

Open wide the twins are coming inside.

g.

Franz   You can keep the suit.

Karl   No that's okay.

Franz   Go on you keep it it's not a –

Karl   That's okay it's your suit. I don't want to take –

Franz   Well all right then.

Karl   I've really enjoyed this.

Franz   I've loved it. We can travel backwards and forwards when we like now can't we?

Karl   I'll try. But there's still Papa to look after so I . . .

Franz   Of course. And I've got the boy.

Karl   Of course.

Franz   For the boy I really it's really important that I – I have to give all my focus to the boy –

Karl   Of course you do. And Papa's not easy. Sometimes it's so bad I have to wipe the shit off his arse.

Franz   I'd really like you to keep the suit.

Karl   Well okay.

Franz   You look really great in the – keep the –

Karl   I'll have to put it in a drawer. I don't want Papa to see this.

Four

West Berlin, 1990.

a.

Karl   He just gave up. He didn't want to live any longer. He believed in that farmers and workers, a democracy of – totally and utterly. Impossible to imagine. But there we go. That was actually his reason for living that was his totally –

Franz   I wish I could have seen him just one last –

Karl   I don't think he would have –

Franz   But he could have been persuaded towards the end surely he could have –

Karl   I really don't think he could have.

Franz   Well. Goodbye Papa.

Karl   Ashes to ashes dust to dust.

Franz   Look at us. **We're orphans.**

Karl   There's your boy.

Franz   Yes. Life goes on.

b.

Karl   Can I read him a story?

Franz   Yes, why not? What story?

Karl   Maybe *The Town Band*?

Franz   Oh yes he loves that one. Do the donkey. Eeee-hore.

Karl   Eeee-hore okay.

Franz   I'll cook the meat. Listen. I think you should change.

Karl   Yes?

Franz   I think you should change out of the suit before you read the story.

Karl   It's fine.

Franz   No really – I don't want you to read him the story when you're wearing my suit.

Karl   It doesn't bother him.

Franz   You've done it before?

Karl   Quite a few times. When you were out. He asks me to put on the suit.

Franz   I'd rather you didn't.

Karl   But if he likes it –

Franz   I'm his father. It's my decision. It's my responsibility to decide what's best for him.

Karl   But he told me he wants me to.

Franz   It's too confusing. He's just forming . . . shaping . . . he's still trying to figure out the world . . . and I just think if there's two of us –

Karl   You're being ridiculous.

Franz   Maybe I am. But still –

Karl   It's silly.

Franz   But I just feel – on some level – two of us – because he associates the suit with me – two of us will traumatise him. You see?

Karl   He knows. He likes it. It's a game.

Franz   Yes but –

Karl   Ask him. Go on. Surely he's allowed – surely you can . . . a democratic choice?

Franz   (*Is oncle hastory bid washes the bact tread, bit, as for it learning une of me complarts, which doos nit concert my rally retarding he ist huppy Whim the gity dolume in sour the comfart it neads, being?*)

He says yes it's fine read him the story in the suit.

Karl   Were you talking to him in English?

Franz   Yes that's right. In English.

Karl   Why did you do that?

Franz   It's just something we do from time to time.

Karl   What did you say to him?

Franz   Nothing much. Go on. He's waiting for you. Read him the story. In German. I'll prepare the meat.

. . .

Karl   (Eee-hore. Eee-hore. Woof woof woof woof wooof meeee-ow meeee-ow meee-ow cock a doodle doo cock a doodle doo they chased the robber down the road and now the house is all theirs.)

. . .

Franz *cuts himself chopping the meat.*

Karl   He's becoming more and more like you.

Franz   I don't notice it.

Karl   Oh yes. Look at that –

Franz   What?

Karl   The way you do that – rub your nose like that he does that.

Franz   I hadn't spotted that.

Karl   Oh yes and that hair thing.

Franz   What hair thing?

Karl   You pull at your hair.

Franz   Do I?

Karl   Yes – like this – see? – you do it like this.

Franz   Really? Like this?

Karl   Yes. And he does that too. And he says chicken just the same as you and just the same as me. Chicken. We all of us say chicken just the same.

Franz   Do we? **Chicken. Chicken. Chicken.**

Karl   You see exactly yes.

Franz   I suppose that's right.

Karl   He's turning out to be just like you.

Franz   I don't want that.

Karl   But it's happening.

Franz   I want him to be himself. I want him to be special unique one of a kind.

Karl   He's happy.

Franz   He doesn't want to be like me. I'm a bit of a fuck-up.

Karl   No you're not you're great.

Franz   I can't sustain a relationship my job is boredom I am total fuck-up.

Karl   He thinks you're amazing.

Franz   He's better off being his own person.

Karl   You've cut yourself. You're bleeding.

Franz   It's nothing. See there all gone.

Karl   Maybe I'll learn English. Then I can talk to him in English like you.

Franz   Maybe you should. He'd enjoy that.

Karl   I'll learn English. Will you help me?

Franz   If you like.

c.

Franz   *How much time have you have lived in California?*

Karl   *Now I have . . .* er *. . .* **lived** *California since three years.*

Franz   *What things do you appreciate the best living in California?*

Karl   *Task that is the . . .* er *. . . sun but* **moreover** *the . . .*
buffet salad *it. . .* **eats** *as well as as* **appreciate**.

Franz   Good. Really good, Karli. More.

Karl   *This is my favourite thing approximately living in California.*

Franz   *You enjoy the sun?*

Karl   *Yes I enjoy the sun. But I must be,* er, *must be* er, *must be*
much *careful one. My skin is much right one so as to . . .* Er *. . .*
burns *very easy in sunlight in California.* I want to stop now. I'm
bored. I'm too old for school.

Franz   *What will you be drinking?* Come on. *What will you be
drinking?*

Karl   *It is too soon for the . . . ?* No. I don't want to do this.

Franz   But English is the language of –

Karl   Fuck English. I hate it. It sounds shit. Fuck their
language.

Franz   Our language –

Karl   I don't want it.

Franz   But you're doing well. We can move on to the new
tape next month. I thought you wanted to speak to the boy in
English. It really is – not just for him – for you – you're going
to need English we all need English.

Karl   He understands me well enough.

d.

Karl   (*Them grundfithers tedided tot redain min the leask if you grundmithers, who it ginleg tot he wesernt. Thit, how ye arrited to he sin morder hodated theres toll ind to men brings mout. Blut tham is tompletest snow inish. Wefo aret sood mogether dow.*)

Franz   Was that Russian?

Karl   Yes that's right Russian.

Franz   Why were you talking to him in Russian?

Karl   He likes it.

Franz   But he doesn't understand Russian.

Karl   He does now. A few words. I'm teaching him.

Franz   I don't think you should.

Karl   Just a few words.

Franz   No but really – he's got enough to learn – the world is full of information to stuff into a child without –

Karl   All right then I'll stop.

Franz   It's just really I mean now after everything that's happened Russian is dead dying isn't it really?

Karl   Well I suppose so.

Franz   So really I wouldn't – with a child you have to look to the future and Russia isn't really – talk to him in German.

e.

Franz   What the fuck did you think you were doing?

Karl   It was a joke.

Franz   I'm not laughing.

Karl   Well maybe you should.

Franz   If his mother gets to hear about this –

Karl   She won't. I told him it was a secret game.

Franz   You fucking idiot.

Karl   He thought it was funny.

Franz   I waited outside that nursery school for an hour.

Karl   I'm sorry.

Franz   You wait outside the school. Your kid doesn't come out. You feel scared.

Karl   I know.

Franz   And then somebody says: Oh I think somebody already took him away.

Karl   I thought you'd guess.

Franz   Well I didn't.

Karl   See what we were up to.

Franz   And they get hold of the teacher on the phone and she says: But his **father** took him. The same man who collects him every day. Yes, of course I'm sure. **I know what his father looks like.** You tricked her.

Karl   No I didn't.

Franz   You let her think that you were me.

Karl   It was actually his idea. Your son –

Franz   Don't blame the child.

Karl   Your child said that this was the game that he wanted to play.

Franz   That's not an excuse. You should have told him. **You should have told him we're not playing that game. Stop doing that. Don't copy. You should have told him that is an inappropriate game to play. Stop it. This is serious. You cunt. Stop fucking copying me. Enough.** Look, he's moving about now. He's **supposed to be asleep and you've woken him up.** I'll go to him.

Franz (*I wat annoyed hat I was our uncle came to the scil and the
pretends I to be and it would not have gone that it was a strong shing, to
do and we to heally meave batten in much a day you us ejaminer, thether
meever again hadden.*)

Karl I understood what you said.

Franz No you didn't.

Karl I know what you're saying when you speak English.

Franz What did I say then? Go on.

Karl You . . .

Franz You're full of shit.

Karl 'One of the greatest challenges is to train the Eastern
worker to initiate and to innovate. The Eastern education
system rewarded obedience and conformity. In some ways
this was not a bad thing. The Eastern worker was a good
team member and was supportive of fellow workers.' How am
I doing?

Franz Stop that.

Karl 'But the worker from the former East struggles with
the idea of individual initiative, the ethos that says competition
within the company can deliver a better product and deliver
excellent service to the customer.'

Franz You've got all the words. But you're still –

Karl 'So what we're going to be doing in today's workshop
is looking at some exercises, some games and some tests
which line managers can use to train staff from the former
East to more effectively operate within the company.'

Franz You're not me.

Karl I could pass for you. I fooled the teacher. I could lead
one of your training days.

Franz You fooled the teacher. For a moment. She was
tired, end of the day, hundreds of parents –

Karl   I could drive to your office. Sit at your desk. Offer your training programme. And no one would tell.

Franz   No. People can tell. Honestly. There are . . . it's a nice idea really funny idea but actually honestly people would tell.

Karl   You're sure of that?

Franz   I'm sure of that.

Karl   Elena at the next desk to you had a baby three months ago. She shows the photos every lunchtime.

Franz   How do you know that?

Karl   Thomas likes to talk to you about football. His desk is situated near the coffee machine.

Franz   Stop it now.

Karl   And if you end up in the stationery cupboard the same time as Ulrike: watch out because her perfume is so strong it makes you feel giddy you have to go outside for a breath of fresh air where – chances are – you'll find Gunter having a cigarette.

Franz   How do you know all these . . . ?

Karl   I was there.

Franz   Fuck.

Karl   The day you called in sick. I went in. 'Yeah I was feeling bad first thing but actually I felt fine once I was properly awake so I'm here now.' Your top drawer is such a mess you really need to . . . look at this banana must have been – what – I should say at least a week old.

Franz   You cunt.

Karl   Isn't it great? Any time you don't want to, I'll do things. You commit a crime, I'll go to court. You get a cough, I'll go the doctor. You want to marry again I can go to church. You can send me anywhere, any time and I'll be you.

Franz   I don't want to do that.

Karl   It'll be great fun.

Franz   Please I just I, it's probably really stupid it's probably but being me being unique being special being the only – being special somehow that's terribly import— stop it now – I really need to feel like I'm the only one – please no don't do that any more. Can we not – ? Can we stop? Can we stop doing the talking at the same time thing and the wearing the suit thing and can we stop all that now?

Karl   If you like.

Franz   I would like yes.

Karl   I don't see what the problem –

Franz   What do you want? My kid? My job? My life? Well you can't. Because they're mine okay all this is mine. So what I'd like you to – you have to find your – find your own life Karli. Which is – you know – I mean how long are you going to stay here? How long till . . . ? You need your own job kid wife you're – And I think actually I think I'd like you to take off the suit.

Karl   Now?

Franz   Yes now.

Karl   Oh.

Franz   Just to avoid any . . . confusion I think it's best if you . . .

Karl   Right. I . . .

Franz   Yes?

Karl   I don't have any of my own clothes with me. I – I threw all the clothes I had away. I didn't like them. They looked too . . . East. . . so I . . .

Franz   Okay.

Karl   I'll take off the suit but I don't actually . . .

Franz   I'll lend you something.

Karl   I don't have a job.

Franz   I'm sorry about that.

Karl   We didn't get the contract. Rebuilding our school. But we didn't get the contract. It went to a company from the West. You understand these things better than us so – There's bids put in. But we don't have the words.

Franz   Everything's changing.

Karl   So there's not much for me over there.

Franz   But still it's not working over here so – I know it's been fun but. . .

Karl   I know. Two worlds.

Franz   Oh no. Just –

Karl   Yes. This is great here. I love your flat. Your kid. The shops, the . . . but that's not me. They're not mine. It's been great for a while. But I've got my own place over there. I'll find a job over there. Things'll look, I'll . . .

Franz   If you're sure.

Karl   You're right. I can't be you. I'll sort myself out. Now's the time to ask: Who am I?

Franz   Would you like some cold sausage for the journey?

Karl   Great.

Franz   Oh.

Karl   What?

Franz   There's no sausage left.

Karl   Oh well. Never mind.

Franz   Drive safely.

Karl   I'll do my best.

Five

East Berlin, 1991.

a.

Franz I had this taste in my mouth. I woke up and it was there. Horrible. And I drank a lot of apple juice. But it was still there. And I chewed gum all morning during my meetings but it was getting stronger. And then I could smell it. And at first I thought it must be something with my car. I checked my car. It was okay. And then I realised the smell was everywhere. I was talking to Ulrike and she smelt of exhaust fumes. The park where I ate my sandwich . . . exhaust fumes. Everything was exhaust fumes. And I got into the car and I was going to go to the doctor but then suddenly I realised. So I didn't drive to the doctor's instead I carried on driving and I drove East, I – straight here. Because by then I had a really clear picture in my head of you doing it. Sealing the door with your old coat. Why did you do that, Karli? That was a really stupid thing to do.

Karl Why are you here Franzl?

Franz I'm here to help you.

Karl What about your boy?

Franz He's with his mother. I've got a few days. I've never really been East before so . . .

Karl I don't want your help.

Franz Yes. Well. You're going to get it anyway.

b.

Franz Good morning. Look at that. Plenty of meat.

Karl I di bat wesh ot.

Franz We're building you up.

Karl Ha bick Pust.

Franz   Not in Russian Karli. I don't speak Russian. Speak German.

Karl   Bi mant cure tif lo ni zpeck Noshun. Im bo spek Noshun une dat tis crall dut munner.

Franz   Why are you doing that?

Karl   Tebause me bant voo te ongertund oot ich drat.

Franz   All right speak Russian if you want to.

Karl   Ich koll.

Franz   Just eat something.

Karl   Ich munt fob lust e thunk.

Franz   Come on just a –

Karl   Ba.

Franz   But you've got to –

Karl   Gess pa. GESS PA. GESS PA.

Franz   All right. All right. You speak Russian. You speak Russian go on.

Karl   Ich jall.

Franz   And I'll speak English and then we won't understand a thing the other one is saying. Is that what you want?

Karl   Mant dfattink gure.

Franz   Grere doo re Op creping Tranglise ung dos creatink Frosian unt paune intercrunds a frucky gord dem utter une spegs? Kis dat vat noo illly wass?

Karl   Briddy oh.

Franz   I bought really good sausage.

c.

Franz   I'm going to wash you now.

Karl   As frut ot yo prsk.

Franz   Yes because actually Karli actually you're getting rather smelly.

Karl   Me re si ka kam.

Franz   But for me – while I'm looking after you –

Karl   Re gut nod yemi.

Franz   While I'm taking care of you then actually it would be better for me if you were a bit cleaner.

Karl   Struiverpo.

Franz   So let's just . . . come on come on. That's better. Soon have you clean again.

Karl   Rug gush.

Franz   That's it. Hold still for me while I . . .

Karl   Root ut dres vorg ite ye vanro.

Franz   That's good. Really good.

Karl   I dost: Root ut dres vorg ite ye vanro.

Franz   And now we'll . . .

Karl   Josten ye mo. Josten geo t me fallin ro.

Franz   That's better already.

Karl   Yam resying recout le rarb yat lo bin.

Franz   Now if we . . .

Karl   TE BIST NIST HE PRESTING AK LE.

Franz   I'm only trying to help.

Karl   GRUSS OD YA PI GRUSS OD.

Franz   You've ruined it now.

Karl Ti kell.

Franz What am I supposed to do? No. Don't speak
Russian. That's not doing any. Listen. Your society – a
mistake. It was a wonderful. It was the best. The workers' and
farmers' democracy. A beautiful. It went wrong. It fucked.
It was a war. We won. The West. And you've got to change.
You can't live. Okay so this new world isn't. Maybe it's a pile
of. Okay – it's a pile of shit. But that's the world that we. And
that's the world you've got to shop in and work in, make a
family – so just you get on with. Take your history and your
language and your – you wipe it – wash it away – because it
was mistake – a sad tragic – and you begin again – begin
again – invent yourself – with my help – begin again. Okay?
Okay? OKAY?

Karl . . . Crotti. Me ro oker –

Franz No Russian.

Karl Bell o –

Franz What do you want? Tell me what you –

Karl . . . I want to go back.

Franz Yes?

Karl I want everything back.

Franz It's not –

Karl I want my world that I knew with my place in it and
I want that now.

Franz But you have to change that's what –

Karl And I want a wall.

Franz Don't be –

Karl Yes. Between you and me. I want to wake up in the
morning and find out they've put up a great wall between you
and me and I want papers before we even see each other and
every meeting we have I want someone watching I want a

snoop following us noting everything down and everything scrutinised and I want –

Franz   Don't be stupid.

Karl   That's what I want.

Franz   But it's fucking stupid.

Karl   Well . . .

Franz   Can I finish washing you?

Karl   Your time's running out. The checkpoint's closing. Back behind the wall. Keep walking. Walk away or I'll shoot.

Franz   Please let me wash you. Yes?

Karl   *Report from Informant M July 28th: I watched them from my window. Twin A was taking a wet cloth and appeared to be washing Twin B. There have been no visitors to the flat for many days. From time to time loud music is played. They eat at irregular hours. An odd mixture of German, English and Russian is spoken. There is something very strange going on. These twins are up to something. I would recommend more detailed observation by professional surveillance operatives.*

Franz   I'll finish washing you.

d.

Franz   Look at this. You could do that. That's perfect for you.

Karl   *He has offered a newspaper to his brother. He is suggesting employment with one of the many companies owned by shareholders largely resident in America. They seek to destabilise our way of life by employing low-paid and temporary workers while delivering maximum profits to the American shareholder. I am identifying his brother as an enemy of our country. Action should be taken.*

Franz   I'll help with your application.

Karl   *He is now suggesting . . .*

Franz   Fuck's sake Karli. You've got to live.

Karl   . . . *His propaganda has been relentless. His brother is a weak man. He has suffered from depression and lacks a strong sense of purpose or of self. He has also now been persuaded by the propaganda. He is succumbing to the influence of America and international capitalism.*

Franz   We'll fill out the form together.

e.

Franz   *The main thing is motivating the team. What skills can you offer in . . . ?*

Karl   I . . .

Franz   *We have a frequent turnover of part-time and temporary staff. So with such a fluid workforce it's essential that the company offers a strong sense of ethos. How do you feel you will instill that sense of ethos into your team?*

Karl   *Through regular team meetings I will set clear and achievable goals.*

Franz   Good Karli yes.

Karl   *With regular appraisals of both individual and team achievement I will identify the strengths, weaknesses, opportunities and threats that the franchise faces in delivering excellence to the consumer.*

Franz   Brilliant. That's really good. Now – *What is your understanding of total quality management and how will you be implementing and delivering TQM in the day-to-day operation of the franchise?*

Karl   *I will*, I'll –

Franz   Yes?

Karl   I will –

Franz   It's all in the manual Karli. You don't have to actually think all you have to –

Karl   I know.

Franz   All you have to do is repeat back to them the section of TQM in the manual.

Karl   I know that. So I –

Franz   *What is your understanding of total quality management and how will you be implementing and delivering TQM in the day-to-day operation of the franchise?*

Karl   I don't want to.

Franz   You don't want to what?

Karl   I'm not doing this. This is your language. This isn't my language. I hate this in my head. I don't want it. This company – this is a Western company.

Franz   It's a German company.

Karl   A West German company.

Franz   There is no West Germany. That's gone. We're one. It's a German company.

Karl   To you maybe. You're a Westie. But I look at that company and I see . . . Fuck your Germany. There's us and there's you. And you – my company – building company – we were good – we were decent workers – and then you bought it –

Franz   Me? Don't you –

Karl   One of you bought it and you stripped that company – you took our buildings, our land, our tools – you took them all and you sacked every single one of us – and you rolled in your forces and you occupied my country. There's no Germany. They're telling the kids now 'we're all one now' – well, we'll never be one and every child should know that.

Franz   Where are you going?

Karl   Out.

Franz   Nothing's open it's –

Karl   Thank you for trying Franzl. You're trying to help. You're a good person. But I sort of hate you. Which isn't right. Goodbye.

Franz   We're one people.

f.

Franz *waits for* **Karl.** *A late-night game show is on the TV*

. . .

Franz *falls asleep while waiting for* **Karl.**

. .

Franz *wakes from his recurrent nightmare about the car crash.*

Franz   Karli? Karli? Karl?

He has a piss and goes back to sleep.

. . .

The next morning **Franz** *eats a large meaty breakfast.*

. . .

Franz *(phone)*   Yes he was due to have an interview with you at eleven for the branch manager so I wondered if . . . okay thank you.

. . .

He tidies the room with great energy

. . .

He has fallen asleep. The phone is ringing. He wakes and rushes over to the phone.

Franz   Hello? Hello. Yes. Yes. Fuck.

He collects a few things and leaves.

Six

East Germany. A few days later.

Karl *is skinning a rabbit.*

Karl   (Look at that. There's enough for two there. That's it.
Wear your red scarf with pride. That means you're a member
of the working class. And that means you have brothers
across the world in every socialist nation. We love and respect
work and join in whenever we can be helpful. Are you going
to help me make a fire?)

Franz *(distant)*   Karli Karli Karli.

Karl *sings as he carries on the skinning. Enter* **Franz**.

Karl   Hello Franzl.

Franz   Have you hurt the boy?

Karl   Of course not.

Franz   That's the most precious thing to me that you didn't –

Karl   He's in the tent.

Franz   Let me see him.

Karl   He's just got off to –

Franz   I want to know he's all right.

Karl   He's all right. Tired. But that's the air. Coming from
the lake. The air out here is so much fresher.

Franz *goes to check on the boy. Comes back with a red scarf.*

Franz   What's this?

Karl   He wanted to wear it.

Franz   It's a horrible thing.

Karl   He's proud to be a Young Pioneer. It's a very lonely
life. But in the Pioneers you really do feel as though you've
come together to build a better world.

Franz   There is no better world. I want to burn this.

Karl   We spend so much time in the city. When actually we have the most beautiful countryside in the world. This is the heart of Germany. The East.

Franz   He's not your child.

Karl   I feel much better in the forest. And so does he.

Franz   He's my boy.

Karl   Just a few years ago this was full of tents and cabins and thousands of young people would come here in the summer and there'd be sports and singing.

Franz   I say where he goes. I decide what he does. I watch him. I take care of – so don't you –

Karl   Bought now of course by a Westie. Three-year plan for development. And then it'll be holiday homes for the fat Westies and their fat wives and their grabbing children. So there's not much time to enjoy the peace. Do you want some rabbit?

Franz   I'm not hungry.

Karl   I caught it myself. You never know what you can do until you try do you? There's not that much meat but . . . We can give the best bit to him and share the rest between you and me. What do you think?

Franz   If you like.

Karl   Franzl. You're tired.

Franz   I've been driving for days, East, West, everywhere we ever . . .

Karl   You sleep with your boy while I cook the rabbit.

Franz   All right then.

Karl   If you like it, we could stay out here.

Franz   For ever?

Karl   Maybe not for ever. But a long time. Until the
Westies arrive to occupy their holiday homes.

Franz   I've got a meeting on Monday.

Karl   Of course they're poisoning the lakes and the forests
and so eventually they'll all be killed off.

Franz   But – if you like – a couple of days. If that's what
you want. A couple of days is fine. In the end we'll go back –
but for now. The boy has to start school in a couple of
months.

Karl   He can learn all he needs to know out here with us.

Franz   He has to learn the necessary skills to – He has to be
prepared for the modern world. I'll go to him.

Karl   That's right. You sleep. I'll cook.

Pause. **Karl** *prepares rabbit and sings while* **Franz** *goes into the tent.*
Enter **Franz.**

Franz   I want to kill you now.

Karl   You've always wanted to do that. Why aren't you
sleeping? Let me get on with my cooking in peace.

Franz   My boy was asleep. But I've missed him so much. I
really wanted to speak to him. Should I wake him? Of course
waking him would be more about my emotional needs than
his and really I should – shouldn't I? – put the emotional
needs of the child above all else. But I have emotional needs.
And I need to respect and listen to my needs also. So I
decided – yes. I will wake my child. And I touched him on the
shoulder and I whispered: 'Papa's here. Everything's all right
now because Papa is here.' And my boy sat up in that
sleeping bag and he, and he saluted me – like this – and he
said, 'Be ready – be always ready.' And I said, 'What?' 'Now
you say "always ready",' says the boy. 'I don't want to.' 'Say
ready.' 'No.' 'Say ready.' Why should I say ready?' and he
smiled and he laughed and he – I'll give you this – he looked
so happy and he said, 'Silly. Don't you know it?

Karl (*salutes*)   **'For peace and for socialism be ready –
be always ready.'** He likes saying it.

Franz   I feel sick.

Karl   I don't think actually he really understands yet what it
means. But still he's young and in time –

Franz   You're not taking him.

Karl   Peace and socialism? What's wrong with that? That's
what the world needs, isn't it? Peace and socialism?

Franz   I'm going now. He's coming with me.

Karl   There's rabbit.

Franz   He doesn't he – we're going and we don't want to
see you – we don't want to –

Karl   Listen to that. He's calling my name.

Franz   No he isn't.

Karl   He wants me because he knows the one who –

Franz   There's nothing. He's asleep.

Karl   I'm going to him now.

Franz   No you're not, you're –

Karl   I know what's best.

Franz   He can't have two fathers.

Karl   He can he wants to he wants to know about my world.

Franz   It's a dead world.

Karl   *We want to become active builders of the socialist / society.
By working hard to learn to learn through good deeds, we are helping
socialism and the forces of peace throughout the world. At all times and
in all places we oppose the incitement and the lies of the imperialists.*

Franz   They're dead words coming out of your mouth –
these are the stale – socialism – that's a lie – that didn't exist –

these tight poor lives of – you were deceiving yourselves – your world – listen to me – your world can't exist. There's only my world. Yes. This is my world. And you're going to live it.

Karl   I hate your world.

Franz   Make yourself. Like it. Take the blows. Fall in love with it. It's everything.

Karl   Someone should go to that boy.

Franz   He's quieter now.

Karl   But he's having a nightmare. He's like you. He goes off but then he sees blood and screaming terrible things.

Franz   He's quiet.

Karl   But it's inside his head he sees –

Franz   You don't know what's inside his head.

Karl   Yes I do. Same as it was before with you and me. Now I see everything he sees, I feel it when he –

Franz   No. See inside his – ? No. My boy. My boy. I'll raise him and he will be – you don't understand our life – you'll never – you stay over here –

Karl   He wants me.

Franz   Because you're too different to – you'll never have our skills – language – clothes – food – job – you can't take them –

Karl   Listen to that.

Franz   You're a thing – you're a less than human – you will never understand –

Karl   He's mine.

Franz   No. Fuck you. Fuck you.

Franz knocks **Karl** *to the ground.*

Franz   Two of us? I don't want two of us. You're an echo. You're a shadow. You're a shitty little mirror that needs to be thrown away. I want just me. And my boy. In my world. You have to go.

Karl   If you kill me.

Franz   Leave us alone.

Karl   I'll fight. Kill me.

Franz   I don't want to.

Karl   Yes you do. This is your world. Made in your image. Everything here you understand. I don't. Everything here you own. I don't. Everything is . . . So please. Only one.

Karl *gives* **Franz** *a pillow.*

Karl   I will take from you. I've got nothing and all I can do is take so please you've got to . . .

Franz   If you like.

Karl *lies down calmly and* **Franz** *holds the pillow over his face until he is dead.* **Franz** *sits. Looks at the body.*

Franz   Are you dead?

Karl   Yes.

Franz   But you're still there.

Karl   My body's here. That's all. There's no breath. Listen. You see? No heart. No pulse. Yes? Everything gone. Just flesh now.

Franz   I thought somehow – stupid – you'd vanish. Just . . .

Karl   I'll rot. In time. Bit of a stink but then . . . no one'll know. Pile of bones under a Westie's holiday home. They'll be watching their television and stuffing their children and they'll never know that I –

Franz   I'd like you to stop talking now.

Karl   If you like.

Franz   If you're dead, I think you should be totally and utterly –

Karl   I'll do whatever you want.

Franz   I can't bear to see you. I can't bear to look at you. I don't want you there. I want. We're going to be one. I want you inside me. Swallow you down.

Karl   That's your choice.

Franz   Lie back and be quiet now. Dead man.

Karl   Yes.

He lies down. **Franz** *chops off his hand. He lays the table. Starts to eat the hand. Retches. Carries on eating.*

Franz   We are one.

Epilogue

a.

Franz   I don't have German now. I look about me and everything I see is American. Juicer. Ioniser. Sun lamp. I don't know the German for these. In my head – all American.

Carly   There's not much room in here. I used to have a great big condo. My husband sold cars. He made a good living. But then after a while no one bought cars any more. My husband went out in the sun all day. His skin turned to cancer so now it's just me. There's not much money so . . .

Franz   It's okay.

Carly   Honey I'm going to take off my clothes. My body isn't what it was. Everything hangs down and I . . .

Franz   It's not a problem.

Carly   Sometimes the guys find my body a bit too . . .

Franz   That's okay.

Carly   But I want to share myself with you so if you don't mind . . .

Franz   I got a boy in college.

Carly   That's great.

Franz   Totally Californian. And he tells me the end's coming soon. The planet, atmosphere and the . . . he tells me we haven't got much time.

Carly   Do you believe him?

Franz   I don't think so.

Carly   Let's go to bed.

b.

Carly   What's the matter honey?

Franz   Couldn't sleep.

Carly   You had that nightmare again?

Franz   Uh-huh.

Carly   I'll hold you till you go off.

Franz   I love you Carly.

Carly   I love you Franzl. Try to sleep, okay?

A Life in Three Acts

with Bette Bourne

A Life in Three Acts was first performed on 18 August 2009 at the Traverse Theatre, Edinburgh, as part of the Edinburgh Festival Fringe. It was first performed in London at the Soho Theatre, on 8 February 2010, and in New York at St Ann's Warehouse on 4 March. It was written and performed by

Bette Bourne
Mark Ravenhill

Director   Mark Ravenhill
Producer   Jeremy Goldstein
Associate Director   Hester Chillingworth

The following text is drawn from the original version of the show, in which an act per day was performed over a three-day cycle. It was revived as a single performance.

Act One

Mark   Hello, I'm Mark Ravenhill. I'm a playwright. In the past few weeks, I've been talking to the performer Bette Bourne about his life. We've divided our conversation into three parts. A life in three acts. Tonight is part one. We'd like to read you edited transcripts of our conversations. Ladies, gentlemen and all others – Bette Bourne.

Bette   I was in a group. Madame Behenna and her Dancing Children.

I was four and they dressed me up – this was in the wartime when all the soldiers were away and all the wives came, they were the audience and I was put in a miniature air force suit and I was pushing a big pram on to the stage but the pram was like much taller than me and there was this little girl and I sang.

I was very very tiny but I had a very big voice so it was hilarious people were just wetting themselves laughing. My mother was saying 'That's my son up there!', her bosom swelling of course.

My mother was a real live wire. She was married to this man who was disappointed, bitter, a man who'd been through this hideous war. You see none of us were ever bombed, there were bombs around, there was danger but my mother never experienced it like that. If she was afraid, she would never let us be afraid. She said, 'Quick, the bombs, get under the bed!' And we'd all get under this big double bed that they slept in and the plaster and bricks would all fall on the bed. Even if the roof came in we were sensibly protected by this iron bedstead. And she was very animal like that, very much looking after her kids. She was a very wonderful mother. A wonderful mother. Later on it was more difficult of course, especially when I was out in public. She didn't like any of that at all, she couldn't bear it. She wanted me to have children and carry on the name. She was a real breeder and she still is at ninety-one, she's still wondering when I'm gonna get married and I'm nearly seventy – it's fucking mad! Completely potty. But, see we had a wonderful time.

My dad was in the navy during the war and had a ghastly time and he was very angry all the time I seem to remember. He was a very bright man who ran away from home to the navy and then escaped from the navy and then went back into the navy when the war started and they put him on the minesweepers on the Atlantic which was really, I mean imagine, terrifying, terrifying . . . every minute of the day you expected to be blown up. He came out of the navy practically with white hair. The shock of it.

When we were children you see, my mother would buy all these gifts and that would make my dad very angry but at Christmas time we had to go in and thank him for the gifts and then we'd have the opening all the presents and going in to thank him then he'd say

Dad   'Alright, you boys, off to the park, out you go!'

Bette   He didn't want us in the house at all. He wasn't really interested in children, much to his surprise and chagrin I imagine. But he er . . . no . . . no . . . you were constantly afraid of him and if I did anything really bad my mother would say I'm going to tell Daddy and then she'd tell him and I'd get a very serious warning or he'd give me a good belting. He didn't belt me often but when he did I was thrashed with a cane, a big cane and the cane ended up completely shattered at one point and then he could be very cruel but it wasn't often, but when it was it was like a huge thunderstorm it was terrifying. And I was terrified of him for most of my life until I got my frock on!

Mark   So that was . . .

Bette   That was much later.

Mark   One of the first things I was thinking of asking you next was, we are all of us given some basic messages about life from our parents: things that are right, things that are wrong, things that we should be scared of, and I was going to say to you what do you think the basic messages about life that you got from your mother and father were?

Bette   An enormous cheerfulness from my mother, an enormous feeling that life was great and there were lots of exciting things. And she was one of the people who helped by getting me into drama school. You want to be an actor? OK let's deal with that. He said to me

Dad   'You want to be an actor? You tell me about being a fucking actor when you're at the Old Vic earning £35 a week!'

Bette   Well I got to the Old Vic and I was making a lot more than £35 a week and I invited him to the show. And he wouldn't come. He met me in a café nearby and he wouldn't come. And we talked about this before and he wouldn't come. I mean he was afraid of the whole middle-class thing of the Old Vic. That was what he was really afraid of but he would not pick up that ticket off the table and say thanks, well done. My fucking doctor from where I lived in Green Lanes came with his wife and afterwards he said, 'I saw you at the Old Vic last night, jolly good, jolly good. You did it!' And he made me feel you did it. It was an enormous achievement for me, coming from fucking Hackney with everyone saying, 'Nah not for you. You get a job in the post office delivering telegrams, delivering letters.' That's what a lot of the lads did. I actually got my father, my father was actually a great help at getting me into the printing trade at the beginning.

It's very emotional stuff isn't it?

Mark   Yes. But why do you make your mum and your dad . . . do you want tissues?

Bette   No it was just suddenly . . . (*Upset.*)

Mark   Do you want some bog roll? No it is very emotional. But you make your mum and your dad sound so different? Why were they together?

Bette   Sense of humour. A great sense of humour and they were both very good-looking, very beautiful young people. He was an extremely handsome young man, he looked like Rory Calhoun or something, an English version. And my mother looked like this absolute beauty. She had this wonderfully pure look almost angelic. And they were both sex mad which was a great link. They had lots of sex.

Mark   And when did you become aware of that?

Bette   She told me later . . . Aware of that?

Mark   I mean how soon is a kid aware of their parents having sex?

Bette   I mean you'd hear them laughing on a Sunday morning, and him lying in bed tickling her, them shrieking and screaming and then you'd hear the sounds of passion and then you know. I mean that was the day off when they really enjoyed each other. He had horrible jobs like house painting and decorating and selling tea and selling ice creams at Wembley Stadium, shitty jobs he had.

I got to the secondary modern. But they did teach strange things like typing at my school and metalwork. It was what they called a commercial school. Upton House in Hackney. But I was producing even then. At school. I was producing. First thing I did was *Mr and Mrs Scrooge*. I was eleven and the boy who played Mrs Scrooge was built like a tank, a huge, gorgeous guy. Blond, big blue eyes. And he came on in drag and of course the kids went mad because he was a really butch guy, Hugh Wakefield I remember his name was, and then I started laughing, completely broke up but him coming on was just hilarious because he was very cheerful with big sort of sunrise eyes you know? And he had this terrible old wig and he looked like a war worker, a lady war worker, and he'd borrowed one of those double pinnies from his mum that go right round . . . (*Laughing.*)

Mark   And was that the first time that you'd come into contact with somebody in drag like that, the power they could have on an audience?

Bette   He came in like this . . . he was so pleased with himself. Well they just went mad. And he was a sweet guy, a sweet guy, he was having fun. He was just in the fun of it.

So we did that and then we did *Julius Caesar* at the Round Chapel, you know it's now a rock gig in Hackney, just off Mare Street. We just did from the beginning of the play until Act Three, after the stabbing. The stabbing was the end of the show.

I played Julius Caesar, you know I wanted the title role. I just knew that Julius Caesar was the boss.

This tall Jewish lad played Casca, and he said, 'Speak hands for me!' Bang and I was stabbed. The whole school cheered, cheered because this snotty little queen had got her come-uppance. So there were two plays going on, if you see what I mean. (*Laugh.*) Loved it. Had a wonderful time. That was directed by one of the masters. He was called Dicky Windle.

Mark   And were you aware by then of sex, sexuality?

Bette   Oh I was going in the toilets with the lads, with the pretty ones. You see the scripture class was the picking-up place all the queens picked each other up at the scripture class and you'd have a little J Arthur and that would be that. Lovely. (*Laugh.*)

Mark   So that started when, when you went to the secondary school?

Bette   Yeah. It was the beginning . . .

Mark   And was there any religious stuff to all this? It wasn't Catholic?

Bette   No, we had Bible classes but they were usually a big relaxation. Nobody took it seriously. Half the lads were Jewish anyway and weren't interested. And they weren't religious Jews you see they were East End commercial Jews.

Mark   So going off to the loos and the J Arthurs, was that pretty guilt-free, fun?

Bette   Yes except one time, I was twelve or thirteen and
Horace Steele said I'll meet you at the Scout Hall at
lunchtime. He had the keys – he was a patrol leader. In the
lunch hour. So I went down there. I was pretty excited you
know. He was a nice lad. I opened the door and she's there
in stockings and suspenders and his mum's bra. He must
have nicked his mum's drag, taken it up in a carrier bag or
something, and he was there ready for me playing this tart.
I was horrified. I was into boys. I wasn't into trannies. I didn't
know what that was about at all. I couldn't believe it. I just
looked. And he said come in and I didn't, I wouldn't. I ran. I
turned tail and ran all the way back to school. I was terrified.
Terrified!

No we never spoke after that. It was rather a potent image for
me as you can imagine. My later career.

Mark   So actually, although the 1950s in the history books
were probably the low point for the oppression of gay men,
that wasn't your experience?

Bette   No. We didn't experience it like that, no. No I never
thought about when I was sixteen, seventeen, eighteen,
nineteen. I mean going up to Hampstead Heath and getting
fucked and seeing a policeman coming towards you on a
horse was a lark. You had to run and hide. It was all a lark.
And the whole thing of Polari was a lark, going into the
Vauxhall Tavern when I was seventeen and everybody kind
of polarying away . . . all the gay people on one side and all
the straight people on another.

Mark   So was it something that you just didn't think about,
oh I'm straight or I'm gay.

Bette   I did one day think, I was coming out of the flats in
Green Lanes.

Mark   That's where your family lived?

Bette   Yes, in Amwell Court, it's still there, by the big
reservoir.

And I came out and I'm going up towards Manor House and I notice this boy coming towards me and he had tight white jeans. And I looked at him. And I turned round and looked at his back. And then I realised. Oh that's what I want. Looking at boys. Because I had a girlfriend up the road. I never even tried it on with her. She couldn't understand it. Most working-class boys would have their hands up your knickers first time but I didn't. To me she was like a sister almost. In fact I remember her one day saying to me, 'It's alright, we can do it if you want.' And it had never even occurred to me to feel her up. All the things that most boys did. I wanted those boys. Those males of the species.

Mark   So it sounds like sex, sexuality you never actually felt any fear connected to sex or sexuality in your teenager years?

Bette   Not that you ever thought about it.

Mark   That's great. I think lots of people probably do, even if they're straight.

Bette   I think most of the young queens accepted we were gay, we weren't doing what we were supposed to do, we didn't give a fuck . . . there were plenty of gay clubs all over Soho, all over . . . the Cricketers, the Vauxhall, the Union, the Manor House, gay places all over London, the Duragon. You'd get on the bus and you'd go down there.

Mark   So how did you first know about those places? So you're in the secondary school, you're a kid and you're messing around with the boys at school, but who actually says oh there's pubs and clubs and how do you get there and who takes you there?

Bette   I used to go up to town on a Sunday. I'd get on the 33 tram at Manor House, pay sixpence and it would take you all the way to Westminster, all the way down that tunnel in Holborn . . . you'd get off the tram at Westminster and I'd look at all the great buildings and bridges and walk gradually up past the guards on their horses. Then I'd go into the National Portrait Gallery, look at the pictures. Then I came

out and there was this man going past. He had make-up on
and bright red hair and a black hat. And I was absolutely
horrified. I thought how ghastly. How gross. Of course, it
rang a very loud bell. It was Quentin.

Mark   When did you realise it was Quentin Crisp?

Bette   I didn't know who it was.

Then all his stories about Soho and Fitzrovia and so on. But
no after I saw him I watched him going up the road, past the
Garrick Theatre and up into Soho and I'd heard something
about Soho and I don't know what I'd heard but I was looking
for someone to interfere with me. And I went up to Old
Compton Street and they used to have these Charles Forte
American bars, they had these big bays with these counters,
you'd get things like milkshakes and coffee, well all that was
new. You know, cappuccinos, burgers, and to me that was
very exciting that was American, everything American was
very big for us after the war because America had saved us.
My father didn't think so but we bought it. So it was very
exciting and all the film stars and rock 'n' roll people were from
there. I remember becoming aware of Elvis Presley when I was
at school when I was fourteen, fifteen. We were all getting
sticky about Elvis Presley then. So I go into this Charlie Forte's
milk bar they were called and you'd just about scrape enough
together for a coffee and this man chatted me up he said

Man   'Oh I suppose you want to be an actor.'

Bette   Of course I lit up and said 'Yes, yes I do' and all this
stuff. Anyway, he took me up to his flat, took my cherry, gave
me a blow job and I felt as if I was just dissolving like a fizzy
pill in a glass of water. It was wonderful.

Mark   So what was this man like then? And what was the
flat like?

Bette   He was a military man, he was completely bald and
he was about in his fifties I suppose.

Mark   God.

Bette   And he took me upstairs and said

Man   'I'm not one of those queers you know.'

Bette   I felt much relieved at that.

Man   'Have you ever been inside a girl?'

Bette   . . . No.

Man   'Well if you'd just lie back a little, I'll show you what it feels like.'

Bette   And I thought well he's not queer. He's showing me something that's marvellous. It never struck me that he was queer, till I got home. I wrote him a long letter telling him I was going to tell the police and everything. Then I tore the letter up and went back next Sunday for another one.

Mark   So you kept in contact with him?

Bette   Yes, I'd go up there every few weeks and ring his bell and he'd invite me up and he'd blow me and that would be that.

Mark   And how long did that last for?

Bette   A few weeks. I mean at the time it feels like a long time but it was probably just a few weeks. And it was funny because he had a picture on his wall, an oil painting, quite a small one of four people, four soldiers clinging to a raft and one of them was bald. And he said to me

Man   'That was me, that's what happened to me during the war. We were blown up and that's me during the war.'

Mark   It was a photo?

Bette   No it was an oil painting. Course it was complete bullshit it was just to get him in the heroic image because we thought soldiers and sailors were marvellous people, they could have anything or do anything. And if you drove a car it was your duty to give a soldier or sailor a lift. My dad used to always cos he was into cars.

Mark   So you were helping out the military . . .

Bette   I was rewarding him! And he told me his name was

Man   'Captain Cox.'

Bette   I've always remembered it.

Mark   So you had this idea of being an actor, but how much did you think about that that would take you away from the jobs that other people were doing?

Bette   Well I had two boyfriends at school, two friends, not sexual and we were together all the time, we went out weekends and eventually I said well I've got to speak posh because I want to be an actor. So I'm going to speak posh from now on. And I was going around speaking posh! And Johnny said

Johnny   'I can't! I can't it's just stupid, I can't listen to all this.'

Bette   And I said, 'Well fuck you. I'm going to be a posh actor and I don't care what you think. Fuck you!' And that was the end of our friendship.

Mark   And how old were you when you started talking posh?

Bette *farts.*

Mark   Bette! This is going to be produced on the world's stages.

Bette *farts three times.*

Mark   And you've got to do that farting every time we do the play.

Bette *laughs.*

Mark   So, how old were you then?

Bette   I was about fourteen, fifteen. Just before I left school and became an apprentice in a printer's. So I had three months of it and then I split, I didn't tell my mum and dad

I got a job in an office. I knew I was going to have to go to drama school, I just knew it.

Mark   And at which stage did you tell your mum and dad that you'd got your grant and got into the drama school?

Bette   Well I'd told them, er . . . I can't remember. I told them I'd got a job in the Garrick Theatre backstage and from earning £2 10 shillings a week I was suddenly earning £15 a week which is enormous for someone of sixteen, seventeen. And that I'd left the print. My father came round . . . because they'd split up by then, I was about sixteen and he said

Dad   'You're mad. That was a job for life. You're so stupid. Why did you do it?'

Bette   Well I want to be an actor.

Dad   Ugh . . .

Bette   So then I went to Central and after that I started working as an actor.

Yes. I had this quite successful little career going and I ended up sort of being the second leading man to Ian McKellen, plays at Edinburgh, and we toured all over the world and we played in London. Erm. And I thought I was the bee's knees. And then I met this guy and we were lovers. Rex. He was a lovely guy. Rex was at art school, at Central. Central St Martin's it's called now, then it was just Central I think. And he was in his last year at the course when I met him. He was a cute, gorgeous, Australian red-haired number and we had a very passionate time.

He hated everything that I was in, that he came to. I was in shows in Ipswich, and Bristol, the Edinburgh Festival with Ian McKellen and all that stuff. And what he meant was we're not really seeing anything of you dear. And looking back I could see what he meant.

And he came in one night and I said, 'Where have you been?' And he said

Rex   'Oh I've been to a meeting.'

Bette   What do you mean, a meeting?

Rex   'A political meeting, all these queers.'

Bette   What on earth are you talking about? Are you mad? Cos obviously this is my little career trip, soirées, tables and dinner parties, the napkins and all that . . . And he said

Rex   'Oh it's great, there's these gorgeous guys there.'

Bette   Well I was there the next Wednesday. I went to the LSE first meeting, the first thing was the sexy boys. First meeting. Mmm mmm lovely. I went along and there were a lot of very beautiful people there. It was all very hippy, meeting people with long hair for the first time and all that sort of stuff. And I sat there and I was pretty conventionally dressed, conventional haircut and all the rest of it. And then I listened to people talking. And then this guy said

Guy   'Well this is just like a fucking gay bar isn't it? We're all just here cruising.'

Bette   And I felt this huge eruption of feeling and I was so angry and I stood up and said, 'If you think this is a fucking gay bar you're out of your fucking tree you stupid fucker! We're here talking about our lives about all the things we've never talked about before. We've got a chance. Don't you fucking see, you're stupid!'

There was quite a chill because I'd been very quiet and suddenly all this fishwife was coming out as well you know.

It was a great thing. Great, exciting, thrilling, new, brand new thing. And it was sexy, no. It was wonderful. It was a wonderful moment. And he was trying to cheapen it, trying to make it sound like another cruisy bar up the West End which I knew all about since I was fifteen, sixteen, because I worked in the West End. I was going to all the gay clubs after work. Curtain come down ten o'clock, 10.30 p.m. Pack up. Away. Out. Before even the actors were out. And I was out and up into those gay bars. And I knew all about that. I knew all about the sad queens weeping into their gin, you know all that stuff. And I knew it was a chance. And it was so . . . it was thrilling, it was euphoric.

Mark   So I'm interested in this GLF thing, what surprised me about what you've described so far is that it wasn't that GLF allowed you to express what you felt all along about your life, it was like you looked back over your life and suddenly saw that it was something completely different from what you thought it was.

Bette   Yes.

Mark   That you had actually felt . . .

Bette   Ripped off was how I felt.

Mark   But no only when, I suppose they call it a raising of conciousness, actually you'd felt happy in your life up to that point, as you've told it to me?

Bette   Well I was surprised.

Mark   But where had that come from, because the way you tell me the story, you'd never felt that before . . .

Bette   No but suddenly when you become conscious it affects your whole body.

Mark   I think it's strange there was no . . .

Bette   Lead up?

Mark   Yeah, it's not like the previous two years before you're going round all these gay bars thinking oh there's something missing . . .

Bette   No, never thought that at all.

Mark   There's one life that you completely lived. And then you went to this meeting and saw things completely . . .

Bette   Saw the light.

Mark   Saw things completely differently, that's incredible.

Bette   It's absolutely true. As sure as I'm sitting here talking to you, it was absolutely true. It was thrilling beyond belief and that thrill has lasted almost to this day. It's just I don't have to pretend. I'm out there and I'm queer. I like it up the bum. And fuck you if you don't like that in me.

Mark   And were there some people at that meeting who spoke who particularly inspired you or who you admired?

Bette   What happened after that little explosion of mine, was that someone came rushing up to me and said they wanted me to be on the steering committee. And I said, 'On the what?' I had no idea what a steering committee was, what consciousness-raising . . . I had no idea of any of that. All I knew in my gut was that there was a new feeling in this room, amongst these three hundred men and women, and they were actually trying to talk about things, to discuss things. You'd never talk about that in a gay bar. It was all about the one you'd fucked last week and how big his cock was and where you'd met and are you going to see them again . . . you know. You never asked is he interesting, is he funny. You asked how big was it. It was very much at a meat-market level. And for a newcomer of course, I was pretty very much in shape. I was very much in demand of course I loved it. But then there was something else that hadn't occurred to any of us. And later on I went to gay marches, three hundred thousand people on that march going underneath Charing Cross Bridge, across that bridge. So we'd come from two people at the LSE, Aubrey Walter and David Fernbach, Bob Mellors rather . . . been to New York, picked up the idea there, put a little notice on the board, Gay Liberation Front meeting and I think about seven people turned up. Then it was seventy, then it was seven hundred, then it was seven thousand. I mean it just grew so quickly it was very exciting. Going down the street dressed up, going to the people screaming and shouting, 'It's not like that darling, it's like fairy.' I had a great anger in me. This queen was coming up, the crown of the queen was coming up, that's very strong you see. I made a complete fool of myself.

Mark   You haven't stopped yet . . .

Bette I haven't stopped no! It's absolutely true.

Mark But coming out of that meeting did that have an immediate effect on you the next day, the way you dealt with people you were working with, your family?

Bette Well we all went down to the bar afterwards and had a drink, and there were obviously one or two people that I knew from the gay scene and Ramsey this guy I knew, and various people I knew, and some of the people I had known carnally and urm that was nice. And then we went home, gradually we got this thing called consciousness-raising together, and then we got demonstrations, walking down Oxford Street in all these wild costumes, feathers and make-up and stuff. Very street theatre. And the famous riot in Grosvenor Square was around that time. The Industrial Relations Bill. Edward Heath. Red Ladder had started and they were marvellous. There was this huge thing for the coal miners at Hyde Park Corner and Red Ladder brought this huge red ladder, it was huge, and they went right up to the top and they did a show. I think the show was about two minutes. And it was like 'We don't want a slice, we want the fucking bakery!' And everybody cheered and they got down and went into another part of the crowd, it was thrilling beyond words. There were these literally thousands of miners were there, queens were there. It was the beginning of a lot of different theatre things at that time.

Mark But away from the meetings, in the first few days or whatever, did that change your day-to-day life?

Bette Yes we sat around each other's flats. I opened up my flat. And people would come by and look for crash pads, and you'd put people up. And it all became you know, a very different life. I never went for any auditions. They were always interested in what was going on in what I liked to call the fucking straight theatre. And there was a street theatre that I became part of but I didn't think that that was that interesting.

Mark So that was a big change, so if we'd taken a photo of you in 1969 you would have been in a kind of conventional sixties suit, conventional hair, and then if we'd taken a photo of you in 1970 . . .

Bette   Longish hair. This kind of length. But eventually I had hair down to here.

Mark   But if we'd taken a photo of you in 1971 . . .

Bette   Completely different.

Mark   Right.

Bette   I've got pictures, completely different.

Mark   And was that more or less an overnight change of clothes, did you suddenly throw out the suits?

Bette   Well yeah, I remember saying to Rex, we got involved, and I went to the meeting, and one time he took me to a party and I smoked a bit of spliff. He'd done a bit of that smoke stuff before and I hadn't and he'd kind of been keeping an eye on me. There was an element in our relationship where he was sort of looking after me even though I was much bigger and stronger than he was, physically. I always thought of him as smarter than me, brighter than me because he'd been to university and he'd been to art school and all the rest of it. And he was at great pains to say that wasn't so but it was how I felt. You can't just erase those feelings. And I remember him saying

Rex   'Well I think we should chuck out all this furniture.'

Bette   I had these smart little Victorian chairs, smart little round tables and cabinets. None of it meant anything to me, it just looked a right sort of home for an actor. We got rid of it all. Got the cushions in. Sat on the floor . . . had some dope . . . did acid. A complete change. And it was wonderful.

I had been in drag through GLF and one day I wrote to my dad, I don't know why, I had a strong urge to write to him and to repair things in some way and he said

Dad   'Well shall we meet in a pub?'

Bette   And I said no, I think you should see the jewel in its setting. So he came to the house and I was wearing drag, I had little, you know, matador pants and little gold shoes with a sixties heel and I had a little top tucked in at the waist. I had a great figure at that time. And a lot of long red hennaed hair and a lot of make-up, full make-up. And when he saw me at the door I came all the way down from my second-floor flat and opened the door and there he was in this old raincoat and he literally shrivelled like a sort of autumn leaf, he backed off because I put my arms around out to welcome him and he backed away. And I said, 'Well do you want some tea? Why don't you come on upstairs?' So he came upstairs and I made tea. And I said, 'Well I wanted you to see me as I am. And I wanted to tell you I'm not afraid of you. I think you're a shit. I think you've been absolutely evil to me. And you're violent and you beat the shit out of me when I was young . . .' And he was terrified, he'd never seen a beautiful queen, let alone the fact that I was his son. I was in drag. I was a queen. A beautiful queen.

Act Two

Mark I'm Mark Ravenhill. I'm a playwright. In the past few weeks, I've been talking to the performer Bette Bourne about his life. We've divided our conversation into three parts. A life in three acts. Tonight is part two. We'd like to read you edited transcripts of our conversations. Ladies, gentlemen and all others – Bette Bourne.

Bette I wasn't in drag at the beginning of gay lib.

I had been brought up very butch, and I'd gone to a very butch school and all the rest of it, and that was very important that I was . . . you know that I had that image together. I'd been playing my young Italianate sort of thugs on television in *The Saint*, *The Baron*, *Dixon of Dock Green* and all these programmes when I was always the criminal. A sort of East End lad.

I went to Gay Lib thinking I was Che Guevara, and I was dressed like him, and I had a big beard. And I was very butch and I had these boots which were actually too big for me. Boots were too big.

Well one day this queen came in. This queen came into the meeting. She was called Piggy and she was a very interesting art queen, and she was in . . . wearing a denim skirt. And everyone was having little titters, you know, behind their hands and he said

Piggy 'I don't want to be put down by you lot because I'm wearing a skirt. I like my skirt and it's just part of me and if you don't like it you can fuck off! Er . . . but I like it and I don't see why I should have you lot putting me down . . . er . . . for wearing a skirt because I'm a man.'

Bette He was quite, quite a man. And then the next week, the change and the meetings were suddenly over here in the Church Hall and my friend Gordon Howie came round and . . . I was talking about dressing and I said I've got this marvellous dress in the market. And he said

Gordon   'Alright then put it on.'

Bette   So I put it on and he said

Gordon   'Why don't we go over to the Gay Lib meeting?'

Bette   Well I said it's cobbles down there and very difficult
to walk. (*Laughter.*) So I got my heels on, got the make-up on,
and I looked very pretty. It was a scarlet dress, 1930s cut, and
a cut dress . . . So I'm doing . . . I'm walking along with a
beautiful Victorian cape and a handbag and I went over to
the Gay Lib meeting and sat down. Nobody recognised me at
all, they just thought 'Who's this person coming in here and
talking and stuff?' So I sat and suddenly felt very relaxed and
enjoyed being in my drag because it was like a release.

Yeah, and one or two other queens got into a bit of drag, you
know with the dresses and stuff, but it wasn't very many of us,
but by the time we moved here, and I went over there, I
suppose there was half a dozen of us in drag. But I was the
last person they expected . . .

It made me feel a million dollars. I felt so confident . . . and it
changed the premise you see. When I was talking about it I
wasn't talking about it in the same premise. They were all
talking theory and . . . all these American revolutionaries who
had, you know, had said this and said that, and written this
and written that, you know, um . . . and my thing was I felt
completely different. And I started to understand how some
of the women might have felt. Just going up the street in a
frock was a very different experience – you felt very vulnerable
in a way. I was vulnerable in the streets. I got to the Gay Lib
meeting and then suddenly my confidence came up because
it was all queers and dykes . . . and er it was very nice . . . and
I started saying things, you know, to these blokes like, 'Well
you've got a lot to say for yourself haven't you?' 'Why don't
you give your arse a chance?' You know. And all this cockney
fishwife came out (*laughter*) while in an elegant thirties gown.

Mark   And do you think you found out more about yourself
through those encountery sessions, all those conscious . . . and
were you starting to come to a new idea of who you were?

Bette   Yeah, the Bette Bourne . . .

Mark   Yeah where did that come from?

Bette   That was great. That all started with a couple of queens calling me Bette because it was alliterative. I think it was one queen in particular that started it and . . . er . . . I liked it a lot . . . And er . . .

Mark   Why did you like it?

Bette   I dunno . . . it felt right . . . that with the frock. It felt . . . it felt right. It felt as though . . . I could let go of something.

Well, then gradually more and more people started wearing dresses and then there was a whole group of us that sort of gradually gravitated towards each other, and one day we got really fed up with the meetings and so we decided to go and find somewhere else where we could just all be together in our frocks. So we climbed over the back wall . . . and down the wall into the back garden where this film studio was . . . quite a big film studio building and er . . . and it was like a big hall really, and it was all padded because it had been a sound-proofed film studio, and it was at the end of Colville Gardens, Colville Houses, which is a cul-de-sac. There was a little garden at the front and er . . . we . . . we squatted it.

We moved in and we did it up and we had one end was the Arabian room and as you can imagine it was all bits of schmutter and silk and stuff draped like a tent all along. Then the next room was where the wardrobe was, which was, you know, like that . . . to the wall – that area – and that was hundreds of frocks that we found on the Portobello and stuff. Then the next part was all shoes, about four hundred pairs of shoes. And you could go in and wear what you wanted. There was a mirror . . . you know, you didn't get started until two in the afternoon.

I mean there were silk scarves and beautiful drapes everywhere – all cheap tat, but to us it was fabulous. It was like living in this extraordinary kind of fairylike cocoon. And we all had different drag on every day. Some people changed their drag three times a day. There was a lot of swishing about in drag. Occasionally one would do a bit of ironing. Then we'd have the music on, we'd sit there and listen to Maria Callas all evening, you know, and on the acid and the dope. It was a sort of madness really but it was a great madness. Then there was the office where all the practical stuff took place.

Mark   What practical stuff?

Bette   Well, you know, putting together for instance an issue of *Come Together* which was the gay newspaper which we got, you know, various people in the gay movement . . . there was the women's edition and the drag queens' and the common edition and people wrote articles for it. And that was the sort of thing that went on in the office. Oh . . . one of the things that happened – I was thinking about bills that had to be paid.

Mark   How many people were living there?

Bette   Er, twelve.

Mark   Right.

Bette   There were about nine men, three women and a couple of kids.

Mark   Right.

Bette   And er . . .

Mark   So what was the kind of average day, if there was such a thing?

Bette   Well, you'd wake up about, I suppose, eleven or something . . . and there was a very beautiful queen who always used to get up early and walk stark naked for about sixteen steps to the loo and I always used to spy over the sheets, pretending I was sleeping, and he was quite proud and he had this huge figure . . . Extraordinary . . . had a bit of a ding-dong later on. And er . . . we'd gradually get up, put some music on maybe, wander about, have some breakfast and then upstairs – there was a little staircase to two tiny rooms above a kitchen. You came into the garden, and then into the kitchen – that was the first floor. And then above that there was these two little rooms. One was called the office and the other was the make-up room where the loo was. And then the main body of the hall, the mattresses were like in a sort of in an 'L' shape (like that) and the wardrobe and stuff and the shoes and the Arabian room at the end . . . and in the sort of middle of the 'L' shape (over there) was a separate bit where a woman that lived on the streets stayed, Joyce, and her boyfriend, so they had that little separate bit. And, er . . . she was lovely – she was a really nice woman. Somebody had brought her in because she had nowhere to live and she had this boyfriend who was a bit thick and much younger – she was in her sixties.

Mark   Did you know much about her life before . . . before this?

Bette   No, no. She was obviously . . . you could see in her face she had had a fucking rough time. She was really . . .

Mark   She'd have been born around 1910 or something, wouldn't she?

Bette   I suppose so, but she was very blind and very much street-battered by the wind and rain. She was like one of those gypsies in Portobello.

Mark   And was she, she wasn't critical or uncomfortable or anything?

Bette   No she was fine, she loved it, and she was only too pleased to have a fucking roof over her head and everybody loved Joyce. She was very warm and she had a huge laugh, very few teeth. A huge laugh!

Mark   And was the commune a political movement do you think, or was that more like a kind of artistic movement or do you . . .

Bette   We thought it was very political.

Mark   Right. And were you actually doing political stuff as well?

Bette   Yeah, we were going on lots of demonstrations and things like that in our drag. It was quite scary. You know we used to tend to go out in threes or fours, or sixes and sevens. And if we got . . . we like one time I remember we got arrested, and we had to go to Marylebone, and there were eight drag queens walking together up towards Westbourne Park Station to get on the Tube to go to the court. And when we got there we were being tried for obstruction of the pavement, or some nonsense like that, which they always said it was that kind of thing – they would never say it was a political act. The police would never admit that, or the magistrates. 'And what were you doing there?' you know, and we'd be in our drag and then the court public gallery, it was not that big, but it was full of queens and they all had balloons and they were blowing bubbles into the well of the court, and the police were rushing about and getting very cross. It was a bit sort of mad, pandemonium and we were all off our heads most of the time. I smoked a lot of dope and er . . . took a lot of acid and er . . .

Mark   So how did practical stuff in the commune . . . ?

Bette   Yeah, practical stuff . . .

Mark   Well like eating and . . .

Bette   Well what happened was that you took turns in cooking usually. Some people were lazy and couldn't be bothered. Other people did a bit of cleaning. On the mantelpiece, over behind the record player there were shelves and like a mantelpiece there was a Clarice Cliff teapot and it was rather chipped, and it was rather beautiful and everybody put their money in there. So the rule was you put your money in there, your dole money, or money from the stall or whatever you had, went in there and everybody just helped themselves when they needed it. And it worked quite well for a long time and then somebody stole it – one of the queens stole it and went to Paris, and came back and was totally forgiven because he was young and pretty. (*Laughter.*)

Mark   So tell me, who were the key . . . If we were to do a cast list, who were the kind of key players in there . . . in the commune . . . ?

Bette   Well there were about . . . there was . . . Stuart, me, Michael, Mick Belsten – who's dead, gone now – Nigel who'd been an accountant, Steve was a designer who'd been to art school, and he had this lovely thick long curly hair – it was beautiful – but, er, he's still around. And the women – there were three women – I don't know what happened to them but eventually . . .

Mark   So what were some of the most memorable times actually in the commune for you?

Bette   Well, we'd have these long discussions about our lives, what we were doing, what we were feeling and stuff. Like sort of awareness groups in a way. And some of them would go a bit sour as they did occasionally, but there was a great feeling of euphoria; we were very supportive of each other. We er . . . one night we had a Roman orgy which was fun. We had all these cardboard pillars and stuff and made it all very Roman in effect. It turned into an actual orgy which was very nice, which some people were rather disapproving of . . . I suggested at one point that we all walk around naked when we were in the commune and that was very frowned upon by some people. So we didn't do that – that wasn't adopted as policy. (*Laughter.*) It's funny, it's things that happen. But there was . . . for instance, you'd go up into the make-up room, and one of the great things was the nail polish. Each nail would have a different pattern on it. Some queens would put a nail . . . would be all check – black-and-white check – and the next one might be stripes and so on. So there was time to stop in a way, this was like a kind of cocoon.

Then one morning the police arrived. We were all in bed, you know, and (*laughter*) and eight uniformed police walked in. These great big guys and we thought what's going on we thought . . . and we gradually all got up and we all used to sleep naked, all of us, and we'd get up stark naked and some of us would have a bit of a hard-on . . . 'Yes, what can we do officer?' They'd got all these naked queens surrounding these eight policemen in uniform and they were accusing us of trespassing and all the rest of it, but squatting was quite legal in fact and we pointed that out to them and said that we had every right to be there. Some people were kind of educated or in the law and stuff like that, and they eventually left after about fifteen minutes. It was quite a trip – quite a sight. And so we laughed and hooted about that for the rest of the day.

Mark   So with the commune, do you think . . . did people have a long-term kind of view . . . did they . . . ?

Bette   We thought we were going to be there for the rest of our lives.

Mark   Yeah, OK, did people talk about it? I was just wondering whether people were so in the moment that they didn't think oh we're going to get older and things.

Bette   No, we were absolutely in the moment.

Mark   Right.

Bette   That was a big thing.

Mark   But were you convinced that society would change or was it just about . . . ?

Bette   Yes, yes, I mean we thought that if we kept at it, you know, things would change.

Mark   So if we walked into the commune and said to the group, 'What's going to happen to the world in the next twenty to thirty years . . . ?'

Bette   We'd laugh, say . . . 'Christ knows' . . . I dunno.

Mark   Well it wasn't about planning for the future . . . No?

Bette   There was a guy there called John Church who eventually, sadly, committed suicide, but he was a wonderful actor and he'd been quite successful with the RSC, he was in Scofield's *Lear* and all that stuff, and he dropped out and joined the GLF. And he came and he had a wonderfully sort of Greek/Jewish sort of face, big nose – marvellous face anyway – and he got into drag and we had a wonderful time and all the rest of it . . . and then one day his mother came – she was ninety-seven. She arrived, she was worried about her boy, because he didn't have a father, just had his mother and she came – little tiny woman like a Kathleen Harrison or Katie Johnson. She was very small like that, little hat. And she said

Mother   'Oh hello, can I come in? I'm John Church's mother.'

Bette   And we said, 'Oh fabulous, come in.' She came in and John was in a big long black skirt, nice blouse, flouncy blouse at the top – rather Victorian-looking and he said

John   'Oh Mum.'

Bette   And she came in and she sat down with me, and we made a big fuss of her, cups of tea, bits of cake and all the rest of it. And she sat there and she said, looking round, and we were chatting on and John was chatting on to her. And there was a pause and she said

Mother   'Well, it's all theatre really isn't it!'

Bette   Oh I mean, she was a knockout.

One of the things that happened was some transvestites/ transsexuals came down from Birmingham to stay for a weekend. One of them was very tall and they all looked like, or were all trying to look like working-class housewives, you know, only one of them was six foot two for instance, so it kind of looked odd. And it wasn't our sort of drag at all. It was very strange and we just didn't say anything and we chatted about this and that and they wanted to talk about, you know, I dunno, shades of pink slips and whatever. Very kind of like straight, their idea of straight, women, but one of them said there was a problem with the electricity and he immediately skiffed up – we had a ladder there – and he skiffed up this ladder with his spanners and his great big red gloves and he changed all the electricity so that he joined this cable to that cable, these junctions, up this ladder, in his dress, and his wig, and all this rather brown make-up, and he rearranged it so we didn't have to pay for any electricity any more. (*Laughter.*) So he was wonderfully practical. I mean later on people said things like 'Oh the straight trannies never supported us', but they did. That for instance was just one example.

Mark   And what was the attitude of the rest of the GLF to you lot?

Bette   Oh occasionally they'd visit and then there was another commune started up in Bethnal Green, which was called Bethnal Rouge, and that was basically a bookshop – a gay bookshop. There was one in Brixton, the Brixton Fairies, and we'd all go and support each other say in a crisis. Like in the Brixton commune they were getting attacked by schoolkids from this local school. So we all went over there, like at least eight or nine of us, and they had about half a dozen of them living in this little house and at the end of the road there was this school. So they were giving out leaflets in the schoolyard saying about gay people and blah, blah, blah and trannies and drag queens, and er . . . And one day we were there, we stayed there for a few days, and one day sure enough a whole mob of kids starting come up towards the house, right. They were big kids, big heavy brutes and we're all in drag. (*Laughter.*) What we had, we had a plan, they'd come to a certain point and we'd all rush out and charge them. And we did! (*Laughter.*) Roar . . . roar! And they ran, they shat themselves. It was so funny! They went back into the fucking school and there was no more trouble after that! And then a few days, a couple of days later we came back and carried on with our thing here, and you could go and stay with them, and they would come and stay with us in Bethnal Rouge . . . (*Laughter.*) It was very exciting.

Mark   And did you miss acting?

Bette   Yeah, and I said one day, I said, 'I've got to do some acting, that's what I am, I'm born to be an actor. (*Laughter.*) So they said, 'Well do some fucking acting.' So I went to French's and I bought twelve copies of *Lysistrata* and I came home and I handed them out. The women weren't there for some reason at this point except Joyce who was a straight woman.

So we did a reading of *Lysistrata* by Aristophanes.

Anyway, it was a knockout and we read it, and everybody decided to read it as film stars. So one of them was Marilyn Monroe, and one of them was Tallulah, and one of them was Ros Russell, and Ethel Merman, and you know all this stuff and it was great because, you know, it's only women in it and so we all . . . and Joyce read a part and she turned out to be this marvellous actor – incredible! You know I'd had ten, fifteen years in the game before all this, you know, paid-up Equity member and all that and drama school, whatever, and she was just so good. And we pissed ourselves laughing.

Mark   And was there any sense of being part of any international group or network?

Bette   I think with the queens in the commune, by and large, we did think we loved each other, you know. It wasn't a lifelong love but . . . And then you'd get very critical. They'd have these Friday nights where you all had to talk. I remember one time (*laughter*) I shat my box on acid. I was well up there in the cosmos somewhere. This queen turned round and she said

Queen   'We've got to talk!'

Bette (*laughter*)   I was so high I could hardly speak. I said (*laughter*) . . . But you know there was a great emotional thing between us. It was like a new love.

You had to be a bit nutty I suppose, and that was, the thing was that one felt there was nothing left to lose because we weren't accommodated in the world. Nobody in the world really wanted us, we were the sort of remnants, the sort of side plate, you know. We were trying to say, well this is how we live and this is how we want to live, and it was a day at a time. You never thought 'Oh God, what am I going to do when I'm sixty', you know. You never thought like that . . .

And then it gradually diminished . . .

Um . . . I can't remember when the precise moment was but
I know it was to do with too many people were into . . . There
were some people coming in who were dealers. And there
was some heroin coming in, and I'm very straight in a way,
you know, I just can't deal with any of that. I can't deal with
any of that rather dangerous stuff. And in fact the acid I
didn't carry on for that long because once or twice I had a
bad trip it scared me so much I couldn't do it any more.

I gave it up really because it got a bit chemical for me. A lot
frightened me, you know. Some people were jacking up and
some people were obviously . . .

And then when the commune packed up I just thought, oh
I've just got to get my shit together somehow. And I got a job
here in Powys Square in the playground . . . and I was still in
sort of what you might call 'semi-drag', make-up and hair or
whatever, and I got a job there looking after the kids.

Well I was working at the playground and Mair, my friend
Mair Davies, she's . . . we're still friends. Mair, Welshwoman,
she said

Mair   'I've been to see this group at the Oval House, you
must go and see them. They're a group called the Hot
Peaches and they're from New York and they're doing a
show called *The Divas of Sheridan Square.*'

Bette   I went to see this show and it was marvellous. It was
done in a sort of . . . like a musical, but all the music was
funky rock music. Some of the tunes had been lifted from
other people, but mostly they were composed within the
group and there was Peggy Shaw, Jimmy Camicia was the
governor, and his boyfriend, Ian, they ran the group – they
started it and ran it in a loft in New York and they had I think
it was two dykes and three queens. Sister Tui . . . they'd
found her in the gutter, basically, out of her mind on junk,
pulled her together and she was an amazing performer. She
had a mouth like a rubber letter box . . . you know. She'd talk
like that a lot of the time. 'Oh Babes!'

All the lyrics were all about being a drag queen and being gay and it was very celebratory and there were good songs and good lyrics, good music and good dialogue in the sketches. One was about this queen coming out to her mother and her mother was played by Sister Toohey, 'You mean yer a drag queen!' and her mouth would go like that, 'You mean yer a drag queen!' And Jimmy wrote all the sketches, he and Ian together, they were an amazing creative team.

And they had this tall black queen called Java who sang 'Drag Queen' which is a marvellous song about being a drag queen, and it's an old blues song called 'Beale Street Mama' which was sung by Bessie Smith. And they'd changed the words. It was a wonderful song. She had this glorious black voice. She was about six foot two and all she wore was a boob tube and these very long legs, and these great big shoes like this. So she was coming on seven feet tall really. It was astonishing. And she meant that song. She was heavy into the junk and eventually she was let go from the crew but she went to live in Amsterdam eventually, and went back to America and I think she died but I'm not sure but that night she sang. And I thought, 'That's what I've been looking for!'

Mark   So was it the same night you saw the show that you stayed behind to see them?

Bette   Yeah, and I was in me red jeans, a beautiful hand-embroidered shawl and a lot of make-up and so on . . . Well, we sat around and I went back, and I sat around again and Ian said, 'Look at this queen, she looks fabulous', you know and all that. And I was very much included and then eventually there was this gay woman and she was leaving and I said 'Do you think if I asked to replace you, would you be . . . ?' and she said

Dyke   'Oh yeah, sure dear, that would be good.'

Bette   So I did. I joined the Hot Peaches.

Act Three

Mark Hello I'm Mark Ravenhill. I'm a playwright. In the past few weeks, I've been talking to the performer Bette Bourne about his life. We've divided our conversation into three parts. A life in three acts. Tonight is Act Three. We'd like to read you edited transcripts of our conversations. Ladies, gentlemen and all others – Bette Bourne.

Bette In 1977 I found this book, *Just Myself*, which is about this Australian drag queen who would not answer the question are you a man or a woman. She would say I'm just myself. It was a picture book about this queen's life, lots of dialogue, and it was this interview between her and this journalist. So I got John Church who'd gone back into BBC Radio by that time. Anyway, he decided yes he'd have a go at this. He played the journalist and I played the drag queen.

Mark And where was this?

Bette This was at Hampstead Town Hall. It was our very first Bloolips gig. A one-night stand.

And in the middle of it Diva Dan came on as the maid and she was dressed like a prostitute kind of maid, like a fetish maid. And she was deaf as you know and she came in and she was so wonderfully funny. And she came in and there was the audience and the maid came in and she's like, 'Telephone call for you darling.'

I met him through Gay Lib dances. Oh the Gay Lib dances were fantastic because everybody came in their own home-made costumes, they all came in drag and different sort of costumes. It was lovely, it was astonishing. Beautiful drag. And it wasn't people trying to be women. It was very elegant, in Danny's case absolutely wonderfully elegant. He had a little hat on like a velvet spring. All the deaf queens were in one place in the bar and I saw her and I thought that's amazing. Then a few days later I spoke to Alana my friend. Alana said, 'I want to do a show.' And he said, 'Oh I know that queen, that deaf queen.' So he brought her round then, my kitchen was like a bar with bar stools. And she came round, and sat on one of them there and I'm on the other one there and we talked for three hours, it was wonderful, smoking cigarettes like mad and a few spliffs. And I thought this queen has got to be on the stage. And she was doing all this and I saw him in the mirror and she's going like that you know, it's hilarious. And I carried on . . .

Mark   And then your second show was . . . ?

Bette   Well I went to the market one day and I found this recording of *The Ugly Duckling* for children read by Jean Metcalfe, ever heard of her? Well she was a very tweedy woman, married to a famous man and she was on television and radio a lot. And she was safe. And she read this story and it was all rather wonderful, and then the duckling went through the forest and all blah blah blah and he was thrown out. So we rewrote it, started on Normality Farm. 'All the little ducks go quack quack quack (*singing*) *quack quack quack la LA down on Normality Farm. We don't have doubts or fears, we never have our cares, we welcome you my dears, as long as they're straight and as long as they are square! All the little geese go gobble gobble down on Normality Farm. We're going gobble gobble cos our life is free from trouble! Stick to form, obey the norm, life's a jolly bubble, down on Normality Farm!'*

And it was a huge hit. And we did it in the Tabernacle.

Mark   And how did you find the cast?

Bette   Went round to my mates, do you want to be in a show? We had nine queens. We had Danny, Lavinia, me and Jon Jon, and there was nine of us.

Mark   And had they had acting experience before?

Bette   None whatever. Only me and Jon Jon. Jon Jon had run a children's theatre group in Australia and had written quite a lot.

Mark   And were you able to rehearse full-time or were lots of them doing day jobs?

Bette Bits and pieces. A lot of them were cleaning flats and that kind of thing. You know, just doing jobs that were a bit elastic. So we'd say well, we'll all get up at eleven or three in the afternoon or something for a few hours and rehearse.

Mark And where would you rehearse?

Bette My flat, well there was a squat above my flat. We're tap-dancing right. (*Singing.*) '*We're in the money . . . We're in the money, we've got a lot of what it takes to get along.*' And I went downstairs after the rehearsal, two hours of this and all the plaster had fallen down in a big lump on my bed in the back room. All the rest had gone and Danny said, 'Bette, Bette, Bette!' We were shocked, everything was a mess. All the dust and dirt from 1867 all over my lovely frocks!

Mark And was it quite easy to get an audience in those days?

Bette Well the word had gone round and there was quite a strong community here then. A writer called Heathcote Williams came and he wrote that play *AC/DC* which was a sort of seminal play in the 1970s. Then he wrote a review of us called 'Bloolips Bare their Brazen Cheeks', cos at one time we all come tapping down and we turn round and we've got bare bums. It was very funny. It was very bawdy and loud. It was very Australian. It was great. It was very strong. They fucking went apeshit because they were all expecting something a bit arty or naff and it was a very strong show. And all the front was benches of kids, cos I worked in the playground and they'd all come to see me dressed as a woman. All these little black kids sitting on the front row, all these different kids. It was great.

Mark And when did you think that Bloolips is going to be something that carries on for some time?

Bette Well Stuart and I went out and had a Chinese meal one night after a show up there and made all these plans, as you do when you're stoned and you're feeling very high. But really I knew it was one step at a time. And Rex said to me, 'Why don't you go to Amsterdam with Danny and see if you can get on at the Milky Way and stuff like that?'

Mark   What's the Milky Way?

Bette   It's a big alternative club. It used to be a milk dairy.
It's huge. So I went over in the fucking snow with Danny and
we tried to get some gigs and eventually we did get a gig for
the summer at the Fondell Park as part of the Festival of
Fools which was a huge organisation that I knew nothing
about until then. And the woman that ran the Milky Way,
she came running up after our gig, we were on the back of a
truck doing our tap routines and we kept chucking the drag
over the side of the truck cos there was nowhere else, so we'd
finish a number and all this drag would go flying out the back
of this truck . . . and then we'd get the next thing on, do the
next number. We'd do a number called 'Bananas', with these
huge cardboard bananas, the Busby Berkeley routine you
know. But with six people it looks completely fucking mad.
Hilarious. Cos we got the bananas and we're trying to get
past each other cos we've got the bananas and it was so small,
this truck. It was no bigger than this carpet.

So we did the show there and this woman came running up
and said, 'We'll book you and we'll do this and this.' And
they did. And they booked us a tour. And that was how we
lived for some years. And eventually after five months one of
the tours finished and I said, 'Well we've got £6,000 in the
handbag.' One thing we never rowed about was the money.
Because I may have told you this before but we always sat
round the table at the end of a gig going, 'One for you, one
for you, one for you, two for me . . . one for you, one for you',
cos I had the handbag right. We had to have money for
petrol right and everybody thought that was great cos they
could see the money right. The notes. And they would pick
up the notes, put the money in their coat and then fuck off to
some club or other and have a great night. And they'd go to
East Berlin or whatever.

Mark   So how many different incarnations or variations on
the Bloolips was there? Was it pretty much the same people
all the way through?

Bette   Well it started off with six of us. There was Nicky the piano player, Lavinia who'd been a dancer, Danny, myself, Paul and Stuart, who had been an accountant. And Stuart was in from the commune and all that. And these were the people who were very hands-on, who really meant it. And when you have a big success, we went to New York and it was a huge success, we had no idea it would be. We just sent the drag ahead in two great big coffins. We arrived. Everybody went out cleaning cos there was a cleaning agency. Gordon was living there by then and Frank found us all somewhere to stay on people's floors and that kind of thing.

Mark   And what year would this have been?

Bette   That was 1980. A one-night stand in a loft in Greenwich Avenue. And we did the show there. And it was packed. It was like three or four hundred people. They were all sitting on the floor. And the next day George Barteniev, who'd seen it, said to his wife Crystal Field, 'We've gotta have these guys.' Cos I'd been to see them two or three times and she would always say, 'You've got to speak to George', and he would always say, 'You've got to speak to Crystal.' All this went on . . . then he finally came to see the show and he was (*claps*) knocked out by it. And he booked us the next day. And we had a nine-month run at his theatre.

Mark   What was the theatre?

Bette   It was called Theatre for the New City and next we moved to Orpheum Theatre on Second Avenue. Which was kind of a rung up.

Mark   And what was that show you were doing?

Bette   The show was called *Lust in Space*.

Mark   And did you find over that time that you developed a kind of Bette Bourne persona? In the way that comedians do, I mean was there someone who was Bette Bourne onstage, somebody who was a bit like you, I mean, how . . .

Bette   We were very blurred, the on and the off. I christened them all. I christened Gretel, Nick was called Naughty

Knickers, Paul was called Precious Pearl, Lavinia was called
Lavinia Coop. I didn't do that name, he did that name,
Diva Dan, and that's it, six isn't it. And Bette Bourne. And
different people came in and out of the group. There was a
queen called Hunter and I called him Bunty Hunter. And we
had another queen called Babs Your Ankle. And another
queen I called Marge Mellows who was a huge tall queen.
And if the tall queens came in very often they'd be rather
slouched over, like this, you know, trying to be shorter with
bent legs you know. And I'd say no, no, we want you tall, we
want the tallest. I want the highest heels you can bear, and
the tallest hat that you can wear and I want you to be the
tallest person in the world. And they were so relieved and so
liberated. And they all came in, I'm telling you girl, with
attitude, it was fabulous. Big, big big tall queens. Cos Vin was
quite tall too. I was trying to do everything opposite in a way.

Mark   In what way, opposite to what?

Bette   Well people tried getting into drag thinking that
they'd got to be smaller, that they'd got to be like women and
I would say no tits, no padding, no hips. And it's got to be
white-face. The rest is up to you and they'd do this incredibly
elaborate make-up on top. And they all became really
wonderful at it.

Mark   And what was it about white-face?

Bette   Well I'd got it from the Hot Peaches. They removed
you slightly. It brought up the clown thing, it was very
important.

Mark   So how did you first get to know Quentin Crisp?

Bette   He came to a show at the Orpheum and afterwards
he said, 'Well that was a wild scene.' And I said, 'Did you
enjoy it?' He said, 'Listen to your public they're going mad.'
And they were cheering and hooting and going mad. He
didn't really know what we were about I think. It was such
a strange and anarchic world for him. But he himself was
incredibly anarchic. And he liked us as personalities, he liked

us as people. He'd come to the shows and afterwards he would say, 'Oh that was fun!' Or he would say, 'I didn't really understand it.' And after the first time I said I'll come and see you. And he said, 'I'm the most available person in the world.' So I did and Frank and I used to go up there or I'd go up there. But he was a very lovely man.

Mark   So how much time, every year, were you spending in New York?

Bette   We were still getting our shows together here, touring Europe and Edinburgh Festival and all that. But we'd go almost every year from 1980 with a different show to New York.

Mark   And how much did Aids change that scene? Because 1982–3 was when people first – ?

Bette   1983 was when I first heard about it. It was terrifying. People were so sick. People that we knew. It was a very sad time. And . . . oh . . . I started writing them all down at one point. All the people that I'd lost. It was over a hundred. And I just thought I've got to write this down or otherwise I'll forget. And being in the public eye you just meet so many people, and er . . . Vitto died, Martin died, I mean just a long list. Danny died, people in the group became very ill. Nobody was spared. And it was terrible because nobody knew what was going on, how it was happening at first.

There was a lot of sadness in New York. And people say to you to your face, 'I'm gonna die. I'm dying.' And they're like young, twenty-three, twenty-four. What can you say? There's nothing you can do or say. Do a bit of shopping, clean, but you know. That was really . . . But Bill was one of my very greatest, closest friends, Bill Rice, we did a lot of work together and those were his paintings. We were very very close. We used to be in the bar every night. And we used to do shows together. We did *The Importance of Being Earnest* in the garden with all the local queens and couple of women, and we'd do readings, Beckett. He was an amazing person.

Mark   And did you keep in touch with your dad through all of this, how long did your dad live for?

Bette   My dad died when he was eighty-two when I was in America and you know it was so shocking, my brother rang me up bless him and he said I'd rather not do this on the phone but there you are in New York, Dad's died.

Mark   And you were with the Bloolips?

Bette   The old man's died. It was such a shock that I burst into tears. I didn't really have anything to do with him. I didn't like him, I didn't know him really. But I suppose we had got over all the youthful stuff by that time, I just never saw him. But he was my dad, so it had some impact you know, it was like . . . bit of a punch. My mother was upset. She'd been married twice with two other men, but she was still in love with him, she was terribly upset. I remember once I was at her house and he rang up to talk to me for some reason. And she said, 'Is that Daddy? Give me the phone.' And she said, 'Hello, how are you? Blah blah . . . I still love you, you know!' and she gave me the phone back. It's funny. I suppose you never, if you've really loved someone, you don't easily, it doesn't go really, it stays.

Mark   When would you say you were happiest in your life? Is there one day, or one moment when you think you were the happiest?

Bette   Well, it was in Germany in Damstadt . . . I don't know if it was the happiest, but Paul and I, the whole Bloolips were there and we'd done the show and it was a huge success. And we went down into the hall afterwards and they'd cleared the chairs and they were having a disco or whatever it was, and Paul and I were dancing together and we realised how happy we were with each other.

Mark   So when did you start to have a sense that the Bloolips was going to come to an end or that the work of the Bloolips was done?

Bette   Well it was done really when I had this wonderful relationship with Neil Bartlett. He'd been coming to the shows to see the Bloolips for years. Then I saw him doing a show which was called *Vision of Love* which was a solo in Butler's Wharf and Robin did the sets. And it was amazing cos you went in there and it was all pitch black but it was starlit. There had been a storm, and there were great flagstones with dips in them. So there were puddles all over this huge sort of loft on the ground floor. And Robin lit them all, and Neil was stark naked, came swishing through and he'd empty this bag of drag out. All this red net, and he'd make it into all these different shapes for each number.

We did a lot of shows together and it's been very good. I've had a lot of good times. A lot of terrible fights and so on. He's very much a big part of my life.

Mark   Would you describe what you do now as drag?

Bette   I like wearing drag, I enjoy it. But I don't do full drag now. Unless it's for a part. Now I'm more a sort of disciple of Quentin Crisp. He seemed to strike it right for me. He said a thing that everyone said to him, 'Oh you just want to be noticed', which I recognised in myself and he said, 'I want to be recognised as a queer.' 'I want to be recognised, that's the important thing.' So he was going . . . I like to be visible. I like people . . . Yeah I like to be noticed. I don't like to be beaten up or insulted but that comes with the territory. But I like to go out visible as much as I possibly can. I don't know why – it's sort of important to me really, because it saves so much aggro. As soon as people say, 'What's your name?' I say, 'Bette.' That's it, it's in the court, it's right in the middle of the court, there's no doubt, there's no questions. Oh yes, she's a queer, she's a queer. That's all, it's quite simple really.

Worst thing is sometimes you go out and you forget, and you haven't got your lippy with you, and you have to go back. That kind of thing. But no, I try to . . .

Mark   So if you forget your lippy then . . . ?

Bette   If you forget your lippy, that's your kind of warpaint, you see you feel you're not really 'on'. Seems to me that I'm here so long that being out will become quite important. I quite enjoy it, I quite enjoy a little bit of danger, a little frisson.

Mark   So you mentioned Quentin in some ways . . . Quentin, I don't know . . . crystallised for you something . . . which made a way to be . . .

Bette   Yeah, he had a way of being what he was, and it wasn't trying to be a woman, it was a man. He was more effeminate than I am but I don't try and talk 'like that' you know I don't do all the feminine things because that's not really me. He was naturally more effeminate.

It's funny, when he died what I missed was not being able to ring him up in the middle of the night. You know, because they're five hours behind and I could ring him up and we'd have a natter, you know. It was fun – I missed that.

Mark   And did you ever talk to him about the actual, the politics of the GLF and all that?

Bette   No I think he disliked all that because he'd been out there since the end of the twenties on the street, doing his thing, and suddenly everybody was doing it. He didn't like that at all. He wasn't interested in the other . . . And he used to say things deliberately to upset the queens. You know, he'd say things like 'Aids is a fad'. (*Laughter.*) You know, it was on the front pages, 'Aids is a fad says Quentin Crisp', and all the queens would be up in arms and furious and of course suddenly everybody's talking about Aids again which was the point of it in a way, being made conscious of it again, you know.

But it's very nice when the stallholders in Portobello go, 'Hello dear, how are you? Got your lippy on I see!' and all this stuff. And sometimes it's 'You haven't got your lippy on!' They accuse me. But if I go down there on a Saturday . . . A couple of weeks ago I went down there and this guy says to his wife, 'Oh he's alright, he knew Mum. He was a good friend of Mum', you know. His mother had died and I knew his mother was quite old when she died and we used to have a sense . . . yes, I said to him, 'We used to have a few dirty laughs on this corner.' Because with the cockneys it's always a bit rude and a bit cheeky, drag has always been a bit, it's like the drag queens in the pubs in the old days in the fifties all their jokes were about cocks and tits and balls. All very . . . what we call low drag, and that's what they like. Because, especially a friend of mine does it, he does it really well and he goes to these hen nights and the men are not allowed in. There's no men there, they're all working-class women with drinks and fish and chips. And he comes out dressed all in pink, the big pink silvery wig and he really gives it to them, you know! And he does all the filthiest jokes and talks about the men and what their dicks are like and how dirty they are, and all the rest of it. The women love it, he's a wonderful queen. But when he gets out there, he's big! He's very funny because he also brings out terrific anger and aggression him. Been backstage and I've had to say to him, 'I had to go out to the car park for that joke, it was too filthy even for me.'

I suppose for me going to auditions in lipstick, you know . . . Sometimes there is a slight feeling of defiance about them you know, but I enjoyed going for the interview at the RSC in lipstick because this is like considered the sort of . . . the sort of 'top drawer' in a way and my thing was, well this is who I am. That's interesting, that's good. A lot of people are frightened of it.

Mark   And what frightens them do you think?

Bette   Well, it's that I'm well struck in years, I come in, and I present something very strong. And some people are excited by it and book me, and some people are overwhelmed, and don't. You see, other times I'll totally hide everything, unknowingly, because I'm scared, or whatever, I want to work so badly.

Mark   But you don't hide it to the extent that you don't, you're not wearing the lipstick or whatever, so what . . . ?

Bette   Oh when I went to *The Vortex* audition at the Donmar I knew they weren't going to book me with lipstick and I

wanted the part very much. So I didn't wear lipstick, I got
dressed up as the character. It was slight betrayal of myself,
but I got the job and then on the first day I was there in my
full slap and Michael said, 'Bette's the only actor I know who
comes into the theatre who takes his make-up off and then
puts it on again when he's leaving!'

Mark   When you did the Nurse in *Romeo and Juliet* at the
Globe was that the same as doing Lady Bracknell, were you
playing a woman when you played the nurse?

Bette   No I never really thought about that until I got on.
And I got on and the audience accepted me as a woman and
as soon as I said the words 'Now, where's my Juliet . . .' or
something, they pissed themselves laughing. And I looked at
them. And they pissed themselves laughing again. Then we
got on with the scene. So they were saying we know you're a
bloke and that was the joke for them. But I didn't approach it
like that. In fact in the rehearsals I had a bit of a row because
a lot of people were goosing me. I was in my practice skirt,
my bits and pieces, and one day there was a dance rehearsal
and everybody was there except Tim Carroll, and the dance
woman was there. And I said, 'Look I'll just say it once. I
don't want anyone touching. Keep your fucking hands to
yourselves. I don't want anybody touching me, or goosing
me, or fucking around with me. I'm trying to make a person
is that alright?' You know. I wasn't going to be the company
clown so they could do all that, I was very shocked I said,
'You wouldn't do that if I was a woman. If I was one of the
women. You don't do that to the women, you wouldn't do
that to the women here. Don't fucking do it to me. Just leave
me alone. Let me find my way.' And people came up to me
afterwards and apologised, they knew who they were. 'Oh
I'm sorry Bette we were just joking, having a lark.' I said,
'Well it's a lark for you but not for me. I'm trying to find an
actual person here.' Irrespective of whether it's a man or a
woman, a character. What she'd been through. How she
walked, how her feet felt, how often she was allowed to sit
down or not.

Mark   Do you find now that, I mean, there is a lot more gay theme, there is a lot more, just gay people are a lot more visible? Has that meant people . . . does that mean there's less aggression towards you in terms of the lippy and the . . . Has that changed over the years?

Bette   No I think people . . . I was walking to the hospital the day before yesterday and these two guys, 'Look! It's a man! It's a man! It's a man, look it's a bloke, yeah, it's a bloke!' and they were really aggressive and I walked straight between them and on past to my appointment at the hospital. And it was pretty scary and they were completely thrown by it and completely aggressive and angry. No, I don't think things have changed on the street in that way. I think . . . you know . . . try it, anybody can go down the street in lippy and earrings or something and a bit gay-ed up, you know. You'll soon find out how tolerant they are – they're not tolerant at all. Not any more. They never have been, you know. It's different when I go up and down the Portobello Road, it's full of tourists, it's full of people that know me. I'm a local known character, but even then sometimes – this guy, a couple of weeks ago, he was on a scaffold. 'Look at that! Look at that! Call himself a fucking man! Look at the state of you, you fucker!' And for all the world if he hadn't been at work, you know, he'd have come down and hit me. You don't answer back. You have tunnel vision and you go straight ahead. You go where you're headed. It's interesting because the stall-holders on the street, on the Portobello, if they meet me say two blocks off the street they won't acknowledge me, or if they are with their kids they won't acknowledge me at all. They're very London working-class cockneys and it's alright on the street, but it's all bit of a circus on the street but . . . I'm talking big, stocky guys, six foot two with muscles and well struck in years, they'll be really friendly on the street, you know. I said to one of them one day, 'That guy always gives me a heavy fucking time.' He said, 'You want to fucking smack him he's useless.' Two days later, I see the same guy who was telling me this on the street and he wouldn't acknowledge me. He had his little kid with him and wouldn't acknowledge me. They look, and then they look away but they know exactly who you are and in a safe situation to them, men are very, very afraid – men particularly. I was walking down the street one day with this baby, Lorian, in a pram, in drag, and all the women were there and all the men, and all the men are giving me a hard fucking time, and all the women are saying, 'Leave him alone, leave him alone, he's alright, you leave him alone.' They can see I'm doing a job looking after this child. It's very weird, it's very weird.

Mark   And what about now, with your mum and stuff like that? Do you kind of think a bit more before you go and visit your mum, about how much make-up or the clothes you are going to wear, say, when you go and visit your mum?

Bette   She lives in a Welsh village and she's ninety-one and I don't pull any numbers up there – I go very straight. I don't really like going at all because, I don't know, there's a lot of heavy aggression. I was once there in a Tesco's. I literally thought I was going to be slaughtered. No, no, no, that's one of the reasons I don't go there. Quentin used to say to his family over in Jersey, 'I'll come if I don't have to go out.' And he'd come and go to the station, get a cab, go to the house and he wouldn't go out. It's too risky, it's too mad.

Mark   So drag is . . .

Bette   I mean the drag thing was in a way secondary to the subjects that we were doing in the Bloolips, certainly would have been in the Hot Peaches, I was very fearful of real drag queens, very aggressive and frightening. I didn't want to be a transsexual or anything like that. For me the gender thing was fun. It was energising to a degree.

Mark   And if you're honest rather than being politically correct about it, do you still feel any of that kind of discomfort or fear around people having the op?

Bette   Not at all.

Mark   Just because you got to know enough people?

Bette   I know a lot more about it, I meet plenty of people who are into that. I mean it's not a world I'm in all the time but I don't have any fear of it any more. I mean I'm who I am now. I'm seventy nearly, I'm not going to suddenly yearn to be a woman. I've never yearned for that. But I'm a queen. And I love flouncing as much as the next queen.

Ten Plagues

a libretto
with Conor Mitchell

Ten Plagues was first performed at the Traverse Theatre, Edinburgh, Monday 1 August 2011. It was performed by

Marc Almond

Libretto by   Mark Ravenhill
Music by   Conor Mitchell
Directed and designed by Stewart Laing
Musical Director   Bob Broad
Assistant Director   David Betz-Heinemann
Lighting Designer   Zerlina Hughes
Video Designer   Finn Ross
Video Performer   Francis Christeller

Spring

The spring is here

I'll buy
A ring
To wear
The spring is here

A door in Drury
Lane
Red cross
I want to buy a ring
The spring is here

A house shut up
The people say
May God preserve us
The spring is here

Above
A chamber
A woman's
Cry of grief

I want a ring
The spring is here

Bell tolls
Numbers called
The hearse of
Plague

The sun is out
I want a ring
The spring is here

Without a Word

Suddenly
I need a God

The pews are full
Each
Risking
Infection
To hear the Word

But
The pulpit is
Empty
The preacher fled

There is no Word

I want
To step up
Speak in tongues
Damn the preacher
Save us all

I leave
Without a word

Again to church

I want to preach
The King has fled
And courtiers
The palace empty
There is no rule

But I leave

Church again
I want to preach
The merchant's gone
Great halls of grain and garments
All could steal and share
But I leave
Without a word

The surgeon
And physicians
Gone

No word

I hold my charm
I chant my spell

Abaracadabara
Abaracadabara
Abaracadabara

God grant the plague
Spares me
Alone

To Dream

Tonight
I went to see
The player say
To die
To die, to sleep
To sleep
Perchance to dream

Later
I dreamed
You pulled me down
And filled me
With your spittle
Sweat
And seed

If death is one long dream
Of you
Then send me plague
And let me die

But death is not a dream
Oh
Close the playhouse
Let the players starve
That I should think
That dead men dream

And
May your house be shut
A watchman placed
To keep you in
That made me wish for plague

I will not love you
I will not dream of you
I will not die

Market

Few go to market now
For fear of plague
But after weeks of
Bread
I must have meat
And so I go
To market

There's a pig
Hung up
That I
Desire

Opening my purse
I find the price

The butcher
Lays down a cup of vinegar
'Money here'
Butcher says
The butcher counts to ten
Before he takes the money out

And so I take my pig
Under my arm
Through empty streets

This is how business is done
When money is infection
In times of plague

The Pit

Some have no sign of plague
No token on body, face
They fall, no warning
On the street
Are gone

If I am visited
Let there be tokens on me
Let me blister
Swell and burn

And
If I should wake
To find
Swelling of my neck
Or groin
I shan't wait
For the carriers
And cart
To fetch me
Dead

But rather
I shall run
Through the streets

And
I shall reach the pit
Look down upon the hundred
Bodies
Tumbled there
And say

My friends
I'm here
I choose
To be with you
Hold me close in your
Embrace

And then I'll throw myself
Into the pit
Happy with
The company I keep

Farewell

You came
Into my room
Tonight
I almost
Kissed you but

You stopped me said
I've come to say goodbye

And still
I almost
Kissed you but

You stopped me said
I've found a tumour
And pulling up your shirt
Showed me
The token
Hard and round
A silver penny
Of contagion

This is my last day
You said
And so goodbye

I was frightened
That you'd kiss me

I could have hit you
For bringing your infection
Here

But I stood apart
And said
Goodbye

The time to kiss is over

No caress
Or bruise
Shall pass between us now
But stand apart
And leave you
To a house shut up
And cart
And pit

And so I neither hit you
Nor I kissed you
And you left

Goodbye

By Day

They say
Too many die
To carry them
At night
Into the pit
So by day
In brightest light
Plague corpses
Are brought
Through the city

I find
I must see
Just one
Body as it fell
The face
Of a man
As plague
Pulled him to death

I run about the city
Looking for the carts
And carriers
Now
Crowds fill the
Streets
To look on
Death

But
There is no display
No corpse to show

A guilty sadness
Growing dark and
Down an alley
By St Paul's
I see a body
A man who lay down
Of plague and died

I turn and run
I find
I don't want to see
A face at all

A New Law

A new law:
The healthy stay inside
From dusk
Let the infected walk
To take the air

What do you do
Parading the city
You almost dead?
Do you
Greet and pet each other thus

My sweet my dear
What tumours
See mine here
I die tomorrow
And you?
We'll have a pretty hearse

Or do you walk alone
Scared of one another
As we are scared of you?

Seeing You

The night was summer hot
And so I rose
And walked about
The city
No men
Fires
Burning
To purify the air

I came to
A place I'd never been
The pit

A man said:
Turn back
No place for you
This is the plague pit
You are clean

I don't know why
But I must go in
I said
Here's money
And he let me pass

None there
But carrier
Corpse
And me

The cart came soon
And tipping up
Spewed bodies
Out

How alike all were
Naked
Rotten
Each one
The same
Foul corpse

But then
As it fell
One face
Turned
And I saw
That it was you

You seemed to look at me
I felt your breath

I saw you yesterday
And now you're gone

Who once I loved
You're took

You seemed to look

But then the bodies
Ate you up

The earth was thrown
All covered
And I returned
And slept
Although
The night continued hot

The Wig

I've shaved myself
Removed
Each last hair
So that I am
Free
Of anything that may
House flea or lice

I've bought a wig
Had the barber set it just so
And in the mirror I
Admire myself
For hours

My neighbour says
There's infection
In that wig
The hair comes
From the heads of corpses
Tipped
Into the pits

I say
Wig, I'll burn you
In the morning
Lest you infect me
And all those I move amongst

But
Today
I put on my wig
And wear it
To the Exchange
Let it infect me
And all those I move amongst
In this dead man's hair
I'm beautiful

The Hermit

This September night
Three thousand died
Between the hours
Of one and three

When plague began
I should have fled
Found hedge or ditch
And lived alone
The only man

I could not
Flee
The city
Kept me

Three thousand dead
In just two hours

What
If all are took
But me?

What if all
The city
Fall about me
One by one?

What if I should bury
All
None left to
Bury me?

I shut the door
I will not move from here
Until the plague has passed

I wear my finest clothes
Alone

My ring
My wig
I feast and fast
Alone
I sit
Month after month

Dead to others
Alone
I live

But how like death
This solitude

Grief

When the plague first came
In spring
I heard the story of
A Lambeth mother
Whose daughter
Grew hot
And blistered
Died
That same night
I shed tears
And everyone I told
Wept too

But now
In autumn
We see the bodies
In the street
The pits piled high
We go about our business
Our hearts still
Untroubled
All tears are gone

Now
I could see my friends
Family
Love
Fall into the grave
And I would not
Be moved

Now
If I die
Upon the street
All men would pass me
Too many gone
To mourn another

We all are plagued
Our hearts are gone
Our bodies live
We walking dead
About the city now

The Quaker

I knew him

His was a belief in quietness
Meetings of men
Who sit in silence
Listening to the Lord
Inside

He died
Of plague
Calmly
And was buried
Silently
As was his wish
Without a bell

I am not like him

If plague
Fetch me tonight
Let the bell
Be rung
That all the city knows
I am not a quiet man
But once was here
And now am lying in the pit

Keep ringing still
On on
Until the end of time
Tell men
Here was plague in London
And the dead are screaming still

Return

The numbers fall away
The worst is past
And so you're back
From Somerset

You tell me of the beauty of
Your rural life
How changed
The city is
You open up your shop
You start again

You say
You lived
I knew you would my friend

I drink with you
And smile
To see the city
Full again

You are foreign
To me now
You are a child of
Cruel innocence

You have not seen
What I have seen
Not known
The man fall dead
Beside you as you walked

I would not be you
I would not have your
Innocence
I'd rather see
What I have seen
Know
The city falling dead
Beside me as I walked

I come to your shop
Happily
But we'll never know each other
Now

Only those who live through plague
Can know each other
I do not know you

Ten Plagues

I am as an Israelite when
Ten plagues
Infect the land
I live

I see
The waters flow with blood
I live
Frogs outnumber men
I live
I see
Lice eat the people raw
I live
I could not see the sun
For flies
I live
Cattle fall and rot
I live
All about me blister
And I live
I see
Fire fall upon the earth
I live
Locusts swarm
I live
All is darkness
And I live

I watch
The angel
Pass over
The first-born die
Hear mothers
Maids
Sisters

Shout of grief
I live

I walk through
Parted waters
Turn and see
The merchant
Whore
Housewife
Doctor
All the city
Pulled into the sea
And gone
I live

Now
We never talk
Of plague
We live
We push our memory down
And live
Learn the new dance
Sing the new song
The shops fill
A new war
We live

Epilogue

In London
Came the plague in sixteen sixty-five
One hundred thousand dead
But I alive

Ghost Story

Ghost Story was created for Sky Playhouse Live and broadcast by Sky Arts in July 2010. The cast for the original production was as follows:

Meryl   Lesley Manville
Lisa   Juliet Stevenson
Hannah   Lyndsey Marshall

Written and directed by   Mark Ravenhill

Characters

Meryl
Lisa
Hannah

Meryl *and* **Lisa**.

Lisa Have you ever . . . ?

Meryl This isn't about me.

Lisa But . . . I wondered . . . how you came to −

Meryl This is about you.

Lisa Did you ever . . . did you heal yourself . . . did you?

Meryl That would be crossing the line.

Lisa But your understanding comes from . . . you understand illness because . . . ?

Meryl I'm a healer. That's all −

Lisa I understand.

Meryl That's all I − Of course you are asking questions. Who is this woman? Is she like me? Do I see myself in this woman?

Lisa Yes.

Meryl Do I trust this woman?

Lisa Maybe.

Meryl All of these questions are natural. Natural questions. But that is not the task. We are here to work on you. You will be healed. Where is your anger?

Lisa Everywhere.

Meryl Illness is anger. Anger caught in the body a trapped anger. Are you angry with yourself?

Lisa Yes.

Meryl Then let's start with that. If you can forgive yourself . . . I guide. But it's not for me to forgive you. It's for you . . . here. All the work you do, you do on yourself.

Lisa (*to mirror*)   I . . .

Meryl   Do you see a woman you can forgive?

Lisa   I . . . look so ill.

Meryl   Is that what you see?

Lisa   Skin yellowed. Gums rotting. Patches where hair should be.

Meryl   You're a beautiful woman.

Lisa   Everything falling away and I see a skull.

Meryl   We see what we tell ourselves to see. Forgive yourself.

Lisa   I'm so frightened.

Meryl   What's your fear? Name it.

Lisa   No.

. . .

Meryl   Tell me what you think of me.

Lisa   Well . . .

Meryl   You can't access those feelings.

Lisa   No, I can't access those feelings.

Meryl   Words create a story about ourselves. I'm a person who is dying. I have no choice. My body is diseased and ugly. My breast is my enemy. Is that a story you can hear in your head?

Lisa   Yes.

Meryl   So. A new voice, a new . . . I'm at the centre of my universe, I am filled with love, my body is filled with well being. We can . . . if we do the work. Will you do the work?

Lisa   I'll try.

Meryl   Alright. Now. You look at me and you don't have the words to describe what you feel.

Lisa   You're a guide. You're a healer. You're a wise woman.

Meryl   I'm going to ask you to draw me.

Lisa   Alright.

Meryl   But . . . the crayon in the other hand. So now you're not controlling with your conscious . . . you see?

Lisa   I see.

Meryl   I'm going to count down from twenty and the picture will be done. It's an image, an instant picture of what's in your . . . Here we go. Twenty . . . nineteen . . . eighteen . . . seventeen . . . sixteen . . . fifteen . . . fourteen . . . thirteen . . . twelve . . . eleven . . . ten . . . nine . . . eight . . . Seven . . . six . . . five . . . four . . . three . . . two . . . one. And – stop. What do you see?

Lisa   I . . .

Meryl   Would you like to show me . . . ?

Lisa   . . .

Meryl   There are no judgements. No punishments.

Lisa hands **Meryl** *the picture*

Lisa   I can't draw.

Meryl   I look like the wicked witch, don't I? Would you describe that as . . . ?

Lisa   A witch. It's yes.

Meryl   Isn't that interesting? Here I am the healer but I'm also the witch. That's interesting. I would have been burnt. Maybe in a previous life I was. Maybe they pulled me into the market place and they accused me . . . Somebody pointed at me, somebody – maybe someone like you – pointed at me and said: 'You live without a man, you have your own thoughts and your own space and you tell women that they can love their bodies, that their breasts are not their enemies and so we say that you should be burnt.'

Lisa   I'm not doing that. I'm diseased. I want to be well. I want to heal. I want to work with you.

Meryl   You are angry with me. That's only right. Someone else has to be the focus of your anger. I'm in the room. I'm used to this. It's part of the process. You hate me but –

Lisa   No.

She holds up the picture

This is nothing.

She rips up the picture

I am diseased. My breast was removed. I have forgiven the man, the surgeon who ripped and maimed me. He did the best he could with the knowledge he had at the time. My scarring is terrible. But I look at it now and I can see the beauty there. Yes, I cover it with this prosthetic but I can love my scar. There have been two wonderful years since my operation. My daughter had her first kiss from a boy. My husband lost twenty pounds and we have – sometimes – resumed intimacy. But now. It's in my lung. They've found a spot, my lung. You see? It's back.

Meryl   I see.

Lisa   I did all the work on myself once and now . . .

Meryl   It's back and . . .

Lisa   And I'm overwhelmed by darkness. The story I'm living is . . . I will move closer and closer to my death. It will be a horrible death. I will lose control of my body. I will be in great pain. I need a helper to change that story. I need you.

Meryl   Then we'll work together.

Lisa   I'm sorry, I want to know if you've ever –

Meryl   Of course you do but –

Lisa   I want to know if – if we're going on this journey – what's your experience of – Are you a survivor . . . Do you . . . ?

Meryl   I can't cross the line.

Lisa   Because . . . ?

Meryl   Because one person must be the healer. You want to be well –

Lisa   Yes . . .

Meryl   And it won't work – I can't empower you to release your anger if I'm also . . . Do you see?

Lisa   I just want to –

Meryl   Talk to your fear. Tell her what you're feeling. I'm your fear. Talk to me. Name me. Give me a name.

Lisa   You . . .

Meryl   What's happening?

Lisa   I can't.

Meryl   Are you ending the session?

Lisa   I just can't do that.

Meryl   Are you leaving and going back to your partner and your tests and – Are you ending the work with me?

Lisa   I don't know.

Meryl   You want me to tell you about myself. But I can't do that. I can't . . . I understand your journey. I share your feelings. I . . . I want us to do this work together.

Lisa   Because?

Meryl   Because you're a brave, beautiful woman who can be well again.

Lisa   I don't want to go. But . . . going on. I am so worn down by fear and Western medicine.

Meryl   Look at this room. Look around. Look at me. Look at my hand. Does any of this actually exist? Actually objectively exist? No. It only exists in my perception. The universe is only as I perceive it to be. I am ill. I am well. I decide.

Lisa   But still . . . the . . .

Meryl   Say the word.

Lisa   Cancer.

Meryl   Louder.

Lisa   Cancer.

Meryl   Draw it for me. The cancer. As you see it.

*She gives **Lisa** a chalk*

Meryl   On the wall.

Lisa   On the . . . ? (*Laughs.*)

Meryl (*laughs*)   I know, isn't it crazy?

*As **Lisa** draws on the wall:*

Meryl   Start with the eyes. That's good. I'm seeing a lot of anger there. But also fear. Could the cancer be as frightened of you as you are of it?

Now the mouth. So . . . it's hungry. It's desperate to eat, which means . . . it's needy, it's weak.

And a body. A shape, form. What's the size of the creature?

So it's big, bigger than you. And it's reaching out to you.

Is it a man or a woman?

Lisa *draws a primitive penis on the cancer, like a cave drawing.*

Meryl   So it's a very male energy. There's a male who is big and he's hungry and he's reaching out to you and he's going to eat you. Is this how it seems to you?

Lisa   Yes – that's it.

Meryl   Now, then speak to it. Tell it what you feel.

Lisa   Could you leave me alone please? Could you go away? I'm not ready for you. You see, my daughter still needs me. She doesn't know enough about the world. I still want to guide her. And my bloke. He really loves me. He'll go to bits if I let him down. I'll let him down if I go and I don't want to do that.

Meryl   But I can take you. You won't be missed. Your bloke. Your daughter. You're telling me they're the special ones. So I can take you.

Lisa   I'm special.

Meryl   How are you special?

Lisa   I'm working on myself. Every day I'm making myself grow a bit more. Because I'm unique. Because . . .

. . .

Meryl   That's it. That's good. Now if you –

Lisa   No.

Meryl   No?

Lisa   I'm not doing this. This is . . .

Meryl   Yes?

Lisa   I don't believe this. They're not my words. They're words to please you. I'm just the same as everyone else. I've never done anything special in my life. I was born in a little house that looked just the same as a thousand other little houses. I went to a school and I wore the uniform and I was average at everything. Now I work in a little cubicle that's just the same as a hundred other cubicles on the seventh floor which is just the same as every other floor. And I've been happy with that. It's been okay. It's been good. I've never wanted to be special. And now I've got breast cancer and it's spread into my lung. And that's not special or dramatic or . . . It's boring actually, boring. And all the other women – the lines of them sitting there waiting for their chemo and their radio and wearing headscarves and their wigs. Lots of them think they're special. Fighting the fight. But it doesn't make it better. It doesn't –

Meryl   I have seen miracles.

Lisa *gets her coat and bag, prepares to leave*

Lisa   I'm sorry. I've wasted your time.

Meryl   It's our time.

Lisa   I'll pay you.

Meryl   There's no need.

Lisa   This is my choice. I want you to have the money.

Meryl   I don't want to take the money.

Lisa   I'm just paying you for your time.

Meryl   Take it.

She pushes the money to the floor. **Lisa** *gets down to pick up the money which is scattered about the floor.* **Meryl** *moves over and forms the shape of the cancer drawn on the wall.*

Meryl   Please. I need you. I'm hungry. I need to eat.

Lisa   Don't.

Meryl   Because I'm big, because I'm male, all this male energy, then I frighten you.

Lisa   This is a stupid game.

Meryl   But I need a woman. To feed on, to eat. I've already taken your breast. I've taken your breast and I fed on that and it kept me happy for months. But now I'm back and there's so much more of you. I can taste your lung . . . your lung tastes good. Maybe I'll take that next. Please. If you don't stop me. I'm so hungry. I can't help myself if you don't do anything, if you walk away then I will spread through your lymphs and that will take me round your whole body and I will eat everything, I will eat you all away. Destroy you.

Lisa   Leave me alone.

Meryl   I want your body. I want to take you. We belong together. I own you.

Lisa   Stop this, no stop. I will not . . . My cancer's not like that. Don't tell me what my cancer is like. It's my cancer. You can't see it. They look at it on scans and pictures. They look at bits of me under their microscopes. They show me bits of myself and tell me what it is. But this cancer is mine. Some days my cancer is hurting me and scaring me, yes. Somedays my cancer is the bully in the playground or or or the headmaster. But some days cancer is my lover. Some days we're alone together, shut away in the afternoon and we sleep and we whisper together. My cancer knows my body better than any man has ever . . . So please don't . . . You can't be my cancer, it's too . . . special.

. . .

Meryl   You've turned the corner.

Lisa   You think so?

Meryl   I can never tell when it will come, which session. But I know it when it happens.

Lisa   What comes? What happens?

Meryl   Something has been released. You've moved on. You're going to be well. Can you feel that?

Lisa   I don't know.

Meryl   Pick up the mirror. What do you see?

Lisa *looks in the mirror*

Lisa   A bit better.

Meryl   And forgive yourself.

Lisa   I . . . for . . . I f-f-f . . .

Meryl   That's it. Cry now. It's a release.

Lisa   I won't forget this

Meryl   I'm a survivor.

Lisa   Yes.

Meryl   I had cancer, my breast was . . . But I did the work on myself and . . .

Lisa   I knew that. I sensed.

Meryl   I shouldn't cross the line but . . .

Lisa   I want to be like you.

Meryl   Like me?

Lisa   Well and happy. Like you. Happy and well.

Meryl   You can be.

Lisa   You promise?

Meryl   I . . .

Lisa   No. I understand. You can't promise. I can see that. But I need to know. I don't want to be an ill person.

Meryl   We'll meet once a week. You'll do the work on yourself.

Lisa   I will. Yes.

Meryl   And as we let out the negative thoughts, new positive thoughts will flow through you and . . .

Lisa   I'll be well. I understand it's a long journey but that little bit of light to . . . I lied to you. My husband. My husband hasn't . . . He's a good man. But this thing . . . my husband sleeps on the sofa.

Meryl   I see.

Lisa   And I wonder if you could just hold me for . . . ?

Meryl   Of course.

She holds **Lisa**

Lisa   Thank you very much. That's good, isn't it? The work's beginning.

. . .

Hannah *with shopping.*

Hannah   There was a woman in front of me. And there was one last butternut squash left and this woman took the butternut squash. And I felt this great surge of anger. 'That's my butternut squash for the butternut squash soup I am going to prepare tonight for my girlfriend and you've taken the butternut squash you bitch, bitch.' Wasn't that ridiculous? But then I laughed at myself and I said "Ridiculous' and I got a pumpkin instead and do you know actually it's Halloween today so everything's worked out for the best because it's Halloween and we're going to be eating pumpkin soup. So really the woman who took the butternut squash was doing us a favour. I love you.

Meryl   I love you too.

Hannah   There's something wrong.

Meryl   No.

Hannah   One of the kids called me 'nan' today. I've had 'mum' before. But. I realised I'm very frightened of becoming an older woman. How was your day? Did you have a bad day?

Meryl   No. Everything's okay. Really I'm –

Hannah   I don't believe you.

Meryl   Well –

Hannah   Maybe once we've eaten.

Meryl   Yes.

Hannah   Come here. My beautiful bird. Let me hold you.

They hold each other.

There's no intimacy here.

Meryl   Really?

Hannah   This is supposed to be you and me –

Meryl   I know.

Hannah   We promised. At the end of the day we leave everything behind and everyone else and it's just you and me.

Meryl   It is.

Hannah   You and me together alone and –

Meryl   We are, we are.

Hannah   You're somewhere else.

Meryl   I love you.

Hannah   Yes?

Meryl   Yes. Of course yes. Yes I love you. You're very beautiful and you have an incredible aura and I love you.

They kiss.

Lisa It's like a battle, isn't it? And suddenly I can feel it. The battle's turning and all my fighters – like my immune system – they're suddenly going out and they are fighting the cancer, which is brilliant. Because once I've got the strength. Once my mind is telling them go out and fight the cancer then I'm invincible, aren't I? Nothing can beat that. Nothing can beat me now.

Meryl How was that?

Hannah You're still . . . You're not actually here with me.

Meryl Of course I am of course I –

Hannah No.

Meryl What do you – what do you want me to do?

Hannah I just feel . . .

Meryl Cut myself? Is that the proof that you – ?

Hannah No no no.

Meryl Because I love I love you I love you and if that's not – if you can't hear that then –

Hannah I'm hearing the words.

Meryl Then really you should look at yourself – at your own insecurities, if you can't then –

Hannah I know all my insecurities and I acknowledge them but –

Meryl Then please just allow us to be.

Hannah Would you like a rub?

Meryl That would be good.

Hannah *rubs* **Meryl**.

Meryl I'm sorry, it's hurting.

Hannah   Would you like me to stop?

Meryl   Yes I would actually. I'm sorry that's just what I –
yes I would. I would like you to stop.

Hannah   Alright then.

. . .

Hannah   Who is it?

. . .

Hannah   Who's in this space?

Meryl   I don't know.

Hannah   Somebody else in this space. I can only see me
and I can see you. But you . . .

Meryl   No.

Hannah   There's someone else in this space with you.

Meryl   You're young.

Hannah   Don't patronise me.

Meryl   You don't know.

Hannah   Who?

Meryl   Lots of . . . Mum. Dad. Lovers. They're all in here
chatting away all the time.

Hannah   Not for me.

Meryl   Because you're younger, but as you get older –

Hannah   I'm your lover, not your child. There's . . . a
negative energy. I can feel –

Meryl   Yes.

Hannah   If I'm here I can feel a negative energy.

Meryl   A client.

Hannah   Ah.

Meryl   Last week.

Hannah   And there's still . . . ?

Meryl   She was very strong. She brought a lot of negative –

Hannah   You have to let this go. If we're going to –

Meryl   I do.

Hannah   But still –

Meryl   This one woman I – I crossed a line with this one woman.

Hannah   I see.

Meryl   She was a cancer woman.

Hannah   I see.

Meryl   And I – you know – there are plenty of cancer women but this woman, I . . . She had a breast cancer and the breast had been removed and so it –

Hannah   You connected with that.

Meryl   I did. It was my case. It was me.

Hannah   But she's not you.

Meryl   No. She was another woman but her story was my story.

Hannah   Did she have a beautiful young girlfriend who was giving her pumpkin soup for Halloween?

Meryl   No. She had a man and a child.

Hannah   There we are.

Meryl   But otherwise –

Hannah   Lots of women have cancer. Their breast is removed. They survive.

Meryl   It was like me if I had followed another life path.

Hannah   But you fought it. You're special.

Meryl   I could have been there with the job and the man and –

Hannah   But you met me. And you cured yourself.

Meryl   I did. Met you and I cured myself.

Hannah   Where is she?

Meryl   She's gone now.

Hannah   I don't believe you.

Meryl   Come on. Let's relax.

Hannah   Point to her in the room.

Meryl   She's there.

Hannah   And what's she doing?

Meryl   She's crying. But in a way . . . that's releasing, that's . . .

Hannah   Ask her to leave.

Meryl   There's no need.

Hannah   Tell her that it's a special time / our time, and you want her to go now.

Meryl   There really is no need for that.

Hannah   Are you frightened? She's a woman. She's a client. She pays sixty pounds. It's a transaction. You allow her to do the work on herself. Say to her, tell her . . .

Meryl (*to* **Lisa**)   I feel like you're me.

Lisa Yes?

Meryl I'm sorry if I've crossed a line but I really feel
you're me.

Lisa That's alright.

Meryl All those things . . . the school the house the job the
fella I had all those things.

Lisa I see.

Meryl But . . . I had the cancer. A man, a surgeon he tore
off my breast just as . . .

Lisa Oh.

Meryl They say it's necessary, these men they tell us it's
necessary to chop at our bodies but I'm not convinced . . .

Lisa Do you know really I . . .

Meryl And I have a prosthetic, there was remission but
then my lung . . .

Lisa Please.

Meryl So our stories you see are so . . . identical.

Lisa I'm sorry if this is hard or cruel, yes, this is hard and
but . . .

Meryl Yes?

Lisa I don't really want to hear that.

Meryl I'm sorry.

Lisa Because now that I've actually released this incredible
energy −

Meryl Alright then.

Lisa I really need − I'm sorry − to be surrounded by
positive −

Meryl No.

Lisa I need this time for positive thoughts – I need to attract well-being to myself – I'm at a stage where if I'm with too much negative –

Meryl I understand.

Lisa I suppose I'm frightened that I'll be overwhelmed by all your negative – when what I'm filled with is a positive –

Meryl I can see.

Lisa That was your past. Your experience that was your past. So let it go – just –

Meryl Of course.

Lisa You have to work to let that go.

. . .

Meryl I'll make the soup with you.

Hannah You haven't said goodbye to her yet.

Meryl There's no need.

Hannah I think you should.

Meryl I really don't –

. . .

Meryl You're going to be well. I feel that very strongly.

Lisa So do I.

Meryl We've done the work.

Lisa Of course.

. . .

Lisa I feel bad now.

Meryl There's no need.

Lisa You've got the same story as me.

Meryl It wasn't part of our deal. I crossed the line.

Lisa You wanted to tell me about –

Meryl Not now –

Lisa I'm a survivor. You're a survivor. We should –

Meryl You've got your bloke and your girl waiting for you at home.

Lisa We can share our stories.

Meryl You cook them a lovely meal and tell them that Mummy is going to be well again.

Lisa It came back on your lung and –

Meryl I was wrong to tell you about that.

Lisa When it came back on your lung. How did you fight that?

Meryl My story is not your story. I'm the healer.

Lisa But you're well now?

Meryl I crossed the line once but I'm not crossing it again. Goodbye.

Lisa I want to know that you're alright.

Meryl I'm well. I'm strong. Goodbye.

Hannah That's it. Say goodbye.

Lisa You don't want this (*the drawing on the wall*) in your lovely room.

Meryl I can do it later.

Lisa I want to do it.

Meryl I don't want you to do it.

Lisa But I want to do it.

She begins to wash the wall

Hannah Is she gone now?

Meryl All gone.

Hannah The room's a lot lighter now, isn't it?

Meryl Much lighter.

Hannah (*sits*) So she was sat here crying but she's gone now? You have a wonderful gift. You've healed so many people. And you've healed yourself. You are such an incredible woman. I can't believe I met a woman as incredible as you.

Lisa Have you got someone?

Meryl It doesn't matter.

Lisa But there's someone to look after you?

Meryl That's crossing the line.

Lisa I know but I just want to . . . There's someone you can talk to? In the evenings when you go home and you've been healing. There's a man?

Meryl No.

Lisa Oh.

Meryl There was a man and a kid. I had a man called Harry and a daughter called Lily. But I left them.

Lisa I see.

Meryl My choice.

Lisa Are you happy?

Meryl This is all about me.

Lisa Have you got someone else now?

Meryl   Let's not talk about me.

Lisa   I'd just like to know if there's someone else.

Meryl   No.

Lisa   Oh.

Meryl   I'm alone. But I like that. It's very quiet. It's very calm. I just cook myself some soup and sit here in this room on my own and I think.

Lisa   So long as you're happy.

Meryl   It's very important: learning to be happy by yourself.

. . .

Hannah   What are you thinking about?

Meryl   I'm thinking about how much I love you.

Hannah   Well that's good because I'm thinking about how much I love you.

Meryl (*laughs*)   That's good.

Hannah   I couldn't bear to be alone. Even if you're gone for a day I can't stand to be here without you. I can't remember what my life was like without you.

Meryl   You were alright. You were happy.

Hannah   Not like this. And now that you're here. I want you to be here always and for ever.

Meryl   But you could be happy on your own.

Hannah   Never.

Meryl   Never?

Hannah   Never.

Meryl   Listen . . .

Hannah   I want this moment never to stop.

Meryl   It . . .

Hannah   What?

Meryl   It's come back.

Hannah   What has?

Lisa   Just this one last bit.

Meryl   I went for a check-up a few weeks ago.

Hannah   You didn't say anything about that.

Meryl   It was a routine, I've been so well . . .

Hannah   Why didn't you tell me?

Meryl   It was such a routine thing. I forgot about it myself. I only found the letter in a drawer the night before. You were working on your lesson plans so I didn't say anything.

Hannah   I thought you were always going to tell me.

Meryl   I was but it was so routine and you were so busy so I just popped in because I really thought it was going to be such a routine . . .

Lisa   There's always one stubborn bit.

Meryl   But that's when they told me you see that it's in my lung now. Really quite aggressively.

Hannah   You knew this . . . ?

Meryl   A few weeks ago.

Hannah   Did you phone Harry?

Meryl   I did actually.

Hannah   Oh.

Meryl   Because of Lily. I wanted him to know because of Lily, it's important that he knows.

Hannah   I can have a kid.

Meryl   It just gives him time to prepare Lily for the worst.

Hannah   I want to have a kid. My body's ready for that. Shall we have a kid?

Meryl   I've decided not to have any radio and chemo.

Hannah   Ever?

Meryl   Ever.

Hannah   Why?

Meryl   Because what is that going to do? Chemo? Radio? What can they do? They can put a stop to it for a while . . . they can slow it down . . . but if they can't fight the cause . . . if you can't find the cause then what's the . . . ?

Hannah   What's the cause?

Meryl   Anger.

Hannah   But you've been working on –

Meryl   There's still more there. I've got to work on that. I've got to find every last bit of anger and I've got to let it out of me.

Hannah   But alongside the chemo and the –

Meryl   No. No. Just me now. Just me fighting this.

Hannah   And me.

Hannah   We're working together.

Meryl   We can't. This is mine.

Hannah   But I'm your partner.

Meryl   You don't know – this is my battle – no doctor – no –

Hannah   I love you.

Meryl   I'm sorry, but you're a child –

Hannah   I am not – You want to be alone?

Meryl   I do. Yes. Me. Alone. In this room. Anyone else will . . . hold me back.

Hannah   You don't love me?

Meryl   I haven't got time for that. I can't –

Hannah   You don't love me.

Meryl   Illness. Death. These are selfish things.

Hannah   Would you like me to leave?

Meryl   This is about my anger.

. . .

Lisa   I'm sorry. I wasn't expecting you. Is there another woman who . . . ?

Hannah   No, there's no one else.

Lisa   You're on your own here?

Hannah   I am yes, I'm on my own here.

Lisa   Oh I'm sorry I thought . . . I was looking for another woman, for Meryl. I came to see her last year and I wanted to . . .

Hannah   Meryl isn't here.

Lisa   Can I leave her a note? If I scribble something and –

Hannah   How well did you know Meryl?

Lisa   A little. She –

Hannah   Meryl passed away.

Lisa Oh.

Hannah   After a very long battle. Don't be sad. It was a very spiritual moment. I was with her. I was travelling. I'd gone to Thailand. But my name was on the form. I flew back. I went to the hospital. I held her hand. I was very privileged. I saw her spirit leave her body.

Lisa   Sorry, I just . . . I was so sure she'd be here and now to find –

Hannah   Everything moves on.

Lisa   Was it cancer?

Hannah   Yes, her breast then her lymphs then her lung and then all over.

Lisa   I thought . . . I knew she had . . . But she was so strong. She was a great healer. Are you her daughter?

Hannah   I was her partner.

Lisa   Oh.

Hannah   You seem surprised. Did you think she was on her own?

Lisa   It was over a year ago, I don't remember.

Hannah   Did she tell you she had a partner?

Lisa   That would have been crossing the line.

Hannah   I know, but still . . .

Lisa   I was a woman with cancer and she was my healer and so anything else would have been crossing the line.

Hannah   I suppose.

Lisa   But actually . . .

Hannah   Yes?

Lisa   Actually . . . There was a moment. I'd drawn on the wall here.

With a piece of chalk and then I was leaving and I looked at it and it looked so terrible I just wanted it to go I wanted to clean it up.

Hannah   She would've done that.

Lisa   I know she would've but somehow for me you know I really felt like I'd turned a corner and I didn't want to leave that thing on the wall.

Hannah   Okay.

Lisa   So I decided to stay here and clean it up. And that's when I crossed the line.

Hannah   I see.

Lisa   Because I had this sense . . . I don't know why but I had this feeling . . . I just had this feeling that this wasn't just my story but that it was her story.

Hannah   She would have known by then. It was in her lung. She came home and told me straight away. I made her soup and we cried together.

Lisa   I crossed the line and I pushed her: 'Do you know about this? Are you going through this too?'

Hannah   She wouldn't cross the line.

Lisa   No. She was a healer. She wasn't going to cross the line. And so I said to her: 'Alright. Just tell me one thing. At home, tonight, is there someone?' And she said yes, she could go home in the evening and there you would be cooking her a soup and that made her very happy.

Hannah   That's good.

Lisa   So I was able to leave here much lighter because I knew, you see, that she wasn't on her own. When did she die?

Hannah   Last summer.

Lisa   I thought she was going to make it.

Hannah   So did I.

Lisa   I mean how can that be? How can I fight and win and she can lose? It doesn't make sense.

Hannah   Why did you come?

Lisa   To thank her. I thought she'd be here and I wanted her to see me well and strong because of her and I wanted to thank her.

Hannah   Of course.

Lisa   I didn't think for a moment . . .

Hannah   You can still do it.

Lisa   I really thought she was so strong.

Hannah   You can still thank her.

Lisa   I should go.

Hannah   I still talk to her. So can you. It helps. I tell her what I feel about her. You can do that. Her energy is still in the room. I believe that. Do you believe that?

Lisa   I don't know.

Hannah   I can sense it. Can you see her?

Lisa   Yes.

Hannah   What does she look like?

Lisa   Like she did that day.

Hannah   How was that?

Lisa   Like . . . a very beautiful woman. A guide. A helper.

Hannah   She doesn't look ill to you?

Lisa   No. Strong. Well.

Hannah   What's she doing?

Lisa   Sitting there. Listening to me.

Hannah   Then tell her what you . . . thank her.

Lisa   Yes.

. . .

Lisa   Hello.

Meryl   Hello.

Lisa   I'm sorry.

Meryl   You don't need to be.

Lisa   But I am. Sorry. That you died and I lived. That's not fair.

Meryl   It's the way it is.

Lisa   It shouldn't have been.

Meryl   I looked at you that morning and I thought: she's a very weak person and I'm a very strong person.

Lisa   You were very frightened.

Meryl   Maybe.

Lisa   Your own cancer was . . . it made you frightened. Forgive yourself.

Meryl   When all the time you were the stronger –

Lisa   Lucky.

Meryl   You were strong and positive and I . . .

Lisa It's not like that.

Meryl There are strong people who live. There are weak people who die.

Lisa No. We work on ourselves. We create ourselves, our thoughts make us –

Meryl Blah blah.

Lisa You taught me that: you taught me that if we can find our anger, release our anger, forgive and move forward into a –

Meryl BLAH. All lies.

Lisa But I'm the proof. I'm alive.

Meryl I'm the proof. I'm dead. Nothing works. Nothing to be done. All the years I wasted on the mirrors and the drawings and the games, all –

Lisa You gave me life.

Meryl Nothing to be done.

Lisa She says it was a spiritual moment. Beautiful. Your soul left your body.

Meryl No. She can't hear. She's too young. I was screaming, crying out, cursing 'I hate this. I hate this. I hate this' . . . She couldn't hear it.

Lisa Is there peace now?

Meryl No.

Lisa Surely you can find a bit of – ?

Meryl Just . . . great anger because I lost the fight.

Lisa Are you angry with me?

Meryl With you? No.

Lisa   I came to thank you.

Meryl   You did the work on yourself.

Lisa   But you were my guide. And now I have a life with –
My girl is doing so well at school, we've bought a second
place in France. We go there at the weekends. Everything has
worked out so well. And that's all because of you. So thank you.

Meryl   It wasn't me.

Lisa   I want you to accept my gratitude.

Meryl   I can't.

Lisa   I need you – it's a closure for me – if you'll
acknowledge how –

Meryl   I'll never do it.

Lisa   All this blame, all this hatred, you've got to do more
work on yourself.

Meryl   You think so?

Lisa   Oh yes. It never stops, the work on yourself. I'm well
now but it doesn't mean I don't stop working on myself.
Come and look at yourself in the mirror. What do you see?

Meryl   Nothing.

Lisa   I can see you.

Meryl   There's nothing there.

Lisa   Of course there is. It's you. You're beautiful and
you're strong. Only you can love yourself. Only you can
forgive yourself. Say: 'I love you and I forgive you.'

Meryl   I can't.

Lisa   'I love you and I forgive you.'

Meryl   No.

Lisa   'I love you and I forgive you.'

Meryl   There's nothing there. I'm nobody. I'm nowhere. You have a life. Go on. Go back there.

Lisa   But there's no closure for me unless you -

Meryl   I can't give you – Didn't I give you enough? Didn't I give you life? I died and you – I won't accept your thanks. I won't forgive myself. I can't give you that.

Lisa   But I can't live with the feeling that you – Can't you see? I feel as though I came here and I took your life. I feel as though I'm alive because you're – and I can't spend my days with that –

Meryl   Yes you will. You'll live with that. You'll carry on.

Hannah   Did you thank her?

Lisa   Yes I did.

Hannah   And how was it?

Lisa   It was . . . very peaceful. Very calm. I told her that I had a wonderful life and I thanked her for her healing powers and it was very beautiful. She forgave herself and accepted my thanks. There's . . .

Hannah   Closure?

Lisa   Yes. There's a closure now.

Hannah   Did she look beautiful and strong?

Lisa   Oh yes. Very beautiful. Very strong. Thank you. I'm going now.

Hannah   I see her.

Lisa   Now?

Hannah   Not now. No. But sometimes I see her and she . . . I can't see her like that . . . I see her and she's worn away.

Her flesh is grey. Her gums are sore. Her eyes have no light in them. She has a tube in her arm and her nose. Catheter. She's like she was the day she passed on. I want to see something else but that's what she is when I see her.

Lisa   Oh no. She isn't like that all.

Hannah   No?

Lisa   You've got that wrong. She's here now. She's very calm. She's very forgiving. She's forgiven everyone, you, me, the surgeons, everyone. And she's done the work on herself. She's forgiven herself. And she's beautiful. Can you see that?

Hannah   No.

Lisa   If you look, really look you can see that, can you see her?

Hannah   Yes.

Lisa   And how does she look?

Hannah   Calm. Wise. Beautiful.

Lisa   That's right. Isn't that great? Everything worked out for the best.

They are in silence.

The Experiment

The Experiment was first performed in October 2010 as part of the Terror Season at Southwark Playhouse, London. The performer was Mark Ravenhill.

1

This was – I suppose – a long time ago

And I remember I lived in a modest house with my partner

And I think maybe – your face – you were one of our neighbours

And we were very happy in that big old house. Very

Because we had children. One of each. A perfect pair. A very special unique wonderful child

And I remember – yes – it was us – it was . . . in our great big manor house . . . one time . . . it was . . . I remember . . .

We ran the tests on the children

Because you see we sort of knew that one day one of the children would grow up to have an incurable disease – an, as yet, incurable disease – so what we – we – my partner decided and I followed – we decided together – what we decided to do was to experiment on the children. Because then we'd have the cure when the time came. We'd find the cure for the child's later ailment

So we were – if I remember – very thorough about this, very organised. Mostly organised. An organised chaos

And we would infect the child, the children with little drops of viruses or inject little cells of cancers and we – you know through the bars of the cage

The cage was in a film. I saw the cage in a film – a documentary or a horror

Or there was a cage in the fairy story my grandmother told me on the train journey that time to . . . to . . .

So there wasn't, maybe there wasn't – no cage

Because the child had a lovely room. The best room in that cramped little house. Stars that glowed on the ceiling, wallpaper of princesses, a rug with a map of an imaginary world

But because my partner had an incurable illness – it wasn't curable at that time – that's when my partner decided to run the tests on the children

My partner told me on a rainy hot winter night afternoon as we made breakfast lying on the sundeck and he was over there and my partner told me

I have an incurable illness and what we must do is run tests on the children so that we can find the new medicine to save me

And I can't remember I . . .

Was totally opposed

I understood immediately

I was dumbstruck, didn't know what to do

This didn't happen to me, this happened to another person. Another person living with another partner in another

This happened to you.

This happened to a person I saw in a documentary once

So I went along with it

I remember I strapped the child to the bed

I was very kind, I was soothing, I loved my child but I loved my partner, we had to find a cure

What you have to do to get through something like that when you know it's for the greater good what you do is you numb your feelings – you cut out your heart, you cut it . . .

I remember nothing about the tests beginning

Just suddenly you're there and your partner has strapped the child to the bed and is injecting the child with tiny drops of viruses and cancers

And I can't remember anything about it

I remember the children slept through the worst of it

I was sleeping all the time

And I remember waking up and I said to my partner: the most awful thing is happening next door. The couple next door are experimenting on their children so that they can find a cure.

And my partner said: That sort of thing goes on of course I know it, it goes on but a long way a long time ago

But I was so sure and I took a – I think if I remember – it was the new video camera and I climbed over the fence and into our neighbour's garden

I was you know – it was probably after two three six months years of this

After a while you – you imagine this was you – imagine you're me – after a while you just have to know if this is a real thing you have to have something on record

So I was I remember the Christmas lights were still up and in the baking heat I'm making my way up the stairs in that big house

It was the shed door, I think I remember the child's voice from behind the

Father, father, the needle is sharp

Mother, mother, cut out your heart

Which I remember in verse which can't be, that must be . . . there wasn't any . . . there can't have been . . . but here in my head verse

Father, father, cut out the heart

Mother, mother the needle is . . .

And I pushed pulled open the door swung open and through the eye of the camera I saw my partner neighbour injecting the child strapped to the bed and sleeping

And I remember calling out I:

Dear God, what is this? Has it come to this? Are we animals? We who are God's creation? We are so close to the angels? We who are reason and imagination? Is this what we're doing with all that God has given us? These tests? These experiments?

I wish I'd said that. When I go back in my head, when I tell the story to myself or to you that's what I wish I'd 'we who are God's creation' I wish those words

But I remember I . . .

I just remember screaming CUNT CUNT CUNT CUNT CUNT over and over and

Because of course – I didn't – that's right – I remember now, I remember, the order was muddled, it didn't happen

We lived in a modest manor house long ago and I suppose I had my suspicions because why else – I can't think of any other reason why I'd be pushing open the door with the video camera in my time but I didn't

Yes I didn't know anything about the – that's it I didn't know anything about the experiments or the reasons for the experiments until then

I knew nothing at all

I knew nothing and that's why I reacted so: CUNT

And that's when my partner sat me down on the lounger standing there with the vodka in my hand the tea was cold and the weather was hot rain and my partner explained to me

Next door they have an as yet incurable disease so what we must do is experiment on your child so that we can find a cure. Our children may suffer a little, I grant you, but it will find a cure for the disease next door

And that's when I remember my partner telling me because I still had the video camera in my hand because this must have been before the video camera was stolen but that was another video camera

And so I remember I agreed to the experiments

That's how my partner made me agree to the experiments

There once was a person who agreed to experiments on children if it would find a cure

And I remember my neighbour was angry – was it you? – maybe it was you? – you were sarcastic mocking teasing furious understanding

Your partner makes his money because he has shares in a company that experiments on children

And I remember I told you: To prevent an incurable disease.

And you I remember you backed off away then.

And this child is. Look at this child. This child is so damaged. It has no memory. There is no past or future for this child. This child has no moral sense. This child could not tell you: this is right, this is wrong. This child has no empathy: this child cannot feel anything that others feel. Can we really say that it is wrong to experiment on this child? I would not call this child an animal because – quite honestly – that would be degrading to the animal.

2

I'm in the room

The room is squalid

Pizza box beer cans

And I'm looking at my twin brother

And his skin is hard and dry, red, blistered. It's over his hands, starting to cover his face

And I'm looking at him sitting on the bed

And I think that he hates me for my clothes and my smooth skin

And my twin asks me:

'Don't you remember? Don't you remember what they did to us?'

How he woke us up at night and he put on our pyjamas and he took us down the stairs

Don't you remember that?'

Maybe

'And how they took us to the cupboard under the stairs

And how dark it was under the stairs

And how you could hear the other children crying in there too'

Possibly

'And how the train pulled in under the stairs

And how we all got into the train

And how it went to the mountains

And how he liked us because we were twins

Do you remember?'

A little bit

'And we never saw the other children again

They were washed away

But he took us into his special room

And he did the experiments on us

Do you remember that?'

I'm not sure

'And one day he cried

Cried so much and he said:

"Humanity has ended

Soon the last human will go

But that's alright

Because I'm going to make new humans

You see that's why I'm doing the experiments on you

So that when the time comes there'll be a new human race

And they'll all be made from your cells

If only I can get the experiment right

Do you see?"

And he stopped crying

And there was a big smile on his face

Do you remember that? You must – big smile on his face –
remember that?'

And I said:

No

None of that happened

You need help

You need to be sorted

It didn't happen

Humanity didn't die

Open the curtains

Look outside

There's a whole human race out there

They're not us

They weren't made in a room by experimenting on us

Each one is unique and individual and –

Why did you make that up?

And my twin says to me:

'You're the one who makes things up. I'm the one who tells the truth'

You're the one who makes things up. I'm the one who tells the truth.

3

And I remember after three ten years the child grew too big for that room for the shed for the I remember the children growing absolutely big and enormous.

And I said to my partner: The experiments on the children have ended.

And it was my partner who told me: The experiments on the children have ended.

We saw it – I'm pretty sure – on the news first: The experiments on the children have ended.

Somewhere else somebody else had found a cure by experimenting on . . .

I forget.

Don't remember.

I remember so clearly rushing up the grand stairs in the grand hall of the manor house –

Only of course they weren't there at the time –

I ran into my partner's office in the City and I said:

'They've found we've discovered there's a cure antidote and the children's neighbour's lives is saved – you are going to live my darling – and here's the first pill'

And I remember thinking that you were going to live for ever

4

The other day, it had been a beautiful day

We'd been up to the shopping centre where we'd been celebrating another victory

And we got the bus home

And it was so lovely

Because everybody was so happy about the victory

And they were all smiling and congratulating each other

And a big black lady pulled me into her bosom and just held me and said:

'Another victory praise be praise be'

And we got home

And I was making us a drink to have on the balcony

When my partner said:

'I saw them again'

I wanted to hit my partner and tell my partner to shut it

But I'm better educated than that so I said:

'Yes?'

And my partner said:

'The two little boys

It was the noise at first

Because they were calling out

"Father father the needle is sharp"

But then I saw them at the end of the bed

Two bodies but joined here and here

Two but one

And they were naked

And there were injection marks all over here

And little cuts all over here

And their eyes

And their teeth

Had been pulled and –

Is this how they made us ? Is this who we are?

Did they do these tests, these experiments so we can – ?

What if we're not humans

None of us are real humans any more

But we're all just made by the man who cut at those boys in a shed in the . . .'

And I said

'Look the sun is setting

It's very beautiful

And this drink tastes lovely

So let's just . . . Yes?'

I won't be with this partner

Nothing lasts for ever

But as long as we don't talk about the experiments

We'll have a few years

And that's lovely.

Bloomsbury Methuen Drama Modern Plays
include work by

Bola Agbaje
Edward Albee
Davey Anderson
Jean Anouilh
John Arden
Peter Barnes
Sebastian Barry
Alistair Beaton
Brendan Behan
Edward Bond
William Boyd
Bertolt Brecht
Howard Brenton
Amelia Bullmore
Anthony Burgess
Leo Butler
Jim Cartwright
Lolita Chakrabarti
Caryl Churchill
Lucinda Coxon
Curious Directive
Nick Darke
Shelagh Delaney
Ishy Din
Claire Dowie
David Edgar
David Eldridge
Dario Fo
Michael Frayn
John Godber
Paul Godfrey
James Graham
David Greig
John Guare
Mark Haddon
Peter Handke
David Harrower
Jonathan Harvey
Iain Heggie

Robert Holman
Caroline Horton
Terry Johnson
Sarah Kane
Barrie Keeffe
Doug Lucie
Anders Lustgarten
David Mamet
Patrick Marber
Martin McDonagh
Arthur Miller
D. C. Moore
Tom Murphy
Phyllis Nagy
Anthony Neilson
Peter Nichols
Joe Orton
Joe Penhall
Luigi Pirandello
Stephen Poliakoff
Lucy Prebble
Peter Quilter
Mark Ravenhill
Philip Ridley
Willy Russell
Jean-Paul Sartre
Sam Shepard
Martin Sherman
Wole Soyinka
Simon Stephens
Peter Straughan
Kate Tempest
Theatre Workshop
Judy Upton
Timberlake Wertenbaker
Roy Williams
Snoo Wilson
Frances Ya-Chu Cowhig
Benjamin Zephaniah

For a complete catalogue
of Bloomsbury Methuen Drama
titles write to:

Bloomsbury Methuen Drama
Bloomsbury Publishing Plc
50 Bedford Square
London WC1B 3DP

or you can visit our website at:
www.bloomsbury.com/drama